Praise for
The Human Value
of the Enterprise

"The Human Value of the Enterprise *masterfully synthesizes theory, research, and practices on measuring human capital. It shows how to measure, track, and invest in human capital in ways that ensure business value. It turns abstract beliefs in the value of people into concrete measures which will enable business leaders to make informed human capital choices and insure that HR professionals act with data not just intuition.*
The 'Human Capital Monitor' architecture encompasses research to date and offers a pragmatic way to assess people performance in a firm. I learned a lot from reading the book and will refer to it frequently as a disciplined roadmap for deriving human capital value."
Professor Dave Ulrich, co-author of *The HR Scorecard*

"A most impressive overview of human value metrics, with very practical references and models, such as the 'Human Capital Monitor' and the 'Human Asset Register', which focus on clarifying people as sustainable value creators, not costs."
Leif Edvinsson, former Director of Intellectual Capital at Skandia Assurance in Sweden and Professor of Intellectual Capital at the University of Lund

The Human Value of the Enterprise

Valuing PEOPLE as Assets

Monitoring, Measuring, Managing

Andrew Mayo

NICHOLAS BREALEY
PUBLISHING

LONDON

First published by
Nicholas Brealey Publishing in 2001

36 John Street
London
WC1N 2AT, UK
Tel: +44 (0)20 7430 0224
Fax: +44 (0)20 7404 8311

1163 E. Ogden Avenue, Suite 705-229
Naperville
IL 60563-8535, USA
Tel: (888) BREALEY
Fax: (630) 898 3595

http://www.nbrealey-books.com

Library of Congress Cataloging-in-Publication Data
Mayo, Andrew
    The human value of the enterprise : valuing people as assets : monitoring, measuring,
    managing / Andrew Mayo.
        p. cm.
    Includes bibliographical references and index.
    ISBN 1-85788-281-4
    1. Intellectual capital. 2. Human capital. 3. Management. I. Title

HD53 .M377 2001
658.3--dc21

2001037663

ISBN 1-85788-281-4

British Library Cataloguing in Publication Data
A catalogue record for this book is available from the British Library.

Printed in Finland by WS Bookwell.

Contents

Acknowledgments

I HAVE LONG HAD AN INTEREST IN THE RELATIONSHIP BETWEEN PEOPLE AND business results. In 1994 I was asked to contribute to a chapter in a book published by the Institute of Personnel and Development in the UK called *Strategic Prospects for HRM*. It was in researching this chapter, "The economic factors of HRM," that I came across the books of Jac Fitz-Enz and Eric Flamholz, tireless thought leaders in this field. I owe a great deal to the comprehensiveness of their work.

More recently I have followed and found great empathy with the pioneers of the intellectual capital movement, through both reading and listening to them: Karl Erik Sveiby, Leif Edvinsson, Thomas Stewart, the Roos brothers, and others. They have significantly influenced my view of the business model for the twenty-first century.

A number of friends have given great encouragement and ideas: Philip Sadler, CK Prahalad, Mick Cope, David Clutterbuck, Marc Baker, Tony Buley, and many others along the way. I am grateful to Geoff Atkinson for his reading of the manuscript and many valuable amendments; to Peter Honey, Michael Pearn (fellow participants in the Learning Symposium Group), and Janice Chalmers for suggestions on structuring the original text. I want to thank Jan Morgan, who helpfully challenged the logic of the arguments and offered many textual improvements.

I would like to thank my colleagues in the Centre for Management Development at London Business School for their practical support and use of facilities, and the continual learning derived from the executives who come on the programs there.

My publisher Nick Brealey and his colleague Sue Coll gave unstinting support and were at the same time my most helpful critic. I am greatly indebted to my professional editors Bronwen Perry and Sally Lansdell for the final presentation. Finally, many thanks to my patient assistant Fiona McDonnell for technical help and to my wife Elisabeth, who has suffered once again the privations that come from "this new book I have to write."

Preface: The Vision

Fortune magazine has just published its 2009 comparison of the leading 500 companies in value generation. No longer do we see columns for Return on Capital Employed and profit per employee. This year's comparison is fully focused on the use of intellectual capital. The first figure is the ratio of intangible to tangible assets. Companies with less than 60 per cent look very bad prospects for investors. Output is measured as the added value that is generated. But the really interesting figures that sort out the exciting companies from the mundane are the investments in R&D, investments in people development, customer loyalty index, and the percentage attrition of professional staff.

The Times Business Supplement, 22 April 2010

The highest paid employee was the chief scientist, who added to her basic salary of $800,000 bonuses totalling $3 million based on the sales from new products introduced in the last two years and on the innovation-culture index of the department for which she is responsible.

Extract from Annual Report, Drugs-R-Us, 2005

With effect from the trading year 2005, all companies registered in Denmark will be required to include in their annual reports information about customer, process and human capital. A minimum of five measures for each is required, and comparison with the previous two years must be shown. Figures for investment in intellectual capital must be shown and compared with the previous two years. A narrative should accompany each set of figures. Information for investors about intellectual capital both current and future should occupy at least one third of the report. Where relevant, information must also be provided regarding care for the environment.

Directive from the Danish Ministry of Business and Industry, April 2002

In the last five years, the HR profession has transformed itself. If we go back ten years, it was a function that agonized about how it could be a real business partner, and yet at the same time peddled soft answers to problems and could not talk in the language of numbers that mattered. Training was fun-oriented, and people were usually valued according to the job they were currently doing. Performance evaluation depended more on demonstrating cloned "competences" than on adding real value to stakeholders. What a difference today!

Back in 2003 HR directors seized the opportunity to spearhead the intellectual capital movement, developing credible measures for valuing people and their contribution. They systematically convinced top management teams that people had a measurable value and that people alone drove value creation. Many human resource directors are now directors of intellectual capital, looking after strategy, knowledge management, R&D, people development, IT systems, and process engineering.

Thanks to their efforts, people are not only recognized as the most important asset in an organization, but private and public sectors alike regard their Human Asset Registers with the same importance as any financial performance summary. The long debates of the 1990s about budgeting and variances have been replaced by intellectual capital planning and monitoring. These have become a way of life.

In the companies that have led this new business model, shareholders have never enjoyed such healthy returns, and other stakeholders have never been better satisfied. Customer and employee loyalty ratios are in the top quartile and new graduates fight to join them.

Thanks to the lead given in Denmark and Sweden, soon after adopted by major global companies, investors can now see the valuable information they need about their investment in intellectual capital and how they use it. The position of power has shifted from the finance director to the director of intellectual capital, and this is reflected in the remuneration packages of each.

Financial Times Review of the Decade, 22 December 2010

DEDICATION
This book is dedicated to the achievement of the vision.

1

A Great Gap to be Filled

Though your balance-sheet's a model of what a balance-sheet should be,
Typed and ruled with great precision in a type that all can see;
Though the grouping of the assets is commendable and clear,
And the details which are given more than usually appear;
Though investments have been valued at the sale price of the day,
And the auditor's certificate shows everything O.K.;
One asset is omitted—and its worth I want to know,
The asset is the value of the men who run the show.

Archibald Bowman, 1938

IN 1960 DOUGLAS MCGREGOR PUBLISHED HIS BOOK *THE HUMAN SIDE OF Enterprise.* He suggested that there were two basic approaches to management. "Theory X" assumed that people are instruments of labor—human resources—and that management is about efficient task fulfillment, with a carrot-and-stick approach to performance. Or, he suggested, you could take the view that what people are actually looking for is challenge and interest, and that the task of management is to maximize commitment and liberate their ideas and abilities. This he called "Theory Y." Most organizations today would say that their thinking embraces more of Y than of X. However, some 40 years later, in a numbers-driven business culture, while we are good at measuring people as costs and resources, we still have no accepted way to value people as assets.

So the gap that Archibald Bowman identified in his piece of doggerel remains. Developing new business models for today's world is one of the greatest challenges we face—and one that this book takes up.

"OUR PEOPLE ARE OUR MOST IMPORTANT ASSET"

Most chief executives would readily nod assent to the frequently heard statement that staff are a company's greatest asset. Yet, the people within an organization do not always experience decisions and policies reflecting this in everyday life. They are much more likely to see the company being driven by efficiency and by minimizing costs. Asking audiences how they perceive reality in the UK, I have found fewer than 20 percent who feel that the decisions made by top management match the espoused belief in the real value of people. The accountant who once described people to me (admittedly with a smile) as "costs walking about on legs" is often closer to reality.

The problem is that people do not fit the strict financial definition of an "asset." They cannot be transacted at will; their contribution is individual and variable (and subject to motivation and environment), and they cannot be valued according to traditional financial principles. And yet, organizations today are as much concerned about the "war for talent" as any other business issue. Why is this so? It is very simple. The valuation of companies has changed progressively since about 1990, putting a much higher value on "intangible assets" such as knowledge, competence, brands, and systems. These assets are also known as the "intellectual capital" of the organization. And it is people, and people alone—the "human capital"—who build the value.

Jack Welch, one of the best-known American CEOs, is famous for saying that "there are three key measures in business—customer satisfaction, employee satisfaction, and cashflow, in that order." More recently, he said that he had the first two round the wrong way—employees should come first. What he recognized was that, at the end of the day, everything depended on people: their capability, motivation, creativity, organizational skills, and leadership. People manage the tangible assets, and they also maintain and grow the intangible ones.

We cannot track intangible assets in the same way as financial and physical assets. We have to learn new ways, but these must have the same level of credibility as well-established systems of accounting. We *must* do this; in an era where knowledge and talent are at a premium, there is no doubt at all about which are our most important assets. Organizations that continue to think of their people as mere resources and costs have not crossed the millennium divide.

There is a growing volume of research aimed at recognizing and proving the relationship between "good people management practices" and "the bottom line." Today, that bottom line is seen as consisting of both profitability and long-term shareholder value. The major consultancies are devising their own systems for assessing the "metrics" of people management. William Mercer, for example, has developed a "human capital wheel," Watson Wyatt has a "human capital index," and PricewaterhouseCoopers has a department called "HR Analytics," which in 2000 won a prize within the consultancy for innovation. Researchers such as Mark Huselid and Jeffrey Pfeffer in the US, and David Guest, John Purcell, and Lynda Gratton in the UK, have done long-term studies to demonstrate the benefits of a positive approach to human resource management.

It is not surprising that there are positive correlations between people and performance. Companies such as Johnson & Johnson and Cadbury knew many years ago that the better people are treated, the more successful the organization is likely to be. However, it is not enough to simply preach the latest research results. These days managers are bombarded with ideas on how to do everything better.

> THE CRITICAL CONTRIBUTION OF PEOPLE—ESPECIALLY HIGH-VALUE, TALENTED PEOPLE—TO ORGANIZATIONAL SUCCESS HAS PROBABLY NEVER HAD A HIGHER PROFILE. IT IS ESSENTIAL FOR ORGANIZATIONS TO HAVE SOUND MEASURES FOR MANAGING PEOPLE AS ASSETS, RATHER THAN MERELY AS COSTS.

What really governs their lives are numbers—so the challenge is to find some quantifiable methods that enable us to understand people's worth and their contribution to "value" in the organization.

SHAREHOLDERS VS. STAKEHOLDERS

Organizations exist to create value for people, either individually or collectively. Charities convert money, expertise, and caring attitudes into benefits for people in many different ways. Public-sector organizations bring value in services and information to different sections of the community. Commercial businesses create monetary value for their owners, and in so doing bring value to many other individuals and organizations. Are shareholders, owners, and investors more important than others with an interest in the success of the organization—the people and groups of people that we call stakeholders? Most CEOs of commercial companies will say that their ultimate goal is to build value for the shareholders. Major decisions, especially about ownership, are taken with this in mind. But, if in so doing they destroy value for other stakeholders, the evidence is that they do not achieve their goal in the long term. If customers no longer want to deal with that company, employees no longer want to work for it, suppliers find it too difficult to trade with, and the community loses confidence in it, then these stakeholders—who are essential to its continuing success—will be lost. Without the support of other stakeholders, no shareholder can achieve sustained returns.

As the song from the film *Cabaret* has it, "Money makes the world go round." But only a myopic mercenary believes that the human condition is all about money, even though it can make life easier. Society needs businesses to provide employment and build financial stability for individuals, to create, make and distribute products and services, and to take a responsible role in supporting communities. Businesses create wealth that can be shared—this is the ultimate "added value."

Therefore in order to create value, we need to know how value is added to *all* stakeholders, both financial and nonfinancial, both now and in the future. We need a clear idea about what matters to them and how to meet their needs, so that they will want to go on working with us.

THE CHALLENGES TO BE GRASPED

Every day we can see the outcomes of a lack of balance between thinking of people as costs and viewing them as assets. Of course, in a sense they are both simultaneously. But let us have a look at some of the challenges we need to grasp, and at how our inability to do so has a serious impact on the effectiveness of our organizations.

Challenge #1

When we make a decision to cut costs from an organization, we have clear numbers to work with. Everyone understands the systems and measures for costs. However, when we talk about their corresponding value (if indeed we do), we may only have words—and numbers always speak louder than words. We lack a commonly accepted framework for assessing the value and contribution of people. It is only when people leave that we miss the value they contributed, often so much so that we hire them again as consultants (who go on a different cost line than salaries and headcount).

Making business decisions purely on cost grounds is yesterday's business model. There are now hundreds of books offering advice on how to create economic value, how to build empowered and innovative organizations, develop visionary leaders, secure evangelistic customers, and win the war for talent. These imperatives are a million miles away from the kind of management accounting that has had a stranglehold on organizations for the last 50 years or more. They require a new language, one about building futures, not documenting the past.

The challenge: **Balance cost numbers with value numbers, so that both have equal status in decision making**.

Challenge #2

Every person brings a different combination of capabilities and contributes to the organization in a unique way. When one joins or another leaves, there is an impact on human capital "stock" that is more than a mere adjustment in headcount. Each individual employee lends the organization their "personal human capital" in exchange for value in various forms: salaries, challenge, development, and so on.

The challenge: **How do we recognize the intrinsic diversity in the worth of people and find a way to value it through understanding their personal human capital?**

Challenge #3

The phrase "adding value" is often used loosely to mean "making a worthwhile contribution." However, adding real value to stakeholders is a serious business—it is the only reason that organizations exist. The phrase is incomplete if we do not specify at least "to whom," and preferably "by doing x." This should be the basis of performance management. Such measures might be either financial or nonfinancial, but it is only some form of *quantification* that enables us to know whether our capacity to add value is increasing or decreasing. Every asset (including individual people) should be linked to the value that is created for one or more stakeholders.

The challenge: **We need to measure the value—financial and nonfinancial—that is added to each stakeholder by each individual in our organization.**

Challenge #4

It would be unfair to accuse *all* organizations of paying much more attention to the short term than the long term, but the reality is that it is easy for short-term pressures to dominate resourcing decisions. People whose role is to focus on the future may be given a lower priority when it comes to restructuring resources. "Shareholder value" is still linked in many minds with *current* profitability. It is true that it provides dividends for shareholders and owners, but the value of a share reflects the collective judgement of investors about the *future* of a company. What they are looking for is the prospect of the revenue streams to come, and historical profits may or may not be a guide to that.

Stories regularly appear in the financial press about CEOs who have tried to set a long-term strategy and yet been brought to heel because quarterly profits have suffered. One headline in 2000 concerned Procter and Gamble, well known for its visionary thinking and excellence in management. CEO Durk Jager, a veteran of P&G, set out his vision for the group in "Organization 2005," but then earnings fell and the share price along with them. Former chairman John Pepper was brought out of retirement and a new CEO was appointed. "I want to express my gratitude to Durk Jager for his visionary leadership and many contributions to P&G over 30 years," Pepper said. "We have an accelerated pace of product innovation that never would have been possible without his leadership. This is his legacy. His emphasis on innovation and a culture that reaches out for breakthrough provides a strong foundation for future progress."

"It was a personal decision to step aside," said Jager with due corporate loyalty. "I am proud of the vision we set out to achieve with Organization 2005, and we've made important progress. It's unfortunate our progress in stepping up topline sales growth resulted in earnings disappointments. I'm confident that with the leadership of AG Lafley and John Pepper and the strength of P&G people, the company will achieve its full potential." He was expressing the difficulty of building for the future and at the same time guaranteeing present financial performance, so readily seized on by financial analysts. One year later under the new leadership, profits were still struggling.

The challenge: **We must be able to value future returns from intangible and people-related investments with as much credibility as the well-tried methodologies for physical asset investment.**

Challenge #5

Organizations set goals, both short and long term, to measure progress. Each of these goals has *drivers*, "input" factors that determine the desired outcome, and they in turn have their own influencing factors. A sound performance management system should monitor all the drivers and influences that affect the goal, just as much as the desired outcome itself. As you follow down the logic of the performance chain, it is not long before you come to people-related issues as a critical dependency. The measures for these are as important as any others in driving success.

A credible set of measures and indicators enables practical, and better, decisions to be taken about important business issues such as:

❏ acquiring new people
❏ rebalancing the workforce
❏ maximizing performance and productivity

❑ developing individuals and groups
❑ resource allocation and options for outsourcing
❑ investing in people and organizational development
❑ benchmarking
❑ setting up partnerships and alliances
❑ managing mergers.

The challenge: **It is as important to measure the drivers of performance as it is to measure the outcomes themselves.**

Challenge #6

The pace of restructuring in organizations always seems to be on the increase, through acquisitions, mergers and disposals, or simply reorganization. However, the rate of failure in restructuring is well documented: for example, research by KPMG in 1999 showed that 53 percent of the mergers studied failed to bring added shareholder value. Although a commercial firm may pay a significant premium for the intangible assets of another company, much of this value is often lost through the pursuit of cost-driven "synergies." Lawyers and accountants focus on liabilities and numbers; meanwhile, the really valuable assets like expertise, experience, customer relationships, and knowledge may be lost in the process.

The challenge: **How do we ensure that value is increased, and not lost, when organizations merge and restructure?** Ch. 10

Challenge #7

Investors find it very difficult to find out the information they need to judge the capability of an organization to deliver value in the future. In a move toward facilitating this, it is almost certain that statutory bodies will soon require more detail to be declared on intangible assets. To prepare for such a move, organizations need to get their internal systems right. A system for regularly reporting what is happening with *selected* and *strategic* intangible assets needs to be set up and to have the same importance and credibility as that for the familiar financial inputs and outcomes.

The challenge: **We need to know how to obtain relevant and reliable data on intangible assets within the organization before we are required to publish it externally.**

THE SLIPPERY SLOPES OF MEASUREMENT

This book starts from the principle that everything can be quantified in a way that enables us to manage it, and cause changes in it. Whether we are talking about the capability or potential of people, the culture in which they work, or their motivation—just to give just some examples—measures for these can be found and tracked. Managers are conditioned to working with numbers and nothing has a greater impact. Nevertheless, numbers that relate to people need to be treated with care and caution, ensuring that the processes used to obtain them are sound and that we are clear what we want from them. A *comparison* over time, or against a particular benchmark or target, is often more useful than the *absolute* measure itself. It is the context that gives meaning to the figures. For example, if an employee opinion survey indicates that 65 percent of people are satisfied, this has little significance in itself. Its real meaning only becomes apparent if we compare it with the same measure in a previous survey or with similar questions in other organizations.

> "IF YOU CAN VISUALIZE IT YOU CAN MEASURE IT, AND IF YOU CAN MEASURE IT YOU CAN MANAGE IT."
> GORDON PETRASH, FORMER DIRECTOR OF INTELLECTUAL CAPITAL AT DOW CHEMICALS

Why are most organizations still so unsophisticated and haphazard in measurement of human assets? There are several reasons.

❑ It is not easy! Unlike buildings or machines, people do not fit consistent patterns. There are many dimensions to be considered, not just dollars or pounds. Attempts to apply well-accepted financial principles to the valuation of people have failed because of the number of assumptions that have to be made. People are not static either, they move around organizations and between them.

❑ Because of the complexity, we need several kinds of measure and processes of measurement. Each measure has to establish its own credibility as a logical driver of, and link to, the ultimate financial numbers.

❑ There are dangers in forming conclusions about measures without fully understanding the range of factors that can determine a particular outcome. We need to understand its *causality*. For example, we might measure attrition rates in the knowledge that our pay rates are below the market, and assume that this is a significant factor. In reality, the dominant cause might be less to do with pay and more to do with the quality of management.

❑ Human resource professionals have often been cautious about championing the need for measurement. Many feel that it is their role to balance the prevalence of numbers with "humanity," and not to try to compete with accountants on their own ground. This is not to say many do not measure the efficiency of their own processes, or create sets of helpful statistics, or attempt to establish return on investment for some programs and initiatives. However, systematically quantifying the worth of individuals and their contribution to stakeholders has generally been neither a priority nor an aspiration.

Since the mid-1990s some progress has been made in this area. Support has steadily grown for the "balanced scorecard," a system designed by Robert Kaplan and David Norton and first published in 1992. This approach does look for measures of the drivers of financial outputs. It balances financial indicators with those for customers, process efficiency, and learning and innovation. Some users of the scorecard have replaced the latter with a more general "people" element—and most find this area the most difficult to find good indicators for. David Norton himself says in his foreword to Becker, Huselid, and Ulrich's *HR Scorecard* (2001):

> But the worst grades are reserved for the typical executive team for their understanding of strategies for developing human capital. There is little consensus, little creativity and no real framework for thinking about the subject. Worse yet, we have seen little improvement in this over the past eight years … human capital is the foundation of value creation. The asset that is the most important is the least understood,

least prone to measurement, and hence the least susceptible to management.

In parallel with the development and application of the balanced scorecard, some pioneering Scandinavian companies have taken a different starting point. They have developed a range of indicators to cover each of the components of intellectual capital, including people. Examples of these will be found in Chapter 3.

THE HUMAN CAPITAL MONITOR

This book provides a coherent model of measures relating to human capital, offering a standalone means of recognizing the vital contribution of people to value creation.

There are three distinctive areas that require measurement, illustrated very simply in Figure 1.1.

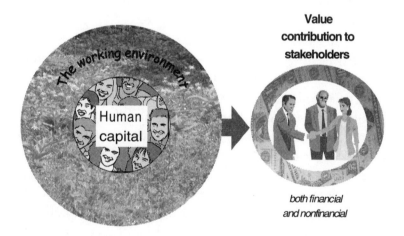

Figure 1.1 *The different requirements for measurement*

People loan their *human capital* to us, and we provide an *environment* in which they can *contribute value* to stakeholders in our organization.

This is encapsulated systematically in the Human Capital Monitor, the three columns relating to the three areas of measurement.

THE HUMAN CAPITAL MONITOR

PEOPLE AS ASSETS		PEOPLE MOTIVATION AND COMMITMENT		PEOPLE CONTRIBUTION TO ADDED VALUE
Human Asset Worth = employment costs x individual asset multiplier (IAM) / 1000 IAM = a function of • capability • potential • contribution • values alignment	**+**	Measures – How successful are we? **The work environment that drives success**	**=**	The value added to each stakeholder • financial • nonfinancial
Maximizing Human Capital • Acquisition ⎮ – How • Retention ⎮ successful • Growth ⎮ are we? ⎮ – What drives ⎮ success?		• Leadership • Practical support • The workgroup • Learning and development • Rewards and recognition		• current • future

Figure 1.2 *The Human Capital Monitor*

People as assets

First, we want to have some indicators of the intrinsic worth of the people and teams who are available to us—not necessarily in any absolute or financial way, but relative to one another. We need to know whether some people have greater human capital than others, and whether our stock of human capital is increasing or decreasing. This implies that we can track the flows of human capital into, out of, and within the organization. When we look at the costs of people, we also need an indicator of value that will enable us to retain a balanced perspective. Also, there may be some people whose cost is greater than their worth to us. These are "liabilities" rather than assets—people who are subtracting value from the organization. In summary, we want a sense of the "balance sheet" effect of human capital.

The formula, which is expanded in Chapter 4, is for a measure called Human Asset Worth (HAW). This combines a person's employment costs (as a starting point of their value) with a combination of four key components, summarized in the Individual Asset Multiplier (IAM). The product of these is divided by 1,000 so that the resulting figure is clearly not in a monetary currency. The four components that make up a person's worth to us are their capability, their potential, their contribution, and their alignment with our values.

Our human capital is maximized through three key activities: persuading people to join us, keeping them, and developing them. There are factors we can identify for each of these processes that influence our success at them and these also require measures.

People motivation and commitment

However good the people we recruit may be, their contribution is strongly influenced by their working environment. This affects the level of their motivation, commitment, and loyalty, and encourages or restrains the full use of their ability.

It is therefore vital to identify the factors that make a difference in the environment and to measure their level of strength or weakness. The Human Capital Monitor chooses five such factors: leadership effectiveness, practical support in the workplace, the nature of the workgroup, the culture of learning and development, and the systems for rewards and recognition. We need continually to take measurements in these areas, to find out whether we are optimizing the value people bring and/or whether these factors are becoming stronger or weaker.

People contribution to added value

Thirdly, we want to be able to measure the contribution of our human capital in terms of how people are adding current and future value to stakeholders.

All the people in a commercial organization collectively produce financial wealth that can be distributed. But they also work in teams and as individuals to provide specific financial and nonfinancial value to one or more stakeholders. We need some organization-wide indicators of their contribution, but also should link every individual with a measure of the specific areas of value their role is designed to add. We also want to distinguish between the current contribution to maintaining value, and those people and activities dedicated to creating increased value in the future. This is about the "profit and loss effect" of human capital.

For noncommercial organizations the same need exists, except that the financial indicators have a value-for-money rather than a wealth-creating perspective.

CHOOSING THE NUMBER AND LEVEL OF MEASURES

If we try to measure everything at every level, we will be swamped and find we have so many numbers that there are too many to manage. Figure 1.3 shows four levels—the enterprise as a whole, organizational units, teams, and individuals—that we want to consider within the context of the two key driving forces in any organization:

❑ the critical organizational goals and strategies
❑ the areas of value that matter most to each stakeholder.

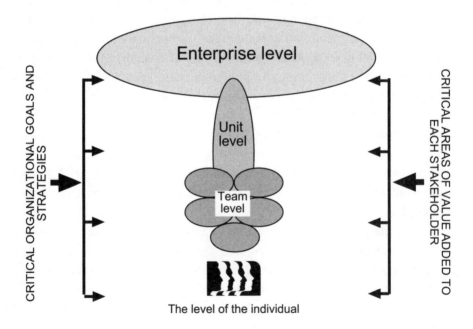

Figure 1.3 *The involvement of different levels with key organizational drivers*

Measures at the enterprise level can be somewhat crude levers for management, since they hide a multitude of sins and virtues in the detail. For example, total attrition figures that include many different categories of employees have little meaning. Aggregated opinion surveys may show common threads that are organization wide, but the many local working climates are the real clues to people's commitment and satisfaction, so we must have data broken down to units and teams. Nevertheless, there are two rationales for measures at the enterprise level:

❏ Indicators we might want to publish year on year as information for investors or stakeholders—for example, financial value added, investments in employee development, community involvement, innovation measures

❏ Those we want to benchmark with other similar organizations—for example, attrition, overall satisfaction, suggestions per person, reward levels.

How do we decide which measures to choose at the lower levels? We start with our goals and strategies, and the final outcome measures that provide their quantitative targets. They may, for example, be growth levels, profitability, market share, service leadership, best value in providing public services, and so on. Each is driven by a number of factors that will influence success, and it is often the case that one or two factors have much more effect than the others. Thus, if we aim at service leadership over our competitors, this may be affected most by the completeness of the customer database (say, 20 percent), call center staff capability (55 percent), and the extent to which a service engineer solves problems in one visit (25 percent). Our prime (but not necessarily exclusive) focus would be on the second, looking then for the factors that influence staff capability, and so on in a "staircase" of cause-and-effect dependencies. Each step leads to the next set of factors, and every factor should have its own measure.

Each staircase may have four or five steps between the ultimate goal and the most basic driver of success. The advantage of this approach is that it leads to very specific areas of the organization's operations, and quite quickly to individuals or groups of people in those areas. We are brought directly to aspects of their capability and the environment that supports them. We can do the same for the key areas of added value for each stakeholder.

Figure 1.4 illustrates the principle. The term "critical input" is used for the most important influencing factor at each step.

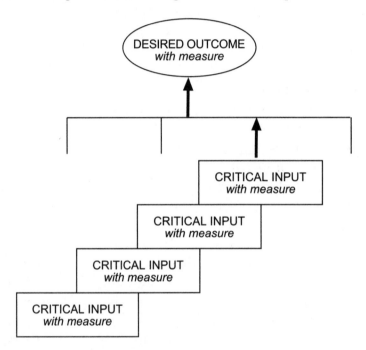

Figure 1.4 *The staircase of cause-and-effect dependencies*

Building critical staircases in each area leads us to the sets of measures that will support our strategies and stakeholders, and defines what we need for each level and for each part of our organization.

These are the principles for selecting the specific measures that form part of a Human Capital Monitor, which itself may be used at any of the levels above the individual.

THE STRUCTURE OF THIS BOOK

This book sets out to answer three questions:

- ❑ Why is it essential to have a system of measurement for human assets?
- ❑ How should we go about measurement?
- ❑ How can this make us manage more effectively and create more ultimate value?

An organization that wants to think and act seriously in the belief that people are its most important assets can be described as a "value-creating organization."

Chapter 2 discusses the meaning of value and the role of people in the processes of creating value.

Chapter 3 looks at the process of measurement in the context of people. This leads us into looking at the components of the Human Capital Monitor in more detail.

Chapters 4 and 5 focus on the intrinsic worth of people as assets— the first column of the Human Capital Monitor. We examine what constitutes their worth, and particularly the challenge in defining levels of capability and potential.

Chapter 6 is about how we can maximize human capital through acquisition, retention, and growth, and related measures.

In Chapter 7 we move to the second column of the Human Capital Monitor, looking at motivation and commitment and what influences these. Chapter 8 discusses how we can build a supportive environment to make the best of people's talent.

Chapter 9 describes the last column of the Human Capital Monitor, showing how we define and track the critical indicators of value to each stakeholder.

Chapter 10 focuses on managing the human side of mergers and acquisitions, and how we can ensure that value is not lost in the process.

Chapter 11 reviews what is happening in relation to the public reporting of human capital measures.

Finally, the Appendix reviews the literature on the measurement of intellectual capital.

2

People Drive Value

WHAT DO WE MEAN WHEN WE SAY THAT PEOPLE ARE "ASSETS"? In this chapter we will explore this concept in the language of accounting and look at the meaning of "value" as it applies in organizations. Traditional accountancy does not serve us well in an era when knowledge is more important than physical assets, and the chapter considers some of the ways in which it needs to be changed.

We cannot talk about value and ignore the prevailing preoccupation with "value for shareholders," so we look at how this is achieved and see why it is the intangible assets—the intellectual capital—of an organization that are its real drivers. This is not just the people; it includes many other generators of future revenues, and we shall see how these can be analyzed and categorized systematically, as well as examining the role of people in contributing to them. This leads us to discussing people as "human capital," reviewing first how others have looked at this, and then forming conclusions about why we need the measures in the Human Capital Monitor to be truly effective.

PEOPLE AS ASSETS

We are borrowing from accountants' language when we talk of people as "assets." Assets have an intrinsic value to the organization, and at the same time they generate value for others. In other words, we add value to our stakeholders through the deployment of our assets. So, when we talk about people in an organization, there are two separate ways in which we can use the concept of value: what they are worth to us and the value they add to others. Both need to be quantified, a dual need that is recognized by the Human Capital Monitor.

Capital appears on the opposite side of a balance sheet to assets. We still debit capital in order to credit assets in line with the tried-and-tested double-entry system invented by the Italian monk Pacioli. Capital is labeled liabilities, because it has to be repaid at some point, but we don't have to "pay back" human capital. We can see it as actually owned by the people themselves, who are "on loan" to us for as long as they choose to stay, or we choose to retain them. Just as we look after and invest our financial capital, so it is logical that we should do the same with our people.

Money is used to fund purchases of physical (tangible) assets and in their day-to-day use. It is also employed by people, both in managing the tangible assets and in building intangible assets, such as brand value, customer loyalty, efficient processes, and new knowledge. An intangible asset, like any other asset, should generate value. We can also have intangible liabilities that *subtract* value: people or processes or reputations can cost money, sometimes adding no value at all and sometimes even inhibiting value creation. Assets can turn into liabilities—we might say that they have a *negative* asset value.

> THE CONCEPTS OF "HUMAN ASSETS" AND "HUMAN CAPITAL" ARE COMPLEMENTARY. IT IS THE INTRINSIC WORTH OF OUR PEOPLE THAT COMPRISES THE HUMAN CAPITAL AVAILABLE TO US, AND AT THE SAME TIME THAT WORTH IS A VALUE-CREATING ASSET.

THE MEANING OF VALUE

The "value" of an entity is in the eye of the beholder. Unlike costs, which are usually expressed in absolute numbers, value goes up and down depending on particular perceptions, so its *worth* can increase or decrease. Money is the commonest currency of value, but it is clearly not the only one. We do not shed too many tears if the burglar only takes replaceable commodity goods. What hurts is when something goes that has unique personal value, an item treasured perhaps because of association with special people or events. Economists (and many finance directors) see value generation in terms of cash transfers, so their measurements are usually expressed in hard financial figures. But when we think of value to stakeholders, we should not think only in this rather narrow way. There is value to customers in receiving excellent service and in the continuity of relationships with our staff; there is value to employees in having exciting challenges at work and opportunities for personal development. Suppliers might well take pride in being associated with us and our good reputation. We add value to the stakeholders en route to an eventual financial outcome. If their needs for value are eroded, the interested parties may begin to lose commitment to working with our organization, which would be bad news for shareholders.

We know how to calculate costs well enough, but linking them to value creation is much more difficult. We cannot often compare them in the same currency. However, in principle all that we spend—including paying for the efforts of people—should have a direct output of greater value in some form. We are certain to find some that do not do this and they have to be questioned. Nevertheless, we can conclude that costs should be (but are not always) an *input* to the process of delivering an *output* called value.

> COSTS SHOULD BE (BUT ARE NOT ALWAYS) AN INPUT TO THE PROCESS OF DELIVERING AN OUTPUT CALLED VALUE.

When costs need to be reduced, management should seek out those that are not value creators. However, they rarely have the information that enables them to do this, and hence value-adding assets can be lost, a loss that is only discovered afterwards.

ADDING VALUE TO EMPLOYEES

People lend their personal human capital to an organization because they believe that they will receive some value in return, in varying forms. They become both an asset—able to generate value for others—and a stakeholder. And, on the assumption that we have selected them well, we shall certainly not want to lose them. Just as a customer only continues to do business with us if they are satisfied, so it is with employees. They are not a mere resource, like electricity, to be turned on and off as needed. They are the most critical generators of value we have, whatever the nature of our organization; if it is purely knowledge based—as many are—they are in fact the only ones of significance.

We add value to people financially. We provide salaries, benefits, bonuses, and maybe equity in the firm if it is available. However, most people look for more than merely financial rewards. They may be also interested in a selection of the following:

❏ Challenging and interesting work
❏ Equipment and resources that would not otherwise be accessible
❏ Being associated with an organization of high repute
❏ Status and self-esteem
❏ Recognition: by the person's managers, or by peers, or even publicly
❏ Opportunities for personal growth and career development
❏ Interesting colleagues to work with
❏ A satisfying and stimulating environment
❏ Social events
❏ Opportunities for travel and perhaps high standards of accommodation.

The way in which we provide this value to people conditions their motivation, commitment, and loyalty—and hence their contribution to adding value to other stakeholders.

Seeing value in merely financial terms seriously inhibits our understanding of the balance that we need. It is worth pausing at this point to note the shortcomings of the accountancy systems that dominate the present business model, which may even work against the maximization of value creation.

THE POVERTY OF ACCOUNTANCY IN THE MODERN WORLD

I have borrowed this subheading from a wonderful article by Alan Dunn, a vice-president of what is now Cap Gemini Ernst and Young, in the firm's house magazine *Transformation*. He imagined he had died in an air crash, but was not allowed to enter heaven because of his dubious associations with management accountancy. He was given a chance to redeem himself in the eyes of the Almighty by taking the (also recently deceased) body of the executive director of the Financial Accounting Standards Board. He proposed three ideas to transform accounting, the first of which was to change the nature of people accounting. His first directive was:

> *The sum of all costs associated with the hiring and continuing development of employees will be capitalised as a year end ledger entry. Accounts normally expensed by period, such as training, employee development and hiring costs will be credited and a new account called "Capitalised Human Assets" will be debited.*

He then contemplated the uncertainties and anomalies in depreciation accounting. His second directive was:

> *Each year, all employees will be evaluated for competency and compared with scores from the previous year's evaluation. The book value of the Capitalised Human Assets will be adjusted accordingly...*

This would be an encouragement, he thought, for all employees to "appreciate" rather than "depreciate" through personal development. His third directive applied the same thinking to building "brand equity."

In *Transforming the Bottom Line* (1995), Tony and Jeremy Hope discuss how traditional systems of management accounting and performance measurement do not provide what an organization and its stakeholders really need to know. The power that many finance functions enjoyed in the 1990s is out of proportion to their relevance. Systems of performance management limited to short-term financial performance against pre-set budgets are inappropriate for the knowledge world. The nonaccountant manager or specialist is a helpless victim of the processes and priorities of accounting practices. They can see clearly the anomalies and stupidities, but they have become resigned to their inevitability.

In business, financial outcomes will always remain the ultimate measures of success; business exists primarily to create wealth. Its success, however, depends on its ability to understand the *causes* of results as well as the results themselves. This leads inevitably into "softer" contributors that can be critical in the staircases of dependency described in

Chapter 1. Here, accounting lets us down. Accountants deal in transactions and this is one reason for costs dominating value.

It is not as if accountancy is a precise science in itself. Despite their appearance of accuracy, many familiar and well-accepted measures—such as profit and capital employed—are the result of judgments and assumptions. Depreciation rates, provisions, classifications of overheads: Judgments on all of these may lead to pragmatic decisions aimed at bringing about a desired financial result.

Table 2.1 shows some of the changes that are necessary to bring accountancy up to date.

Table 2.1 *Summary of the changes necessary in accounting*

From	To
Tangible asset management	Plus intangible asset management
Valuation of physical and financial assets	Plus valuation of intangibles
Criteria for physical capital investment	Plus criteria for intangible asset investment
Departmental cost focus	Process and customer cost focus
Past oriented	Plus future oriented
Cost measurement	Plus value measurement
People related costs all treated as expenses	Distinguishing between expenses and investments
Work measured as salary costs	Work measured as activity costs and % added value
Cash flow oriented	Plus future revenue streams
Indirect cost allocation to department	Indirect cost allocation to value streams
Fixed budget periods	Dynamic budgeting
Financial data as outcomes	Plus nonfinancial data as inputs
Regular period statements	Continuing access to company data
Profitability focus	Added value focus

A number of initiatives exist toward making these shifts. Work is going on in the valuation of intangible assets, and various consortia are looking at alternatives to budgeting. In 1999 in the UK the Beyond Budgeting Round Table (BBRT) was formed. Since then some 45 companies, including Barclays Bank, Bass Brewers, Diageo, DHL, Novartis, PricewaterhouseCoopers, Sainsbury's, SKF, Unilever, and the Chartered

Institute of Management Accountants have sponsored its research. The following quotation gives an indication of their thinking:

> *Traditional budgeting is a serious handicap, particularly when firms need to operate at high speed, continuously innovate, and compete with e-business strategies. Budgets are barriers to devolution and more effective management, yet it is entirely feasible to manage without them.*
>
> *Jack Welch of GE has called budgets "The bane of Corporate America"; Bob Lutz of Chrysler "A tool of repression"; and Jan Wallander of Svenska Handelsbanken "An unnecessary evil". There are two fundamental problems. Budgets are barriers to (1) the devolution of power and authority to the front line, and (2) the implementation of more effective performance management processes. While most companies are dissatisfied with their budgeting systems, only a few pioneers have really addressed the issue. The most mature case is the Swedish bank, Svenska Handelsbanken, which adopted a devolved management model and abandoned budgeting 30 years ago. It is now one of Europe's most successful banks. In recent years many other companies including Volvo, IKEA, SKF, Borealis, Schlumberger, Air Liquide, Bull, Carnaud Metalbox and Boots have (to varying degrees) followed its lead.*

The BBRT has produced a 240-page guide and 10 detailed cases illustrating an alternative approach. It visualizes the changes as in Figures 2.1 and 2.2 opposite.

The flexibility and responsiveness of the model in Figure 2.2 are much more appropriate to a value-creating organization. This approach enables us to use money and resources much more intelligently, and removes the need to spend "because we have the money and we don't want to have our budget reduced next year."

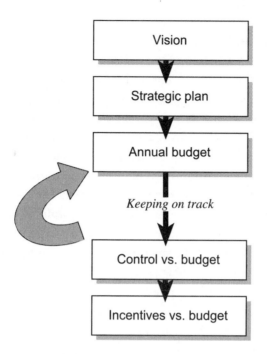

Figure 2.1 *Traditional budget control*

Figure 2.2 *The emerging dynamic approach*

VALUE FOR SHAREHOLDERS

The *delivery of shareholder value* is the dominant goal of the Anglo-US capitalist philosophy, which is progressively modifying the more stakeholder-conscious capitalist models of continental Europe and Japan. In any discussion of value, however, our starting point must be the return, in the form of dividends and capital growth, that shareholders can anticipate. Dividends come from current (or past) profits, but for investors to buy or hang on to shares, what matters is their *confidence* that the particular company will provide continuing profit growth. The investors with influence in today's world are mainly large institutions like pension funds, and an organization's managers often have a vested interest in the same outcome through their share options.

If you ask how shareholder value is increased, people usually say "by focusing on profitability"—which is hardly surprising. So much emphasis is put on profits and their forecasts by senior management, and by the analysts who comment on company performance. We see immediate, albeit often temporary, changes in share price whenever an announcement is made that might affect profits.

The response of senior management to "bottom-line" performance problems is usually to cut: cut projects, cut staff, amalgamate, centralize, streamline, outsource, and so on. They often give insufficient thought to the parallel loss of current and future value-creating sources. Studies repeatedly show how heavy cost cutting batters morale and has many "hidden costs," causing good people to leave, and reducing levels of customer service. Voluntary redundancy programs, although perhaps a mark of a caring company and undoubtedly benefiting many individuals, can lead to a devastating loss of valuable skills and experience—unless the organization retains the right to say "No, we cannot lose you."

It is nearly always easier to reduce than to grow and the effects are more speedily seen and celebrated. Yet, even the architects of reductionism in business process engineering had to admit that it can lead to what they called "corporate anorexia." James Champy and Michael Hammer had to add a human element in the sequels to their original 1993 book *Reengineering the Corporation*. Geoff Armstrong, Director General of the UK's Chartered Institute of Personnel and Development, said in his 1996 keynote speech to the Institute: "Does anyone stop to think of how the billions spent in firing people might have been otherwise invested for growth, and the effect that would have had on our companies?"

The legacy of the short-term and narrow approach to shareholder value is well described in Alan Kennedy's *The End of Shareholder Value* (2000). He describes it as leading to a "me-first" mentality, which spreads through the attitudes of all stakeholders as they reciprocate. Employees respond to their unpredictable level of security by losing loyalty to the organization, and job mobility becomes the norm. Many suppliers are more interested in their own organization and internal cost management than in what matters to customers, and the latter can also vote with their feet. Loyal suppliers are squeezed out by the vicious cycle of demands for ever lower prices. All of this one might regard as the inevitable progress of the capitalist ethos, but Kennedy argues that these are the direct fruits of the short-term desire to enhance the stock price at any cost.

Good companies have always paid attention to the long term and to their stakeholders' interests. Porras and Collins of Stanford University took 18 examples of what they called visionary companies, with an average lifespan of nearly 100 years. They compared them to similar companies that had experienced roughly the same opportunities but had not achieved the same reputation or performed so well. The authors said they were looking for timeless management principles. What did they find? The visionary companies demonstrated a continuing focus on "intellectual capital" in the following ways:

❑   A consistent and strong core ideology, with clear values that formed the foundation of their infrastructure
❑   A clear vision for the future and "Big, Hairy Audacious Goals" that went beyond the current financial year
❑   A high premium on innovation: "Try a lot of stuff and see what works"
❑   A focus on employee development, and growing their own senior managers.

Not many organizations have managed to maintain the optimum balance between short- and long-term gain through their systems of management and performance measurement. The forces for the short term are strong and easily dominate. Many managers are very conscious of this dilemma but feel powerless to solve it.

THE POWERHOUSE OF VALUE: INTANGIBLE ASSETS

The starting point for assessing value—and its message is powerful enough on its own—is this equation:

MARKET VALUATION = VALUE OF NET TANGIBLE ASSETS + VALUE OF INTANGIBLE ASSETS

The market valuation of a company—its share price times the number of shares—is what a stock market says it is worth at a point in time. It never has been exactly what internal accountants calculate it as, although it used to be pretty close, since it was their duty to provide shareholders with their best estimate. Unfortunately, their system of calculating the net assets ("book value") no longer serves shareholders well. A yawning gap has arisen in the last ten years between this and the value placed on the company by the market.

This gap represents the increasing value allocated to intangible assets. According to Microsoft chairman Bill Gates, "Our primary assets, which are our software and software developing skills, do not show up on the balance sheet at all." In fact, less than 3 percent of Microsoft's value is accounted for by tangible physical and financial assets.

The term "intellectual capital" is often used for an organization's intangible assets. The first thinkers to realize the significance of this intellectual capital came from Scandinavia: Leif Edvinsson of Skandia and Karl Erik Sveiby of one of Sweden's most successful publishing companies, Affärsvärlden. In the USA it was Thomas Stewart, a journalist with *Fortune* magazine, who highlighted this valuation dilemma in a 1994 article. In this era, Stewart says, wealth is the product of knowledge and he defined intellectual capital as:

> *Intellectual material—knowledge, information, intellectual property, experience—that can be put to use to create wealth.*

The confidence that causes a share price to be sustained, and to rise over the medium to long term, is built through a belief in future earnings streams. It is true that there are variable market factors that affect a share price at any point in time—we saw that particularly in the "dotcom bubble" of late 1999 and early 2000. But over time, that confidence comes from a sound strategy, from continuing innovation in products and services, excellent people, loyal and satisfied customers, a reputation and image in connection with the community that create a positive company "brand," synergistic partnerships, and so on. All of these come under the category of intellectual capital.

Each time a balance sheet is prepared, the figure for intangibles can be calculated as an absolute amount by comparison with the prevailing market valuation. There are valid criticisms of the simplicity of such a formula, the most obvious being the volatility of the market value, as well as the fixation of a balance sheet "snapshot" on a particular day that can be out of date immediately. Better, one can take a three- or six-month moving average of both of these and calculate each month the *ratio* of intangible assets to market value. This is our best indicator for comparison with other organizations, and over time.

Valuation and depreciation of tangible assets follow different rules in different countries, so global comparisons have to be treated with caution. Nevertheless, however sophisticated we become in devising a formula, the fact remains—and this is what matters—that a very large part of value is unaccounted for in most enterprises.

Figure 2.3 overleaf shows the gap that has arisen over the years between the book value of an enterprise—as measured through traditional accounting practices—and the market valuation. A ratio on the left-hand side of 1.0 indicates a book value equivalent to market value. As the importance of intangibles has grown so this ratio has come down. The proportion of value attributable to tangible assets has continued to fall, and in 2000 was about 0.2 for the S&P 500 in the US. A radical change happened in the early 1990s with the growth of information technology, together with a newly focused emphasis on quality and customers. Today, high-technology and healthcare companies will probably have over 90 percent of their value in intangible assets. Even in manufacturing and engineering companies we will find figures of between 50

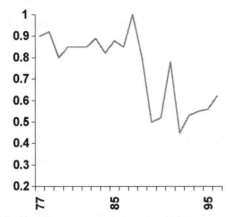

* For firms with comparable earnings, a value of 1.0 means
that differences in share prices depend solely on differences
in book values

Leif Edvinsson, Source: Baruch Lev, New York University business school

Figure 2.3 *The change in equity valuations over time*

and 80 percent. In late 2000, for example, BP showed a figure of 74 percent, 3M 82 percent, and ABB 85 percent.

Why has this happened? Although it is fashionable to distinguish between "old" and "new" economies, the fact is that practically every organization in the developed world has seen a growth in the importance of services, and in the competitive advantage of knowledge in all its forms. Managing "talent" and managing "knowledge" have become the imperatives of the new millennium for all organizations.

The inescapable conclusion is that valuing and quantifying intellectual capital form perhaps the greatest challenge facing businesses today. Investors need methods of understanding how value is being created in the organization and assessing what confidence they can have in the future. Management needs measures in order to manage these assets more coherently and effectively. And accountants need ways of achieving a more complete asset valuation. We should expect *more* activity and attention to be given to managing intellectual capital than to managing the tangible assets.

Accounting bodies and academics have recognized this need for some time. The Appendix reviews some of the available proposals for measurement and valuation of intangible assets/intellectual capital.

THE COMPONENTS OF INTELLECTUAL CAPITAL

So far we have treated intellectual capital as a whole, but it is of course composed of many parts. In order to understand the part that people play in the overall picture, we need a means of looking at the various components. In the few years that authors have been thinking and writing about intellectual capital, a broad categorization has emerged, as follows.

> HUMAN CAPITAL IS WHAT PEOPLE TAKE HOME WITH THEM, AND STRUCTURAL CAPITAL IS WHAT THEY LEAVE BEHIND.

Structural capital

Structural capital falls into two parts:

❑ *Customer (external structural) capital.* This includes assets that enable and/or stimulate people outside our organization to work with us, and—in a commercial organization—to buy from us. It includes customer contracts, relationships, loyalty, satisfaction, market share, image, reputation, brands, distribution networks and channels. In the public sector we would talk, for example, about service levels, accessibility, reputation, or the popularity of revenue-generating activities.

❑ *Organizational (internal structural) capital.* This includes all that relates to our internal operations and efficiency. It embraces strategies, systems, methodologies, and operational processes. All the recorded knowledge we have is here: patents, know-how, databases, and technology. We would also place here the culture of the organization.

Human capital

This is the people themselves, loaning their personal "human capital" to the organization, their individual capability and commitment, their personal knowledge and experience. But it is more than the individuals alone: It includes the way in which they work together, and the relationships they have both inside and outside the organization.

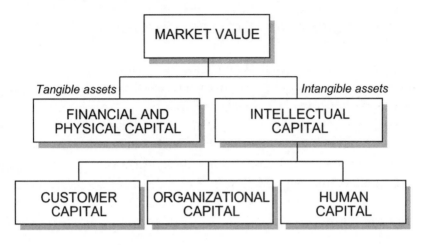

Figure 2.4 *The constituents of market value (adapted from Skandia)*

PEOPLE: THE MAINTAINERS AND CREATORS OF VALUE

When we look at Figure 2.4, are there any grounds for saying "people are our most important asset"? If we were able to divide the total financial value calculated as attributable to intellectual capital between the three categories, would the largest sum be in the human capital box? We would not be able to do this—and to do so would miss the point. The "snapshot" approach of a valuation at a point in time diverts us from the reality of the continuing change and dynamics of an organization. Yet, the truth is that all intellectual assets are maintained and grown by people and without them will wither away.

> ALL INTELLECTUAL ASSETS ARE MAINTAINED AND GROWN BY PEOPLE AND WITHOUT THEM WILL WITHER AWAY.

The unique contribution of people comprises their command of information and experience, their ability to integrate these and use personal judgment, to be innovative and intuitive, and to develop relationships. These are the vital dynamics of a progressing organization. Without people, all the structural elements—customer related and organizational—might decay, and certainly will not grow. The only possible exception is well-documented methodologies or patented knowledge, which Annie Brooking, in *Intellectual Capital*, put—with some justification—in a separate category of *intellectual property*. Even then, people are needed to exploit it. Gordon Petrash convinced Dow Chemical that it was sitting on a mass of potential revenues with its accumulated intellectual property and this led to his setting up a department to manage and market it more effectively.

COMBINING THE HUMAN CAPITAL OF INDIVIDUALS

Individuals bring their own human capital to us, and through working together they are able to create more value for the organization than as isolated contributors. They thus build structural capital, and various terms have appeared to describe this.

Social capital

People are mobilized into teams to create new intellectual capital. If they trust each other and are enthused by the work itself, they will want to work together and to share and exchange knowledge and ideas. They will find reasons to come together, to seek and give help, and exchange ideas. Building such trust may become an investment in itself, through providing opportunities for people to meet. Project teams, working groups, seminars for exchange—all of these are activities that promote social capital.

Emotional capital

Kevin Thomson writes in *Emotional Capital* that "assets like passion, obsession, motivation, desire, innovation and knowledge will be critical in creating the products, services and relationships which produce lifetime loyalty from customers and colleagues alike." He rightly emphasizes the need to harness intellectual capital assets through belief, enthusiasm, and passion. When revising its "business competencies" in the mid-1990s, IBM placed "a passion for the business" at the center. It recognized that the most potent driver of success was a love for the IT world and what it could do. This kind of passion has driven many entrepreneurs and leaders to great success, and their enthusiasm is transmitted to others.

Relationship capital

This term has been used to describe the network of relationships that exist within, and beyond, an organization that make it function effectively.

The most obvious and important example is the relationships with customers. Customers can interact with a firm quite impersonally, and many transactions take place without any intervention of a human being other than in a mechanical way. But in many businesses it is the personal touch that makes such a difference to customer loyalty. It is not surprising that when some salespeople or consultants leave they are made to sign an agreement that they will not take any clients with them for a period of time. It is also well known how difficult this is to enforce, especially where the client has the choice of whom to deal with.

The same principle applies to suppliers. Firms like Marks & Spencer (in its heyday) and Procter and Gamble were always known for seeing suppliers as real partners, for creating relationships with them with a view to maximizing their common interests. Frequent visits would take place, joint projects and experiments were entered into, and data on quality and product effectiveness shared. By contrast, the cold, adversarial, clause-enforcing relationship that characterizes the construction industry produces no loyalty, only a continual and expensive struggle for contracts.

Today's businesses invariably involve a range of partnerships and alliances. These may cover research, marketing, manufacturing, or shared technology. Each has its own network of key relationships of trust that make it work.

The importance of both external and internal relationships is such that a firm should be aware of them and be very careful before breaking them. Restructuring in the interests of cost saving often takes no account of such capital, and as a result precious customer loyalty may be lost. Copious written explanations of why the change will be "better" for the other party are unlikely to make up for the loss of a relationship of trust.

It is one thing to look for the positive side; equally important is the removal of discord and destructive relationships. Enmity between departments that need to cooperate is found all too often and is clearly a liability. Job rotation, interdepartmental "team-building" sessions, secondments—these are some of the ways of creating trust and working more effectively together.

Knowledge capital

Firms have begun to wake up to the fact that knowledge is a precious asset that is frequently underutilized and poorly managed. Knowledge is an important component of our overall intellectual capital and it is intricately linked with human capital. However, considerable confusion exists as to terms and what constitutes knowledge; academics pour out papers seeking to clarify this critical area. More and more case studies appear demonstrating both constructive and value-producing ways of managing knowledge, and also illustrating the mistakes that have been made.

Hubert St Onge, a major Canadian contributor to thinking about knowledge management, sees the generation of knowledge capital as *the major* contributor to corporate value. His model is of human, customer, and structural components all working together, in a positive environment of organizational learning, to produce this knowledge capital.

A distinction needs to be made between knowledge and information. The initial answer of many organizations to the challenge of knowledge management was to make more and more information available, on for example an intranet. Much of this was merely digitized information such as telephone directories and procedure manuals. It has extended to shared databases, such as customer and product information, and to external links with the internet for news and market data. Of course this does have value, particularly in saving time when accessing facts and being able to keep information up to date much more readily.

However, knowledge is the result of *processing* information, what is learnt from it. It is what the various pieces of information, perhaps culled from multiple sources, are telling us. For example, people pay subscriptions for investors' broadsheets, buying the conclusions and recommendations the writers have reached from studying as many facts as they can acquire.

Knowledge also comes from experience. New experiences are the most potent form of acquiring new knowledge. They arise every day, from problem solving, experimentation, mistakes, market and environmental change, projects, new ideas, and so on. Each person involved is enriched through the extension of their existing knowledge. This can be expressed visibly and explicitly, for example in new products and services, revised processes, or manuals of best practice. These may be retained within the group that generated them (for whom this is certainly enhanced knowledge "capital") or made available to the whole organization. One of the key challenges of knowledge management is creating this availability to others. Through sharing:

❏ We avoid duplication of mistakes.
❏ We avoid duplication of projects.
❏ We can update to best known practices.
❏ We stimulate more new ideas.

This all makes such good sense that one wonders why organizations have taken so long to wake up to this priority. The large consultancies were among the first to realize how vital this activity was for their business success. Tom Peters uses some 50 pages in *Liberation Management* (1992) to describe the system set up by McKinsey. Karl-Erik Sveiby wrote many pioneering texts focusing on how knowledge should be managed in the knowledge-based organization. Arthur Andersen produced its first CD-Rom of "Global Best Practices" in 1992, describing ten core established consultancy processes.

Technology has been a great stimulus, but it is not enough. Whereas people will readily supply information and facts, giving their knowledge to others runs into several barriers. Time, availability, motivation, and fear of losing personal power are some of them.

So far we have looked at making knowledge *explicit*. This is distinguished from knowledge that is *tacit*, which cannot be expressed in a way that others can use. Experience produces knowledge, which leads to sound judgment and wisdom—the "knowledge" that is used in making future decisions. This is a complex area, intricately tied in with personal attributes such as analytical thinking and intuition. It forms the core of an individual's personal human capital. The way in which the collective tacit knowledge of individuals is harnessed is a critical success factor in a value-creating organization.

Gordon Lackie, a consultant based in the Netherlands, has captured the importance of people sharing their knowledge in his concept of "Mobilizing Collective Intelligence" (MCI). He argues that mobilizing people to use their collective tacit knowledge is far more important (and likely to succeed) than attempting to "manage" it. Although storing knowledge and making it available are clearly helpful activities, he argues that more effort should be put into adapting, improving, and applying what is known *together*. This makes much sense and integrates the concepts of knowledge and social capital.

SUMMARY

People are a unique form of asset. They possess their own personal capital that they can withdraw from an organisation at any time. Nevertheless, we can make it attractive for them to join and stay, to use their capital for our advantage, and at the same time add value to themselves.

Delivering "value" is why organizations exist. This is clearly about providing "sustainable returns to shareholders" for those companies that have owners and investors, but not-for-profit organizations also create value for their stakeholders even though it may not be measured financially. Value is in the eyes of the beholder, and a stakeholder will only want to continue their association with an organization if their expectations of value are being met.

The obsession with value to shareholders is seen at its extreme in the US and countries that have embraced that style of capitalism. It has been associated with many short-term decisions, especially in reducing costs—whether they are value-producing costs or not. Traditional management accounting, designed for the industrial era, often causes decisions to be made that are inconsistent with a value-creating organization, which needs to build the strength of its intangible assets. Even the sacred cow of budgeting is under attack, as the pace of change demands control *with* flexibility.

Today's markets look for value beyond the traditional net book worth, which reflects only the physical and financial assets. Even heavily capital-intensive companies are valued at two to four times this book value, and knowledge-intensive organizations up to 20 times. The gap represents the "intangible assets," those that have no coherent system of measurement, such as customer relations, unique knowledge and systems, talented people, and clear visions and strategies. It is these that will generate *future* profits. As yet, there are few agreed ways to assess the value of these intangibles.

However, these are what drive *continuing* value for all the stake-holders of an organization. The time and attention given to the planning and monitoring of these assets are generally much less than their importance justifies. Unlike the finance director who coordinates through common systems and standards, intangibles are generally distributed across many functions and monitored in varied ways—sometimes not at all.

The intangible assets of an organization are more generally known under the heading of intellectual capital, although this is often confused with intellectual property (in a legal sense) or with the people and their knowledge. However, the emerging categorization distinguishes, first, assets that relate to the external world, to do with customers and the community; secondly, those that are part of the internal infrastructure of the organization; and finally, the human capital. Although referred to commonly as assets, there are aspects of all these areas that can be negative, "liabilities" that subtract value rather than add it.

The term "capital" is being applied to many concepts. Emotional, social, and relationship capital are all in use and represent different aspects of the softer side of an organization's infrastructure. Knowledge capital is more substantial, and represents the cumulative codified knowledge, wisdom, and experience on which the organization can draw.

CHALLENGES FOR ACTION

good questions!
(for practitioners)

- ❏ In which contexts is the word "value" used in your organization? What meaning would people give to it?
- ❏ Assuming you have a quoted market valuation, do you know and track the percentage of value that is intellectual capital in your organization?

❏ Do you have any way of evaluating how well the market is seeing your intellectual capital compared to that of your competitors?

❏ How well is it understood in your organization that it is the continual addition of value to all stakeholders that is the fundamental source of maximizing shareholder returns?

❏ What messages are given to managers and other employees in your organization about what really leads to long-term success?

❏ Do you have a language in your organization for describing intellectual capital that people naturally understand and that fits with your normal work terms and expressions?

❏ How would you categorize intellectual capital in your organization?

❏ In what ways does your organization have measures relating to human capital?

❏ Have you mapped key relationships held in the organization?

3

Measuring Human Capital

IN THE LAST CHAPTER WE DISCUSSED THE IMPORTANCE OF INTELLECTUAL capital and how it could be categorized and visualized. People, human capital, are the foundation of value creation. We defined the Human Capital Monitor in Chapter 1, and three areas of necessary measures. In this chapter we look at the measurement process itself, and at the ways in which measurement has been attempted to date. There are many difficulties, of course, which is one reason we are still struggling. The different types of measure available are discussed, as is how we can balance the positive value adding (an asset) and the negative value subtracting (a liability). We survey the different approaches to measurement in current use, including the balanced scorecard, and expand the idea of cause-and-effect dependencies as a means of choosing which measures to track.

WHY THIS IS NOT AN EASY AREA

It is no accident that people-related measures have less presence and impact in everyday performance measurement than do financial or even customer-related ones. We know that people are important; perhaps this is so self-evident that measurement seems almost superfluous. And yet, most will agree that this area is significantly underdeveloped. Why has it been so difficult to get people measures taken seriously?

❑   Since as we know it is difficult to quantify most intangible assets in a monetary way, whatever measures we have will compete with financial measures' apparent credibility and appearance of accuracy. People are mobile, subjective, changeable, variable—and as far from an accountant's concept of an asset as one could be. The new International Accounting Standard IASC 38, which deals with the valuation of intangible assets, excludes the whole area of human capital (and others too, such as brands) as not conforming to the definition of an asset.

Jeffrey Pfeffer, writing in the journal *Human Resource Management*, provides an excellent summary of the pitfalls in human capital measurement. He argues that most human resource measures focus on costs or link in with existing accounting systems. He notes that when people are the denominator in a ratio such as productivity, the way to raise it is to shrink the number of people—a "pernicious way to make people appear more productive." He warns that HR people should not "become more skilled at someone else's game." We need to find a different measurement framework. It cannot be the same playing field as that of the accountants.

❑ A number of HR professionals are uncomfortable with the need for measurement where people are concerned. They regard it as both unnecessary and essentially inadequate to describe people in terms of numbers: "It should be self-evident that people are the most important asset we have; we don't need numbers to prove it." This thinking has restrained professional HR bodies from making measurement a priority. Despite the concern of many HR departments to be seen as more and more business linked, this area has not received the attention it deserves. One persuasive and tireless advocate, however, is Dave Ulrich, professor at the University of Michigan.

❑ Senior management has acquiesced in the lack of insistence on measures by being relatively undemanding of any information other than headcount or cost-based data, rarely asking, for example, for return-on-investment calculations on HR initiatives. Faith in what seems the right thing to do has triumphed over evidence of benefits achieved. They would not dream, of course, of investing in capital equipment without detailed consideration of the return on their money.

❏   This lack of demand means that something that is difficult anyway will inevitably be squeezed out of the priorities of most HR functions. The effort required may seem to go relatively unrewarded, or perhaps attempts to do it in the past may have lacked credibility— or the results may even have been uncomfortable.

❏   Much as managers love numbers, they can become very fed up if more and more measures are foisted on them. Because they represent more paperwork and bureaucracy, the question is always: "What's in it for me?" This is a fundamental question that must be addressed. Unless top management is visibly committed to new measures and makes clear that they are important, we cannot expect interest and attention, particularly from managers further down the organization. Measures must be carefully chosen to reflect what is strategically important, and also what is helpful in achieving organizational goals.

Some practical difficulties

There are problems with many measuring processes and those used in accounting have their own difficulties. It is worth reminding ourselves of some of the traps in our way.

Measures designed to reflect the contribution of people will rarely have total "causality," that is, they will not be exclusively linked to the people themselves. The efforts of people combine with other factors such as market conditions and the effectiveness of internal systems and processes. Intelligent interpretation of the measures is therefore more important than the numbers themselves.

The "consolidated measure" that is often seen at the top level of management is certainly useful for benchmarking. However, it hides a range of data that has more meaning as it describes what is actually happening in different functions or units. When several results are consolidated, the danger is that a sweeping solution is applied across the board, which may be quite wrong for some.

A classic case here is a profitability crisis that results in a universal headcount cut or recruitment ban, which may be counter-productive to growing units. Likewise, a corporate attrition rate may on its own look quite acceptable, but hide undesirable losses in critical areas of the enterprise.

"Headcount" is the simplest measure of people and is commonly used as a denominator in ratios such as revenue per head. There are at least three dangers arising from the use of the word "head." First, it is rare today for the human contribution to the enterprise to be confined to the so-called "permanent" payroll, whether full or part time. Temporary staff, for example, or contractors and consultants might be contributing to the added-value output. Secondly, a focus on heads leads to a tendency to manage headcount down in order to improve ratios. Hard-pressed managers soon find ways round it by hiring people who do not show up in the figures. The outcome is that actual costs are not reduced, and human capital that should be "committed" to the organization may not be hired or even retained. And thirdly, one "head" is certainly not the same as another, in both cost and capability. For example, the cost of a software specialist in India might be one twentieth of that in Silicon Valley, but accountants would count each in the same way—one head.

HR people are often required to spend an extraordinary amount of effort reporting on the state of the headcount. People budgets are frequently set as the number of heads. I once argued strongly the imperfections of this approach to a particularly wise and sanguine CEO, and his answer was: "I know. But it is simple and everyone understands it, and it works." In the twenty-first century and the era of understanding value, we need to progress beyond that.

Measures are frequently presented as static, absolute numbers. In fact, they often have little meaning expressed in this way, and at a given point in time. Business is dynamic, so trends, comparisons, and directions provide more meaningful data.

A CHECKLIST FOR GOOD MEASURES

Many of these will be familiar, but it is worth having a reminder. Effective and useful measures have the following characteristics:

- ✔ They are simple to understand.
- ✔ They are clearly defined so that people interpret them in the same way.
- ✔ Data can be collected in a way that ensures that the effort required is proportional to the resulting usefulness of the measure.
- ✔ The process of measurement has integrity: Measures are made in a consistent way and are seen to be reliable.
- ✔ The measures are not the result of one person's judgment.
- ✔ They do not have built-in biases, such as "leading" or "loaded" questions in a survey.
- ✔ They make sense in the context of other measures—for example, if we measure a person's skills through an off-job assessment center, how does this match with the perceptions of colleagues in the workplace?
- ✔ They are credible as "roughly right, not precisely wrong."
- ✔ They focus on what is important and comprise key outputs or are linked to them.
- ✔ They are at the right level of detail to enable appropriate action to be taken.
- ✔ They can be used for tracking change.
- ✔ There is clear ownership of them by an individual or team.
- ✔ They are taken at the right frequency, chosen to provide useful trends and comparisons.

EVALUATING MEASURES

How do we know whether to be pleased with the results of our measurement or not? When is a measure a "good result" and when is it a "bad result"? Often it will be obvious, but there are three means of evaluation to help us answer the question:

❑   Is it *increasing or decreasing* compared to the previous figure? Whichever way it is going, we want to understand why. Some measures will vary over short periods (for example, attrition rates may be quite different month to month) and we need to look at trends such as three-month moving averages.

❑   How does it compare to similar measures in other organizations? We will want to carry out *benchmarking* with competitors and other organizations in a similar sector; we may also want to compare with others whom we particularly admire or who are known for "good practice." To do this we may utilize some measures that are not perfect for our own use but that enable benchmarking. An example might be "training days per head," which may carry little weight internally, but externally enables us to look at comparative investment levels in people development. I recall using such data in front of a board (knowing that it was an inadequate measure of learning investment) and successfully making the point that competitors appeared to be investing much more than we were. The desired concern was raised and such an investment measure became part of the budgeting process. Another example of inter-firm comparison would be general satisfaction measures; here a core of questions can be shared by collaborating in "survey clubs."

❑   How does it compare against an *internal target* we have set?

Value adding and value subtracting

Clearly, when we are measuring we need to identify the "liabilities" that subtract rather than add value. Sometimes we can actually calculate a bottom-line cost resulting from some characteristic we have that causes problems. For example, unwanted attrition has a very real cost, as do processes that consume time for no added value. Perhaps we just do not have essential knowledge or capability and this constrains the revenue we could earn. If we have a culture that does not support knowledge sharing, repeated mistakes can be estimated as a cost or loss of revenue figure. Low levels of employee satisfaction lead clearly to a lack of productivity or to people leaving.

We can draw up a scale representing our best knowledge of the "ideal" and the opposite of that ideal. Below the midpoint we believe that we are subtracting value from one or more stakeholders. It is actually—in all measures of intellectual capital—a critical management task to know where the dividing line lies between an asset and a liability in this sense.

Let's take an example. One measure might be our "replacement ratio," the percentage of roles in the organization for which we have a ready successor. The ideal is 100 percent, but we know that this is unlikely to be achieved. However, if we were forced to go to the market for every vacancy we would be subtracting value from shareholders through the sheer cost involved, and from employees who saw no means of promotion. Low morale also may affect performance. There is a level below which the lack of succession becomes a real liability and we must be above this. Figure 3.1 illustrates this principle.

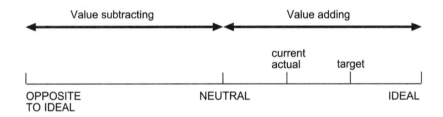

Figure 3.1 *Adding and subtracting value*

Alternatively, when we compare ourselves against a desired standard or goal, or against the competition, we may find we fall short. We may still be adding value positively, but not as much as we could or should. So long as we are below our best competitor, or our target, or both, on balance we have a *relative* liability.

For example, "the number of experts in a particular technology" will always be positive. But it is enough? (See Figure 3.2.)

MEASURES SHOULD HELP US UNDERSTAND WHETHER WE HAVE AN ASSET OR A LIABILITY IN AREAS OF HUMAN CAPITAL, AND/OR TELL US WHETHER VALUE IS BEING ADDED OR SUBTRACTED FROM STAKEHOLDERS.

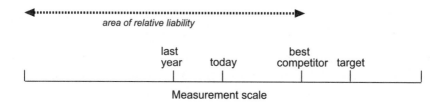

Figure 3.2 *Sample measurement scale*

These kinds of scales could be used with most of our measures. With them we can manage performance, compare with others and with time, know where our "liabilities" are, and set targets for improvement.

EXISTING APPROACHES TO PEOPLE MEASUREMENT

Before going into detail on the measures that support the Human Capital Monitor, it is worth looking at the various approaches that others have taken in the area of human capital measurement. These fall into five categories:

- ❑ Attempts to value people as assets. This applies accounting valuation principles to people and is known as human resource (or asset) accounting. (This is discussed in detail in the next chapter.)
- ❑ Creating an index of "good" HR practices and relating these to business results.
- ❑ Statistical summaries analyzing the composition of the workforce and measures of the productivity and output of people.
- ❑ Measuring the efficiency of HR functions and processes and the return on investment for "people" initiatives and programs.
- ❑ Integrating people-related measures in a performance management framework.

INDICES OF GOOD HUMAN RESOURCE PRACTICES

There is now substantial research that has set out to study whether good people management practices are directly linked to parameters of business success. For example, a study in the UK sponsored by the Institute of Personnel and Development with Sheffield Business School and the London School of Economics looked at 110 manufacturing companies, and related a variety of supporting processes to profitability. The researchers calculated that "employee commitment" accounted for 12 percent of the variation between companies in their profitability, and 17 percent in their productivity. Those firms with a strong human relations ethos showed more consistently good results than the others.

Mark Huselid of Rutgers University in the US has been studying the relationship between a company's personnel policies and its business performance for many years. One set of data he collected in 1995 from 968 firms related HR practices to attrition, productivity, and financial results. His analysis showed, for example, that one standard deviation in the "index of work practices" accounted for a 16 percent increase in productivity. Organizations that make development of their people a fully strategic goal performed spectacularly better than others.

Jeffrey Pfeffer of Stanford University, in his book *The Human Equation* (1998), argues eloquently for the "seven practices for successful organizations" that made a difference, according to his research. These are listed as employment security, selective hiring, self-managed teams and decentralized decision making, comparatively high compensation linked to organizational performance, extensive training, minimal status differences, and extensive openness in sharing financial and performance information.

The Corporate Leadership Council worked with Coopers and Lybrand in 1992–6 and surveyed 1,500 companies on "high performance work practices," a range of HR systems and approaches. The findings were matched against criteria of business alignment and financial results. The researchers computed that each standard deviation improvement in their index of good HR systems led to an increase of $40,000 per employee in market value and $27,000 in sales.

Lynda Gratton at London Business School has worked with seven major companies and one large hospital since 1992 in the "Leading Edge Consortium." This is a very deep study, involving hundreds of managers and employees, into the relations between people processes and business strategy and results. The better-performing companies were those that placed significant emphasis on communication, managed change, and employee involvement.

Watson Wyatt's Human Capital Index (HCI)

Watson Wyatt, a firm of consultants, has developed what it calls the "Human Capital Index" (HCI). The consultants surveyed over 400 US and Canadian companies in 1999 and linked human resource practices with market value by tracking shareholder returns over a five-year period. They found a strong correlation between their index, a consolidation of 30 key HR practices, and increases in shareholder value— acknowledging that correlations are not the same as direct causal links. Over five years the third of the sample showing the lowest index had risen 53 percent in market value, as compared to 103 percent for the upper third. The 30 practices were split into five groups. The figures shown in brackets below are the increases in shareholder value creation over give years associated with one standard deviation of improvement in that part of the Human Capital Index:

❑ Recruiting excellence (10.1%)
❑ Clear rewards and accountability (10.2%)
❑ A collegial and flexible workplace (3.8%)
❑ Communications integrity (5.0%)
❑ Prudent use of resources (–10.0%)

Not all HR initiatives were found to be effective. The last category is particularly interesting and was somewhat of a surprise to the researchers. It covered some popular HR initiatives, such as 360° assessment. Watson Wyatt concluded that undue investment was put into practices that in fact yielded very little benefit and could even be counter-productive. Importantly, the research found that there is a negative impact where the activity is not directly supporting the objectives of the organization.

In a separate study on employee attitudes, again in the US, Watson Wyatt also found a clear direct link between "high commitment" and enhanced three-year shareholder returns.

Watson Wyatt uses its index as a diagnostic instrument for organizations wanting to check their own "human resources health" and benchmark against others.

The European Business Excellence Model and the Malcolm Baldrige criteria for performance excellence

Originally a model for quality management from the European Foundation for Quality Management, the EFQM Model (Figure 3.3) enjoyed widespread popularity with organizations in Europe, and is now often used as a monitor of organizational excellence. It balances "enablers" against "results," and comprises audit questions resulting in a set of scores placed against an ideal. The relevant areas for human capital are Leadership, People, and People Results. The latter is assessed through opinion surveys of people satisfaction.

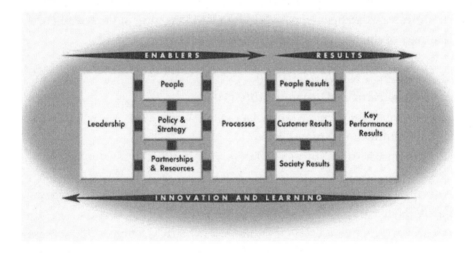

Figure 3.3 *The European Business Excellence Model*

The model is closely related to the Malcolm Baldrige National Quality Award in the US. This has a series of criteria for performance excellence, in Business, Education and Health Care, aimed at:

❏   ever-improving value to customers
❏   improved organizational effectiveness
❏   organizational and personal learning.

Seven categories are used and 1,000 points are distributed between them: 550 points are shared between Leadership, Strategic Planning, Information and Analysis, Customer and Market Focus, Human Resources Focus, and Business Results; the remaining 450 cover Business Results, with 80 allocated to Human Resource Results.

The Human Resource Focus covers:

❏   works systems, aimed at high performance
❏   employee education, training, and development
❏   employee wellbeing and satisfaction (focusing on the work environment).

Applicants for this quality award describe in detail their processes and the data regarding their effectiveness. Self-assessment can be made against detailed check questions, and a library of good practice is available.

William Mercer's Human Capital Wheel

William Mercer, another leading specialist HR consultancy, has developed a "wheel" divided into six segments entitled "people" (capability and experience), "structure" (hierarchy and organization), "processes" (how work is organized), "decision making," "information flow," and "reward." Concrete measures exist for each.

Changes that have happened in each sector over the previous three to five years are plotted on the wheel. These are then related to measures of performance and quality such as added value per employee or another measure of productivity. In a large organization, separate business units can be compared on the relationship between their success and their positioning on the sectors of the wheel.

Arthur Andersen's approach to human capital management

Friedman, Hatch, and Walker, three partners in Arthur Andersen, published a book that topped the US bestsellers lists in 1999, entitled *Delivering on the Promise: How to Attract, Manage and Retain Human Capital*. Their system is known as Human Capital Appraisal™ and is a matrix of systematic intervention steps vs. five HR areas of activity. The steps are clarify, assess, design, implement, and monitor, and the areas of activity covered are:

❏   recruitment, retention and retirement
❏   performance management and rewards
❏   career development, succession planning, and training
❏   organization design
❏   human capital "enablers"—compliance, employee relations, communications, IT.

These two dimensions of steps and activities result in a 5 × 5 matrix that effectively acts as an audit checklist for good human capital management practices.

Potentially of more interest for our purpose is Arthur Andersen's Fit–Cost–Value™ framework. Each program or initiative is plotted on two dimensions of high/low strategic fit and cost > value/value > cost, as in Figure 3.4. "Strategic fit" rates each HR approach against business strategy, best practice, and (where relevant) the market. However, value is determined by the consolidated impressions of employees in each of the five areas, which does not take us much further forward than employee satisfaction surveys. We are measuring only the value to one stakeholder, and in a rather generalized way.

THE VALUE-CREATING ORGANIZATION STARTS WITH THE STREAMS OF ADDED VALUE PROVIDED TO STAKEHOLDERS, AND *THEN* PUTS IN PLACE PRACTICES THAT WILL MAXIMIZE THAT VALUE.

All the above approaches start with the structural capital of HR processes and initiatives, and with the existing culture. They are particularly useful in benchmarking people management practices. It is good news—though hardly a surprise—that treating your human capital well yields good results. In our terms,

Figure 3.4 *Arthur Andersen's Fit–Cost–Value™ analysis*

we would say that adding value effectively to employees as stakeholders will in time yield a return on financial outcomes. Nevertheless, this must be the wrong starting place for a system of measurement for human capital. We do require diagnostic instruments, but they should be supporting our particular needs to provide added value to stakeholders. They should focus on measurable outcomes rather than on the mere existence of systems and processes.

STATISTICS, EFFICIENCY, AND RETURN ON INVESTMENT

Organizations will almost certainly want to report in some way on the breakdown of their workforce, looking at diversity statistics, qualifications, lengths of service, and so on. They will also have data on movements, such as attrition ratios and recruitment. How far they go in tracking productivity and the effectiveness of human resource functions and activities varies considerably.

Jac Fitz-Enz and The Saratoga Institute

In the middle of 1984 the Saratoga Institute, founded by Jac Fitz-Enz, assembled 15 HR professionals under the sponsorship of what is now the

Society for Human Resource Management, to develop a set of measures for the work of the HR function. It has since established itself as the leading authority on comparative measures in human resource management worldwide, with some 2,000 subscribers covering every kind of organization. It collects thousands of pieces of data regularly, by sector and company size, and subscribers can compare themselves with similar companies. This is a valuable service, provided that intelligence is used in interpretation and in knowing how the data is collected and appreciating any consequent limitations.

In 2000 Fitz-Enz published a comprehensive summary of people-related measures under the title of *The ROI of Human Capital: Measuring the Economic Value of Employee Performance*. He organizes the measures on three levels, all of which need to be integrated:

❏ The overall enterprise—the relationship between human capital and its contribution at the level of the whole enterprise.
❏ By process or function—leading to service, quality or productivity.
❏ The human capital itself—how it is managed.

The level of the enterprise

The most common comparative measure in use has been *revenue per employee*. FTE (full time equivalent) used to be calculated based only on employees, full and part time. However, in acknowledgment of today's flexible labor market, it now embraces all "contingent worker" contributions (American government statistics in 1998 estimated that 14 percent of the workforce was in the "contingent" category). The term now used by Saratoga is the *human capital revenue factor*.

Other ratios divided by FTEs that reflect the contribution of people include overall intellectual capital value (as calculated by subtracting net book value from market value), financial value added, and economic value added. These last two are calculated according to standard accounting formulae.

We outlined above the problems of measures that have "headcount" as a denominator; one head is not the same as another in contribution, nor in cost. This factor therefore differs widely between types of organization, depending on the makeup of their workforce and their geographical distribution (salaries vary widely between countries). Thus, we would much prefer to look at ratios where the denominator is the total cost of people remuneration, or compensation as it tends to be called in the US. One such is the *human capital return on investment*, which looks at the financial value added related to compensation costs. This is calculated as:

Revenue – (operating expenses less compensation) / compensation

At the overall enterprise level, Fitz-Enz also outlines various ratios that are useful for planning and costing. These are not linked to any output, and could be categorized as statistics. Examples are:

❑ Total employee costs per FTE
❑ Remuneration per FTE
❑ Percentage of specified types of employee
❑ Employee costs : contingent worker costs
❑ Training and development costs as a percentage of payroll costs
❑ Training days per FTE.

Statistics of workforce movement would include attrition rate and hiring rate.

Cultural and process norms are recognized as critical aspects of the working environment. Saratoga studied some 1,000 companies over four years in the 1990s and concluded that there were eight practices of exceptional companies to be tracked and measured: balanced values, commitment, culture, partnering, collaboration, innovation and risk, communication, and "competitive passion."

The level of the process or function
Fitz-Enz is here concerned with the human contribution to outputs such as service, quality, or productivity. He lists performance metrics for each typical organizational function, which enable change and improvement to be managed. In the terms we are using, this level is about the human contribution to increasing *structural* capital.

The level of the human capital itself

The focus here is not on measuring the value of human capital, as in Chapter 4 of this book, but on the effectiveness of six human resource management functions. These are planning, acquiring, maintaining, developing, retaining, and evaluating. According to Fitz-Enz, the middle four of these activities should be measured against the following:

❏ Costs—per unit of activity
❏ Time—elapsed per activity
❏ Quantity—numbers handled
❏ Error rates—percentage of "right first time"
❏ Reaction—levels of satisfaction.

These are mostly about the effectiveness and performance of HR professionals, and as such provide a useful framework.

ROI: Return on investment

Whereas Arthur Andersen's model described above recognizes that value is in the eye of the beholder, i.e., in their approach to employees, others put their focus on evaluating the financial return against the costs of a particular activity. Paul Kearns of Personnel Works in the UK is an ardent advocate of this concept, and has many fellow thinkers in the US. Kearns founded the Profitable Human Investment and Resource Management Network in 1991, which researches and promotes the link between every individual and financial organizational goals. His methodology is called Human Contribution Management, and he claims that its distinction is that it starts at the bottom line and works backwards. His exclusive focus on the financial bottom line, however, misses the value given to other stakeholders.

Various formulae have been put forward to measure return on investment. One such is from the Corporate Leadership Council in the US, as follows:

❏ Calculate all the costs of the intervention, including the time of specialists and participants

❑ Multiply the number of employees participating by:
—the percentage of the job related to performance changes
—the performance change (in standard deviations)
—the value of one standard deviation in performance
—the duration of performance gain in years
❑ Subtract the costs
❑ Divide the result by the costs to give return on investment.

Some of the factors here will be very difficult and time consuming to quantify. They also assume that financial benefit is the only goal, and that the resulting changes can be isolated to one cause, the intervention itself.

If we adopt the approach that value given to a stakeholder is a valid outcome in itself, we will not look immediately for purely financial measures from training and HR programs, even though we expect an eventual financial return in the long term. So, a program may be about better communications, or cultural change, or improved benefits to employees, where the financial benefit may be some way ahead. Too many other factors are likely to dilute any attempt at a direct link. In this area we need to distinguish between *validation*—did the intervention meet its objectives?—and *evaluation*—did it actually influence a key business measure? Often the first is difficult enough, especially if the objectives of the initiative are vague or unquantified.

Investment in personal development has a long-term return; graduate trainee programs and apprenticeships, for example. Computer company ICL (now part of Fujitsu) had a Eurograduate training program, hiring graduates from various European countries and training them together. Much of the 10 months' training took the form of work assignments, but these were essentially a vehicle for learning. The cost was about £30,000 per person. The return from this investment started after the first year but the long-term benefit—the creation of a group of cross-national friends who would use their network and cross-cultural experiences in leadership roles—was 10 years ahead. Sadly, 10 years on, only 15 percent of the graduates remained in the company. Many factors had led to this significant loss of human capital, but nobody was tracking the assets.

When we move outside of the simple arithmetic of a financial return, we are faced with the question of an *acceptable* level of added value. We do know the costs of the activities; we have to ask whether the outcome is justified by the cost. For example, for a program aimed at improving relationships with the community as a stakeholder, how much is a reasonable cost input for a measured change in image? One way to evaluate this is the cost of not doing the program or taking an initiative. Not investing in some environmental issues could have devastating future effects on image, cleanup costs, and lawsuits. Likewise, not providing opportunities for people to explore their career development could lead to frustration about personal development and consequent unwanted attrition.

INTEGRATING PEOPLE-RELATED MEASURES IN A PERFORMANCE MANAGEMENT FRAMEWORK

The Saratoga approach and others like it are closely linked to accountancy thinking, analyzing numbers and history. A better way is to start with the organization's goals, because all stakeholders contribute to value creation, and, without looking after them all, the ultimate goal of financial wealth will not be achieved. There are two main approaches in use, those based on a balanced set of measures that reflect the different stakeholders (scorecards), and those derived from the starting point of the organization's intellectual capital. The former looks for a relatively small number of key measures that are essential inputs to the strategic goals. The latter starts from human capital as a major component of intellectual capital, and asks how this can be effectively tracked and managed. It may yield a larger number of measures, but is much more closely aligned to our Human Capital Monitor.

The Balanced Scorecard

In 1992 Robert Kaplan, a Professor at Harvard, and David Norton, a consultancy CEO, wrote an article in the *Harvard Business Review* called "The Balanced Scorecard: Measures that Drive Performance." This was built on a research study exploring whether running companies on the basis of financial measures alone was becoming increasingly obsolete.

The scorecard sets out to balance four "perspectives":

❏ Financial—To succeed financially, how should we appear to shareholders?
❏ Customer—To achieve our vision, how should we appear to customers?
❏ Internal business process—To satisfy our shareholders and customers, at what business processes must we excel?
❏ Learning and growth—To achieve our vision, how will we sustain our ability to change and improve?

Kaplan and Norton distinguish between outcome measures (which they term "lag measures") and performance drivers (termed "lead measures"), and emphasize that a good scorecard should have a mixture of both. Although organizations may have hundreds of performance measures scattered through the various functions, they are frequently unconnected with the (usually) financial outcomes that govern decisions at the top level.

The Balanced Scorecard does not specifically focus on people—it is implicit that each of the four sets of outcomes are generated by them. However, some company applications have changed the name of the learning and growth perspective to "employees" or "people." Kaplan and Norton did include in this perspective two sets of people performance drivers, as follows.

Employee capabilities
In this area, three outcome measurements are identified as:

❏ Employee satisfaction
❏ Employee retention
❏ Employee productivity

and these are driven by the following enablers:

❏ Staff competences
❏ Technology infrastructure
❏ The climate for action.

Motivation, empowerment, and alignment

The outcome measures described here are:

❑   Measures of suggestions made and implemented
❑   Measures of improvement (in processes)
❑   Measures of organizational and individual alignment (this refers to individual and team goals being consistent with and supportive of the overall business goals).

In their book describing the concept and some applications, Kaplan and Norton say: "We can supply many fewer examples of company-specific measures for this perspective compared to the financial, customer and internal process perspectives." They comment rightly that this reflects a failing of companies to understand that all their strategies and goals are in the end dependent on people.

Mooraj and Oyon, at the University of Lausanne, combined with Hostettler of Tetra Pak to analyze the use of the balanced business score-card in an article "The balanced scorecard: A necessary good or an unnec-essary evil?" (1999). They were unreservedly positive, but made some interesting observations: For example, that national and organizational cultures have a big influence on both what is chosen and how effectively it is implemented. The approach sits comfortably with well-controlled, process-centered organizations. Many have found that, despite their com-pleting scorecards, the emphasis continues to be essentially financial unless the balance is reflected in managerial incentive plans.

The Skandia Navigator

Leif Edvinsson, for many years director of intellectual capital at Swedish financial services company Skandia, adapted the balanced scorecard to form the "Skandia Navigator." He placed "people" in the center as the dri-ver of all four outcomes and thus had five sets of measures. In his pas-sionate and highly readable book *Intellectual Capital*, he lists 32 measures for "Renewal and Development" and 23 for the "Human Focus". Figure 3.5 shows the concept and a few of the measures used in each category.

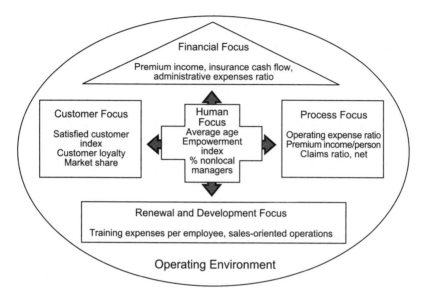

Figure 3.5 *The Skandia Navigator*

Skandia reported 119 percent increase in sales for the first quarter of 2000 with a doubling of its profits. It has transformed itself from being a traditional composite insurer to one focused on long-term savings products. Its shares rose 207 percent in value between April 1999 and April 2000.

Dave Ulrich and the HR Scorecard

Dave Ulrich of the University of Michigan has long been a champion of making HR activities measurable and closely linked to business results. In 2001 he published his *HR Scorecard*. Such an instrument, he says, enables two important things: "managing HR as a strategic asset" and "demonstrating HR's contribution to your firm's financial success." The scorecard has four components, designed to balance the twin HR imperatives of cost control and value creation:

❑   HR deliverables, such as talent, stability, optimal staffing levels—people-related outcomes necessary for business success

❑   High-performance work system—a set of systems and processes designed to achieve the deliverables

❑   Identifying HR system alignment—measures of how effective the systems are in practice

❑   HR efficiency measures—measures for the HR function in assessing its own productivity and efficiency.

The HR scorecard lists many possible measures; over 50 are suggested as possibles for HR efficiency alone. The danger of trying to be comprehensive for its own sake has to be avoided. We may be able to measure many things, but the checklist of good measures (page 44) must be taken into account.

The Intangible Assets Monitor

Karl-Erik Sveiby, one of the fathers of the intellectual capital movement, developed an intangible assets monitor for Swedish consultancy company Celemi. He took the three standard components of intellectual capital and chose measures for each under three headings, as in Figure 3.6.

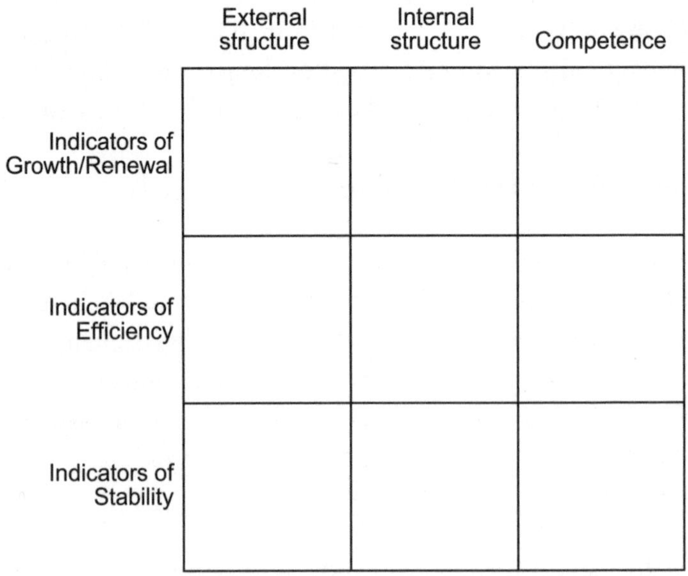

	External structure	Internal structure	Competence
Indicators of Growth/Renewal			
Indicators of Efficiency			
Indicators of Stability			

Figure 3.6 *Structure of the Intangible Assets Monitor*

Sveiby recommended having only one or two measures in each box. He uses the term "employee competence" for human capital, and he confines this to "professionals." This seems appropriate for totally knowledge-based companies like consultancies, but could overlook the very real added value provided by others. Under *competence* his measures include those shown in Figure 3.7.

Indicators of Growth/Renewal	Indicators of Efficiency	Indicators of Stability
• Numbers of years in the profession • Level of education • Training and education costs (including cost of time) • Grading • Competence turnover • Competence enhancing customers	• Proportion of professionals in the company • The leverage effect • Value added per professional	• Average age • Seniority • Relative pay position • Professional turnover rate

Figure 3.5 *Intangible Assets Monitor as used by Celemi*

Sveiby's *leverage effect* is a formula that looks at the effect of the firm's own professionals in generating revenue, in the context of all the human capital available. The formula goes as follows:

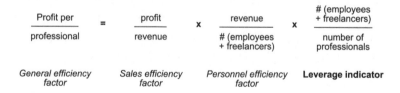

Under the "internal structure" category several measures relating to human capital are included:

❑ Proportion of support staff to total employees (efficiency)
❑ Sales per support person (efficiency)
❑ Values and attitudes (efficiency)
❑ Age of the organization (stability)
❑ Support staff turnover (stability)
❑ "Rookie ratio"—number of people with less than two years' employment (stability).

Sveiby compares the Balanced Scorecard with his Intangible Assets Monitor. He notes that there are clear similarities between the nonfinancial areas of focus and their links to the strategy of the firm. The two developed independently, but both recognize the importance of intangible assets.

However, Sveiby sees the Intangible Assets Monitor as based on the notion of people as an organization's *only* profit generators, and as assets because they drive revenue streams and hence value. Because the monitor focuses on intangible assets as "stocks" and the interactions between them as "flows," it relates more to traditional accounting theory for physical and financial assets. By contrast, the scorecard is an extended performance management system.

The Balanced Scorecard and its variations have revolutionized performance management in many organizations. However, two possible problems are:

❑   the constraints of the four specific perspectives
❑   the focus on balance in itself.

It may well be that a particular area deserves much more attention than others, and to "fill every box" for the sake of the model serves little purpose. However, devotees would argue that if the scorecard is derived systematically from the business strategy, this will not happen.

CHOOSING MEASURES FOR THE HUMAN CAPITAL MONITOR

An HR department exists to support the creation of value for all stakeholders, but especially the employees themselves who have chosen to invest their human capital with the organization. Like all functions, it should have its own measures of efficiency and process effectiveness. But its ultimate measure is the extent to which it builds quantified value.

The Human Capital Monitor, as we saw in Chapter 1, is designed to link the intrinsic worth of the human capital available with the work-

THE HUMAN CAPITAL MONITOR

PEOPLE AS ASSETS		PEOPLE MOTIVATION AND COMMITMENT		PEOPLE CONTRIBUTION TO ADDED VALUE
Human Asset Worth = employment costs x individual asset multiplier (IAM) / 1000 IAM = a function of • capability • potential • contribution • values alignment	**+**	Measures – How successful are we? **The work environment that drives success**	**=**	The value added to each stakeholder • financial • nonfinancial

Maximizing Human Capital
 	
• Acquisition | – How
• Retention | successful
• Growth | are we?
  – What drives
  success?
		• Leadership
		• Practical support
		• The workgroup
		• Learning and development
		• Rewards and recognition
				• current
				• future

Figure 3.7 *The Human Capital Monitor*

ing environment, which includes the systems and processes that guide and condition people's behavior and the value that people create. It is not specifically designed for the HR function to monitor itself, even though it would be used as the main measurement tool to guide the department's priorities and goals.

The first area of the monitor is the worth of people themselves, and it is recommended that the Human Asset Worth of *every* individual should be evaluated and monitored regularly.

When looking at measures of *contribution* and the *working environment*, a combination of the following is required:

❑ A set of high-level measures that reflect the prime needs of each stakeholder.
❑ A set of very specific or local measures that reflect the needs of business goals and strategies.

Both of these can be derived from using cause-and-effect staircases, as introduced in Chapter 1. The concept of the staircase is to identify the connecting steps that lead to an ultimate desired outcome, one step feeding into the other in a series of dependencies.

Let's look at an example that might come from a typical business. It starts with a business goal of "to increase the sales growth in Asia by 25 percent." There may be several inputs to this outcome, each with a different strength of influence or weighting. For example:

❑   Sales productivity (45 percent)
❑   New products and services, ready as promised (20 percent)
❑   Pricing strategy (15 percent)
❑   Marketing promotion (20 percent).

It makes sense to focus on the factor with the highest influence, although in some cases we might want to take two that are both significant. The staircase of dependencies will then be built up as in Figure 3.8.

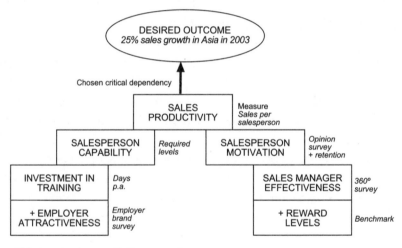

NB Each measure has a specified frequency and owner

Figure 3.8 *Example of dependencies for a business goal*

In addition to our key organizational strategies, we should draw up chains for each stakeholder, taking the two or three most critical areas of value added to each. Again, we may find several factors contributing to the desired outcome. In Figure 3.9 we have taken *customers*, and looked at the value added goal of on-time delivery.

Some of the input factors might be (with their weighted influence):

❏ Accuracy of sales estimating (20 percent)
❏ Manufacturing alignment with forecasts (20 percent)
❏ Logistics effectiveness (60 percent).

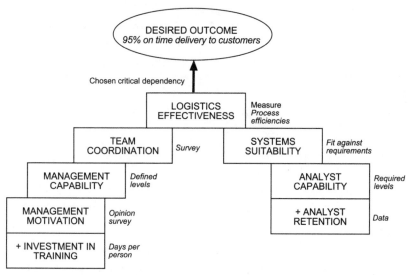

Figure 3.9 *Dependencies for generating on-time delivery to customers*

As we take each business goal and each stakeholder in turn, we will build up a set of indicators—owner by owner—to form the set that we will track and manage. Many of these will be valid for a long time, but they should be reviewed for relevance each time we replan.

PRESENTING THE DATA

Whereas the Human Capital Monitor is a comprehensive model for combining all the measures that apply to the management of human capital, we cannot present all the results on one slide. There are many techniques for presenting data, and it is helpful to combine a number of indicators to see where our positive and negative indicators lie. The matrix in Figure 3.10 relates "assets" and "liabilities" to "current" and "future" value. This in effect is a SWOT matrix, giving strengths, weaknesses, opportunities,

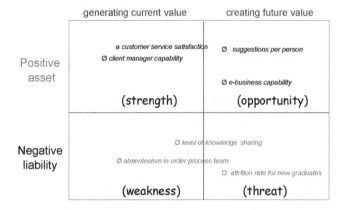

Figure 3.10 *Balance of factors influencing added value contribution*

and threats. It shows us clearly where we need to focus attention.

Another way to display the information is as in Figure 3.11. Several diagrams can be prepared for particular groups of measures. The perimeter represents the ideal or targeted state, and the scales should be fixed in such a way that the halfway point is the dividing line between "asset" and "liability."

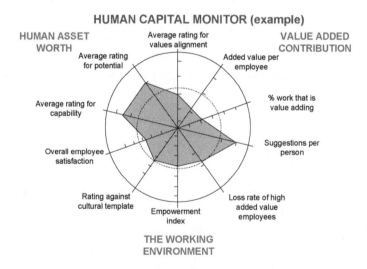

Figure 3.11 *Graphical display of Human Capital Monitor measures*

SUMMARY

Measures are essential to managing effectively; this is a fact of organizational life. Managers are overwhelmed with numbers already, and will resist yet more unless they see a clear purpose for them.

When it comes to human capital, we are dealing with a great deal of complexity. Choosing the right measures is one challenge, but the *process* of measurement also must have integrity. We believe that everything can be quantified, but some areas relating to human capital will be based on perceptions or how well a template fits reality. In these cases, the *relative* movement over time will be more important than an *absolute* measure. We also need to know whether an indicator is on the asset side of the intellectual capital balance sheet, or on the liability side. It will be the latter if it is below an acceptable target level, or is below a similar measure for a competitor.

A number of researchers and consultancy firms have been working to show that good people practices have a positive impact on the bottom line—and, indeed, on long-term shareholder value. Such studies invariably prove their point. Nevertheless, we would not start with the HR practices themselves, but with the requirements of the value to be delivered. "Practices" tend to be consistently applied across an organization. By focusing on the specifics that are key for each stakeholder and each business goal, we will be led by the business needs to what is essential for success. The use of cause-and-effect dependencies (depicted as staircases) will lead to focused measures for specific groups of people.

Somewhere in the history of studying the measurement of people almost all aspects have been considered. The greatest gap is in the area of understanding the intrinsic worth of individual human capital. The Human Capital Monitor combines this with more traditional measures to provide a fully coherent framework.

okay, but still not clear what this actually contributes

CHALLENGES FOR ACTION

❏ How many of the stumbling blocks to measurement can you identify in your own organization?

❏ What people-related measures are currently in use in your organization and where? How many fit the characteristics of a good measure? How many are useful in leading to action?

❏ Is there any attempt to have a more balanced approach to strategic performance management in your organization? If so, what measures are in use on the people side and how seriously are they taken?

❏ Are there important areas of human capital management that have no quantified measures in your organization?

❏ When you look at the added value that stakeholders demand, which areas have credible measures that are in use in the organization?

❏ If you draw out the cause-and-effect dependencies on key strategies, how many steps have or do not have related measures in your organization?

4

The Worth of People as Assets

THE HUMAN CAPITAL MONITOR STARTS WITH THE INTRINSIC WORTH OF people, since this is the "raw material" of the human contribution. There have been several attempts over the last 30 years to value people, going generally under the heading of human asset (or human resource) accounting. However, none of the methods proposed has become widely adopted. One has to conclude that attempts to use financial valuation methods in respect of people have too many pitfalls.

In this chapter a way of calculating the relative worth of people is proposed based on a combination of their costs (this being some indicator of their market value) and an "individual asset multiplier," looking at four aspects of personal human capital that bring value to an organization. Very few organizations at the time of writing have a systematic, integrated way of balancing the costs of their people with a measure of the value they are able to contribute, and this is the goal of this chapter.

> RESOURCING DECISIONS SHOULD BE MORE ABOUT VALUE THAN ABOUT COST.

Why should we bother to find a way to describe the asset value for people, individually and collectively, given the difficulties attached to such so-called assets? After all, many organizations have delivered increasing value over the decades without solving this dilemma—is it a real problem?

Years of growth and progress may yet hide a multitude of poor decisions that have subtracted potential value from stakeholders, including the owners and shareholders. Precious assets and knowledge may have been lost through restructuring. To manage effectively for value creation we need to:

❑   Be able to counter the one-sidedness of "people are costs" with "they also have worth as assets and they add value." It will always be necessary to adjust manpower levels, but resourcing decisions should be more about value than about cost

❑   Understand the *relative* value of individuals and teams, and make choices regarding who we must retain if at all possible. It is not just performance over one year that should shape our judgment; there is much more to our human capital than that

❑   Make informed and intelligent investment decisions, and understand the relative benefits of investing in people compared to other assets

❑   Most of all, "keep stock" of talent and expertise in a much more meaningful way than counting heads, and know whether the human capital available to us is increasing or decreasing. The management of talent has rightly become one of the great priorities in this era of managing intellectual capital.

Very few organizations can say that they know how to balance the expense of people with their respective value. They may have lists of people with potential, perhaps also of key players who make a special contribution. Most are conscious of their significant talent and where it resides. What is lacking is a systematic, rigorous approach to understanding the value of people.

CALCULATING THE ASSET WORTH OF PEOPLE

The problem of finding a satisfactory method of accounting for people has never been solved in a way that has led to its widespread use. In the context of society, the law places a value on lost lives and limbs, and this varies according to earning power and benefit to the family. Soccer clubs value players through transfer fees (for example, Real Madrid bought

Zinedine Zidane in July 2001 for a record £46 million), and increasingly firms pay "golden hellos" to secure individuals they really want. The amounts indicate that they are valued assets, but they are not calculated in any formal way, being the result of negotiation.

Analysts and investors are conscious of the value of businesspeople who have a public profile. Readers of daily stock market reports will frequently see a price rise or fall if a key player joins or departs—not quite the same as football transfer fees, but the principle is the same. When Robert Ayling left British Airways in 2000, the company's share price went up; fairly or unfairly, the perception was that he had become bad for the airline despite his tough stance on cost cutting. More commonly we see the opposite. A typical headline found in the *Financial Times* read "MOL shares plummet after chief resigns." Hungary's biggest company, in oil and gas, lost its chief executive after a dispute with the government. The shares fell by 10 percent and had to be suspended.

Human resource accounting

The father of this niche of study is Professor Eric Flamholz, Professor of Management at the Anderson Graduate School of Management at the University of California. He has worked for 25 years in the field and published many articles, as well as the definitive work, *Human Resource Accounting*. Flamholz's methods and formulae have not been taken up widely in practice. This may be for the following reasons:

❏   There has been very little pressure, either from accountants or from elsewhere (including statutory bodies), to look at people in any way other than as costs

❏   HR people generally prefer to work with "softer" issues

❏   Applying many of his concepts introduces a level of complication beyond the patience of many practitioners

❏   The method relies on predictions and probabilities about the future that are increasingly difficult to make.

Interest in human resource accounting blossomed in the early 1970s, when several committees were set up by accounting bodies on the subject. However, it has waned since then, and was overtaken in the 1990s by some of the other approaches outlined in Chapter 3.

The economic concept of value has two dimensions, usefulness (or utility—value to the owner) and exchange (value to another owner). Flamholz suggests that there are three criteria for defining any asset:

❑ It possesses future service potential
❑ It is measurable in monetary terms
❑ It is subject to the ownership and control of the firm, or it is rented or leased.

When it comes to valuing assets, there are three traditional ways:

❑ Cost based—this method typically looks at acquisition or replacement cost
❑ Market based—the price to be paid in an open market
❑ Income based—the cash streams to be expected into the organization related to the contribution of the human asset, calculated as the present value of the expected net cash flows.

Cost based

There are variations of this approach. One method looks at all the costs of *acquiring* a human asset—recruiting, selecting, hiring, training—and amortizes the total over the expected future service of the person. The full replacement cost includes the actual costs of replacement itself, which can be substantial, plus the loss of contribution while a new person is being retrained up to the same level. A host of problems arise with this: It denies the impact of personal experience and development, and implies that value and contribution will be directly related to recruitment cost alone.

Another very simple way is to take an individual's gross remuneration. This includes salary and related benefits, and should also include taxes on employers such as social security, which vary considerably from country to country. Variable bonuses based on performance should not be included as they do not reflect the basic value of the individual. The only exception to this might be positions where the mix of fixed and variable pay is designed to provide a certain figure for on-target earnings, in which case we would use this instead of salary. This method is really equating value with cost, and does not add much in relation to our purpose.

A variation proposed by Lev and Schwartz (1971) is to use discounted future remuneration levels. This is more of a traditional asset valuation approach, and has all the problems of predicting future earnings and choosing a discount rate, as well as assumptions about the length of careers. Also, being cost based, it makes the assumption that cost and value are closely related. In its intellectual capital report for 1998, Skandia calculated this and called it the "human capital base value," using five years and 20 percent discount. It rose from SEK9 billion in 1995 through 10.6 billion in 1996 to 12.7 in 1998. Lev's methodology has not generally been taken up by US companies, but has been adopted by several Indian companies, such as Infosys. Its annual report for 1997 showed its 1,700 employees broken down into production, technical support, and others, and calculates the human asset value for each group. The value of the total human resources in 1997 is quoted as R278.56 lakhs against costs of R51.63 lakhs and added value of R99.41 lakhs. The ratios are interesting, the value calculation being more than five times costs.

Market based

Every employee has a figure in their mind of their own market value, which often represents a bigger job than they currently hold, believing that they could successfully apply for such. Although remuneration specialists try to assess market rates for a particular role, a job-based approach does not take account of the variable value of individuals. It does provide a broad guide to what one might have to pay for a role through recruitment. Another way to look at this is the cost of buying the capability and experience through interim management or consultancy. However, such costs vary with the supplying organization, depending on its reputation and overheads. The rates are always higher than would be paid for a fully contracted employee, because the flexibility of the variable resource has a value in itself.

Market value would be a good base to take for our purpose. In practice, however, it is a difficult and time-consuming exercise to assess this with any realism for every individual.

Income based

Instead of seeing value as closely tied to costs, this method looks at the money that a person might bring into the organization. This is the closest to accepted valuation techniques. Unfortunately, it is particularly difficult to apply to most employees, except in certain roles; consultants or salespeople, for example. In a consultancy, one might choose to take the discounted expected revenue streams for, say, five years ahead as the base of an individual's asset value.

A time has to be chosen for the expected future life of the person and this will significantly affect any numeric answer, because, needless to say, it is difficult to predict. Many of the models in the literature assume a relatively steady state of employment, which has been largely replaced.

The method takes no account of value added other than financial.

Flamholz's approach

Flamholz asserts that the aim of human resource management is to optimize human resource value. He defines the measure of individual value as resulting from two interacting variables: a person's *conditional value* and the *probability* that they will stay with the organization. An individual's conditional value is the present worth of the potential services that could be rendered if they stay with the organization for x years. The conditional value is a combination of productivity (performance), transferability (flexible skills), and promotability. The latter two are heavily influenced by the first element. This is then multiplied by a probability factor that the individual will stay for the x years. This gives the expected realizable value, which is a measure of the person's worth.

Flamholz extends the principle to evaluating the effectiveness of development programs. If a program produces a measured change in productivity, transferability, or promotability, this translates into an increase in the value of the individuals concerned.

There are a number of difficulties with this approach, not least of which is the estimation of potential future services. It also leads to lower values for older and more experienced people who have less time to render future services. There is a case for looking at them this way if we consider value over a future lifetime, but it fails to take account of the wealth of value in past experience.

Walgemoed

Walgemoed is a management consultancy in the Netherlands. In 1999 it was commissioned along with three other major consultancies by the Dutch Ministry of Economic Affairs to examine "Balancing Accounts with Knowledge." Each consultancy analyzed a small number of companies and reported on how it believed intangible assets should be evaluated. The initiative was prompted by a previous 1996 study showing that over 50 percent of national investment in the country was intangible. Of the four companies, only Walgemoed made a concerted attempt to look at the valuation of human resources.

It first analyzed the costs of recruitment, replacement, training, and so on and proposed allocating them to individual balance sheets. It acknowledged that these "input costs" say little about the ability of people to generate value for the company, and suggested that the input costs should be compared with the income generated by the individual as a personal "profit and loss account," although this is clearly not possible for every person.

After discussing the difficulties of individual financial evaluation, Walgemoed finally suggested a points system based on the importance of the role performed, qualifications, experience, and age.

Giles and Robinson

Giles and Robinson (1972) also came to the conclusion that a points system was needed. They developed a factor called the Human Asset Multiplier, which is applied to gross remuneration. An average multiplier is derived from a financial formula based on the market value of the organization. This is then weighted for different categories of employees, by assessing their personal value using a weighting that reflects qualifications/expertise, experience, attitudes, promotion capability, loyalty, replacement scarcity, and an estimate of expected future service.

We can conclude that, whereas it would be neat if we could have a realistic, generally accepted, absolute financial formula, this is unlikely to be achieved. There are very real problems in following definitions and methods that fit the principles of economics in valuation. Furthermore, the variables to be considered are very complex, and the uncertainty of future predictions immense. We should end up with formulae so complicated that they would be unusable—and to some extent this is what has happened to human resource accounting as a discipline. It has rested largely with the academics.

Our conclusions are allied to those of Walgemoed and Giles/Robinson; that is, that there are characteristics of people that enable value to be delivered to stakeholders. What we need is to identify those characteristics, and then find ways of measuring and tracking them. We want at least to start the search for a relative asset value, even if an absolute financial value is beyond us.

HUMAN ASSET WORTH: A PRACTICAL FORMULA

What is it that makes one person more valuable than another? The answer is very organization specific. For some, it is finding people who will fit in well and make good team members. For others, the ability to get certain kinds of results is all that matters. So any approach has to have some flexibility to meet different situations.

The formula suggested in the Human Capital Monitor for calculating Human Asset Worth is as follows:

$$HAW = EC \times IAM \ / \ 1,000$$
(Human Asset Worth = Employment Cost × Individual Asset Multiplier / 1,000)

We divide by 1,000 so that the end result will not look like a monetary amount that can be directly compared with cost, as this would be misleading. The purpose is to be able to understand *relativities* and provide a guide to taking appropriate actions.

Although one might naturally start with a person's market value, as we saw above this is hard to ascertain and is not going to be readily at hand. What we do know is people's remuneration and we keep close track of this. It may well reflect accidents of history (either positive or negative) and be under- or over-rated in respect of the market, but it provides the best starting point.

EC—Employment Cost

This is the cost of employing a person, including taxes such as social security or national insurance, and the value of the benefits package. It should exclude bonuses unless they are in whole or part guaranteed. It also does not include the overheads of providing space and equipment, as these are so variable and are likely to be averaged out on a per person basis.

Employment Cost =
Base salary + value of benefits + employer taxes

IAM—Individual Asset Multiplier

Every person is an individual, not just another "head." They bring a different level of present and potential value to their current role and to the organization. The Individual Asset Multiplier is designed to reflect this.

Some people we are happy to lose. There is a replacement cost, but no real asset loss. What factors make the difference? There are four that predominate and determine the worth of an individual to us, as follows:

Individual Asset Multiplier
Weighted Average assessment of:
Capability—the cumulative skills, knowledge, experience, and useful networks
Potential—to grow and contribute at a higher level
Contribution—to stakeholder value
Alignment—to organizational values

Capability and potential are discussed in more detail in Chapter 5. To calculate the IAM, each of these factors is assessed on a scale of 0.1 to 2.0.

Personal capability profile: breadth and depth of experience, personal skills, technical and professional know-how, personal network

The value of an individual is in *all* their cumulative knowledge, skills, experience, and their relevant network of contacts. It is more than whether they have what is required by their current role. Their breadth is a measure of their flexibility for deployment in different roles—and this makes them more valuable. Whereas it is difficult to encapsulate this in numbers, it should be relatively easy to make judgments, as follows:

0.5 Has some noticeable deficiencies compared to expectations for this role

1.0 Generally has the balance of capability expected for this role

1.5 In several areas exceeds the level needed for the role; has unique knowledge and experience, and capability that can be applied in various other roles

2.0 Has considerable breadth and depth beyond the basic needs of the role; known for unique expertise or has a range of capabilities that can be applied very flexibly

Potential to grow

An individual invests their human capital with an organization with the expectation that they will grow and progress. The organization also wants to maintain continuity and provide ongoing succession, as well as build its expertise. The potential to grow beyond the present role is a source of value in itself. It could be for managerial positions, or for growth in any area that is strategically important.

The scale for this factor would be as follows:

0.5 Probably overpromoted at current level

1.0 Expected at the very least to grow within the role, or to stay up to date with a specialism, or to move laterally to different roles

1.5 Able to grow to at least one higher level of responsibility, or to one or two further levels of specialist depth

2.0 Considered high potential for management positions or technical/professional leadership

Q: why .5 - 2? (impact of this?)
-1 - no effect

3) *Personal contribution to stakeholder value*

It would solve many problems if we could quantify the financial added-value contribution that each person makes—this in itself would be a better basis for asset value than the remuneration figure. However, it is not possible. Nevertheless, we need to reflect the fact that individuals add different amounts of value to stakeholders. This is due partly to the opportunities presented by their role, and partly to their personal performance. This factor should be based on specific measures of value added, not on competences or performance measures (such as achieving milestones) that a stakeholder cannot see. Chapter 9 discusses this in more detail. (third column)

The evaluation scale for this factor is suggested as follows:

0.5   Makes some measurable contribution to nonfinancial measures
1.0   Makes an average level of contribution to either a financial or a nonfinancial measure, or a combination
1.5   Makes an above-average contribution to either a financial or a non-financial measure, or a combination, with a significant proportion being aimed at future value creation
2.0   Contributes considerably more to both financial and nonfinancial value measures than the average employee, with the majority aimed at future value creation

4) *Alignment to values*

We are using "values" in the sense of the philosophy or ethos of the organization, which may be expressed formally in written (or espoused) form, or in an accepted unwritten understanding. In some organizations, but not all, this would be a key factor. Managers make judgments about "chemistry" and "fit" when they hire people. Good-performing, capable people who comfortably align themselves to our values have particular worth. They become "part of us" and are likely to be loyal to the organization.

0.5   Shows little alignment to corporate values
1.0   Behavior does not explicitly conflict with values
1.5   Makes considerable effort to live as many of the values as possible
2.0   Known throughout as a role model for the organization's values

Weighting   *(good)*

These four factors should be assigned a percentage importance out of 100, i.e., if all were equal, we would assign 25 percent to each. In some companies, and for some groups of people, potential may be deemed less important. Companies with powerful, well-established cultures may find it hard to acquire people who are firmly aligned to their values and therefore put more emphasis on this area. In some, getting results is so dominant that it outweighs all others. In a highly technical organization, capability—especially technical knowledge—may be given the greatest weight.

Examples of calculating Human Asset Worth

Harriet Smith is a purchasing manager. Her total remuneration package is £60,000 per annum, made up of £45,000 plus benefits of £15,000; social security costs average 9 percent of the combination of salary and benefits.

We thus calculate EC as $(45,000 + 15,000) / 1,000 \times 1.09 = 65.4$.

Harriet is an excellent performer with 10 years' experience of the business she is in. She consistently exceeds money-saving targets and at the same time maintains and builds sound supplier relationships. She does not have the potential to rise another level in the organization, but is expected to continue to deepen her expertise in her specialist area. She makes considerable effort to live the values of the company.

The relative importance of the four factors for her organization is shown below. Results are deemed more important than working with common values; lateral flexibility and adaptability more than potential for growth.

Harriet's Individual Asset Multiplier is calculated as follows:

Component	Factor value	Weighting	Weighted value
Capability	1.5	0.30	0.450
Contribution	1.7	0.35	0.595
Potential:	1.0	0.20	0.200
Values alignment	1.5	0.15	0.225
Individual asset multiplier			**1.470**

Harriet's HAW is therefore $65.4 \times 1.470 = 96.1$.

Gerry McDougall is the customer service representative for West Scotland with an engineering firm. His total remuneration package is £35,000 per annum, made up of £28,000 plus benefits of £7,000; social security costs average 9 percent.

We thus calculate the EC as $(28,000 + 7,000) / 1000 \times 1.09 = 38.15$.

Gerry is a role model of what the organization aspires to be and has very high customer loyalty. He has no potential to grow further in the organization and his knowledge and skills are very much aligned to the role he has had for many years. He could take another region, but much of his value is in his natural empathy with his own compatriots.

Gerry's Individual Asset Multiplier is calculated as follows:

Component	Factor value	Weighting	Weighted value
Capability	1.0	0.15	0.150
Contribution	1.9	0.40	0.760
Potential	1.0	0.15	0.150
Values alignment	2.0	0.30	0.600
Individual asset multiplier			**1.660**

Gerry's HAW is therefore $38.15 \times 1.660 = 63.33$.

The IAM is a valuable metric in its own right. These two examples show how a salary gap in cost can be narrowed in value terms when other factors are taken into account.

Many organizations will not have all the information for the four factors; however, it would be hard to argue that they are not important. Is it necessary and practical to have these indicators for every employee? We should focus our attention primarily on those individuals and groups who form part of our strategic cause-and-effect dependencies. However, nobody queries the need to regularly value a physical asset that appears on the capital register, which begs the question of why we would not want to know the worth of our more important human assets.

> THE COMPONENTS OF THE INDIVIDUAL ASSET MULTIPLIER ARE UNQUESTIONABLY AS IMPORTANT AS A PERSON'S JOB GRADE OR BENEFIT COSTS.

It is likely that some form of performance ratings may exist, and there will be potential evaluations for some people but not all. A holistic evaluation of total capability will be rare, as will any systematic approach to values alignment. These are challenges to be grasped.

Jobs become redundant, through restructuring or technical progress. We could say they fall out of any value-creating chain. So many good individuals have been lost to organizations because their *role* is no longer needed. A value-creating organization would see the value primarily in the person rather than in the role, hence the importance of the factors we have suggested. Although costs may well need to be reduced, understanding the relative value of people enables more intelligent decisions to be made.

COLLECTIVE HUMAN ASSET WORTH

The purpose of an organization is to organize the human capital of individuals in ways that produce more than they would as individual contributors. A team should be more than the sum of the individuals that make it up. When we look at the working environment, *workgroup effectiveness* is picked out as one of the contributing factors to value-adding contribution. But for the purposes of asset value comparisons, we can look at teams by combining the Human Asset Worth of all the members. If we have evaluated each individual in the way suggested, we have the basis for some important analysis of our human capital. For example:

❑   *The relative value of teams and departments*. Our efforts on the retention of talent can be focused through seeing the relative value of different groups of people. This value may then be compared with the contribution that the group is making—and, indeed, their costs. Arguably, there should be a more or less linear relationship between "asset value" and "value added" for most groups.

❑   *The distribution of potential*. We can get an understanding of how potential is distributed and where we may have continuity problems.

❑   *The extent of values alignment*. We can look at the factors that have been judged and get a feel of how values alignment is distributed, in functions and in areas. This may lead to some action to shift the culture more toward the espoused values.

❑ *The flexibility of our workforce.* The higher the average factor for "capability," the more flexible our people are. In times of restructuring this may save unnecessary redundancies and it also gives us more options in career management.

IS ALL OUR HUMAN CAPITAL INSIDE?

Should we assume that our human capital is only those people with an exclusive contract to us, those we would regard as employees? Boundaries are breaking down in many ways: Previous competitors collaborate, customers and suppliers interact electronically and share knowledge databases, and individuals work for a variety of organizations. Former employee departments become outsourced suppliers. Are they still part of our human capital? Or is our asset value confined to the management activity of them as a supplier?

Exclusivity is not a satisfactory criterion, since consultants and associates may be able to add significant value to stakeholders through their capability, and still apply themselves uniquely and confidentially to the organization just as if they worked for it. Their services have a cost, as do employees; the main difference is the continuity of their contribution and the tenure of their services.

The HAW formula cannot be applied in the same way for non-employees. It is better to see them as service providers, as suppliers of temporary human capital, in the way that a bank loan provides temporary financial capital. They are certainly stakeholders in their own right, even though their input may or may not be adding value to others. Consultants advising on restructuring, for example, are probably not adding value to any other stakeholder, even though the cost may be felt necessary. A contractor on a customer project hopefully will be adding value. It is important to be clear about what each subcontracted human cost is contributing.

SUMMARY

This chapter studied the intrinsic worth of people as assets. People bring their own "human capital" to an employer, and that employer has the opportunity to develop it for mutual benefit. In a value-creating organization, it is vital to have some way of systematically distinguishing the worth of each individual, and also of teams.

Attempts at human resource accounting, which began in the 1970s, have not been widely taken up. This has happened for various reasons, but mainly because accounting rules cannot be rigorously applied to people, especially in turbulent times. We concluded that any indicator should not pretend to be financial, and has to be based on some factors that can be rated. *(interesting after Coens + Jenkins)*

We recommended the measure Human Asset Worth, a combination of employment cost and an Individual Asset Multiplier. The latter reflects the distinctive value a person brings to the organization, a combination of capability, potential, performance, and their alignment to organizational values. These factors need not have the same weighting—what brings value to a particular organization must be assessed. Although there are sound arguments for calculating and monitoring the Individual Asset Multiplier for every employee, in practice our attention will go first to those individuals and groups who feature in the vital links leading to achievement of business results and key added value to stakeholders.

This formula enables a great deal of helpful analysis to take place. We can not only distinguish between individuals but also look at teams. We can monitor the "health" of teams, particularly those in the front line of strategy. It enables us to manage our stock of human capital, whether generally or for specific groups, and has particular application in managing mergers and acquisitions.

CHALLENGES FOR ACTION

❏ What information do you currently have that relates to the value of the individuals in your organization? How would you practically set up a system to maintain the data for each component in the IAM?

❏ If you were to employ the four suggested components of the IAM, what weighting would you give them?

❏ Why not try out the HAW approach on two or three groups in your organization and see how useful it could be to you in managing the human capital concerned?

very interesting questions!
(would be good to try)

5

(first two factors in IAM)

Capability and Potential

WHAT AN INDIVIDUAL BRINGS THROUGH THE DOOR OF AN organization is essentially their accumulated capability, and their potential to grow, given the right nurturing and opportunities. These two components—capability and potential—must be understood, regularly assessed, and updated.

The systems generally in use for measuring levels of capability are far from consistent, however, and often not very comprehensive. This is an area that deserves more attention, since a sound framework for describing capability provides a vital bridge between people and job roles. Capability encompasses the strengths a person has at a given point in time and it has six components. This chapter looks at these and how they can be measured and assessed. We also discuss how the potential for growth is described and evaluated, and consider the question of openness.

CAPABILITY AS PERSONAL CAPITAL

"CAPABILITY" MEANS ALL THAT A PERSON BRINGS THAT ENABLES THEM TO ACHIEVE BOTH THEIR GOALS AND THOSE OF THE ORGANIZATION. IT IS SUCH AN IMPORTANT INPUT TO THE PROCESS OF ADDING VALUE THAT IT REQUIRES SERIOUS ANALYSIS AND MEASUREMENT.

Capability is the essence of an individual's *personal* assets—their own human capital. It is that which they can hire out or sell to an employer, or capitalize on through self-employment. It is more than competency, which has come to refer very much to personal traits and attitudes.

The focus in this chapter is very much on people's strengths. Of course, everybody has weaker areas, and some of these can be corrected or developed. Rarely, one weakness can be so critical, or the sum of the strengths so small, that we might have to acknowledge that a particular person is more of a liability than an asset. Appropriate action then needs to be taken. But in the main, working with people's strengths is the way to grow them.

Six components of capability

Many frameworks that concentrate on competences combine everything a person knows about the business into one competence called "business awareness" or "technical knowledge." The test of any framework must be its perceived usefulness in the eyes of managers and employees. In interviewing, managers generally are at least equally concerned about what and who a person knows, and what experience they have, as they are about personal behaviors.

A framework for understanding and measuring *capability* is the most fundamental tool we can have in facilitating all those processes that require comparison between a person and a job profile. These include:

❑ *Performance appraisal*: How does the person match the requirements of the current role?
❑ *Recruitment and selection*: How does the candidate match the specification of a prospective job?
❑ *Career planning and potential assessment*: How does the individual match the profile of a different job in the future?

All this comes together in:

❑ *Development planning*: In which areas and to what levels do we plan to increase a person's capability?

To make such a framework useful, we must have a systematic way to describe distinctive levels—What is high and what is low? What is needed and is it enough?

There are six components of a person's capability, encapsulated in Figure 5.1. The three circles of *personal behaviors*, business and profes-

THE HUMAN CAPITAL MONITOR

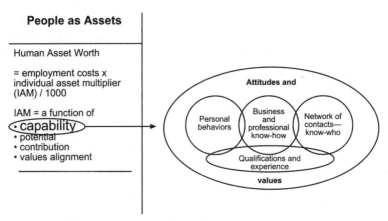

Figure 5.1 *The components of capability*

sional *know-how*, and their network of contacts or *know-who* are the core, and they are developed primarily through *experience*. Know-how can also be developed through systematic study or *qualifications*. The way in which the core is demonstrated is then conditioned by the *attitudes and values* that the person holds—these being the most difficult to change.

Personal Behaviors

This area covers personal traits, attitudes, and behaviors that are demanded by a role, or that generally characterize "high performance." They are undoubtedly important and very individual.

In many job roles, aspects of personal behavior can be extremely pertinent to the likelihood of success. As one goes up the management ladder, these behaviors gain increasing importance and can outweigh the technical knowledge that might have been more important in junior jobs.

Nevertheless, this aspect needs to be kept in proportion when thinking about a person's value. Paul Dobson of City University Business School in the UK argued this persuasively:

❑ *Personal competencies alone are unlikely to deliver superior performance outcomes. This is because of the influence of the environ-*

ment in which people work, and the fact that they are only one component of capability.

❏ *There are severe limitations in the way that competencies are chosen, validated and assessed, and they lack the flexibility needed to cope with change and diversity.*

❏ *Results can be achieved successfully in many different ways. Moreover each area of adding value demands its own set of behaviours for success.*

Measurement

The concept of "universal competences for all" conflicts with the knowledge that men and women achieve results in different ways, and that different national cultures have effective leaders with their own distinctive approaches. Also, requirements and priorities change with time, so companies are finding that competency frameworks are out of date three to four years after they are developed. Instead, many organizations find creating a dictionary helpful. This lists the range of behaviors that have importance in the organization in different roles and at different levels, from which those that are important for a specific role can be selected. A dictionary can be added to, and enables each role to be specifically described according to the critical attributes.

Figure 5.2 overleaf shows a three-level approach that would be applied to each "job family" in an organization. The center has a small number of core behaviors that reflect the common values of the organization. These are a passport to entry for all and a condition of retention. They relate directly to the Individual Asset Multiplier component of "values alignment." Then, each "job family" has its distinctive set of personal and know-how components.

Most organizations do not have more than six to eight distinctive job families. For example, a large software company identified the following:

❏   Business leaders
❏   People managers
❏   Technical specialists

❑   Market development
❑   Professional and administration support
❑   Customer support.

Finally, within a job family are specific roles where some additional specialized capabilities may need to be added.

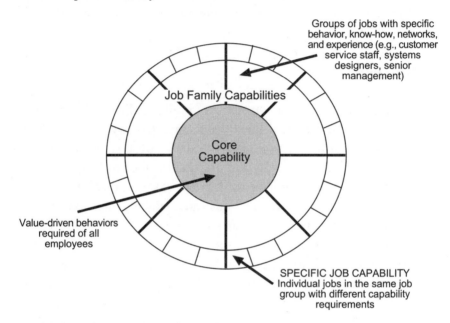

Figure 5.2 *Modeling capability*

The same software firm identified five core capabilities, which would be typical of many other organizations. They were:

❑   Customer orientation
❑   Teamwork
❑   Change orientation
❑   Integrity
❑   Business orientation.

Personal behaviors are described in different ways. Here are some examples:

A description of behaviors represented by the capability

Enabling change:

❏ *encouraging an environment where continuous improvement is seen as an integral part of everyone's responsibility*

❏ *personally demonstrating and visibly rewarding creativity, innovation, and willingness to question what is current*

❏ *recognizing and addressing the effects of change on people and working to maintain their commitment, motivation, and performance in a practical and compassionate manner.*

A description of positive and negative behaviors

Teamwork

Seeking and fostering opportunities for synergy and cooperation between the different parts of the company.

+ *think company, multicultural, and multinational*
+ *celebrate success with all functions involved*
+ *seek to improve own ideas by discussing with other teams before implementation*
– *think internal company, own country, own culture*
– *celebrate success only with own immediate team*
– *deliver own ideas without seeking improvements from others*

Hierarchical levels of expectation of the behavior

Delegation

Level 1: Allocates staff according to their strengths in order to achieve objectives

Level 2: Gains agreement on the delegation of tasks by negotiating with subordinates

Level 3: Delegates projects or major responsibilities that challenge and develop people

Level 4: Allows subordinates freedom to set their own targets and priorities.

This example was designed to illustrate expectations from junior manager through to executive.

Levels of demonstration of the behavior, not linked hierarchically

This example shows increasing breadth and depth of creative and conceptual thinking.

Creative and conceptual thinking

Involves generating ideas and recognizing innovative solutions to business problems. The ability to identify patterns or connections between situations is not obviously related.

Thinks "within a box"
❑ *finding limited solutions to problems*
❑ *fails to identify the links between pieces of data*
❑ *is not open to ideas*

Shapes ideas
❑ *assesses and adapts ideas by putting them in the context of their own work*
❑ *is open to ideas*
❑ *sees possibilities to shape ideas to suit a range of applications*

Constructively challenges the status quo
❑ *spots links and connections*
❑ *questions self and others to see if there is a better way to do things*
❑ *identifies where things could be improved by doing them differently*

Sees and clarifies the bigger picture
❑ *connects ideas together that are not obviously related*
❑ *creates frameworks to make sense of ambiguous or unfamiliar issues*
❑ *thinks "outside the box"*
❑ *makes complex ideas clear and understandable*

Creates new ideas for the business
❑ *develops and evaluates ideas that represent new ways of thinking*
❑ *improves performance by doing things that are leading edge*
❑ *radically rethinks traditional ways of doing things*
❑ *creates an environment for others to generate new ideas*

The preferred approach to describing behaviors is to provide a series of specific examples that typify the behaviors at all levels and against which people can be assessed for their strength and consistency.

Often, data from 360° surveys is averaged so that individuals can match themselves against a mean for their organization, or even a more general population. Summaries provide a means of understanding collectively the strengths and weaknesses of teams, and particularly those behaviours that are "mission critical" in respect of business goals.

TECHNICAL, PROFESSIONAL, AND BUSINESS KNOW-HOW

The most important aspect of capability is the core business, technical, and professional know-how that brings value to the organization's customers in new products, services, and processes. Knowledge is knowing and understanding what has to be done; skills are actually being able to *apply* the knowledge. At management levels, the business know-how overtakes the professional and technical in importance.

This is a complex and wide-ranging area, and can be broken down by job families or functions in line with Figure 5.2. Components can be defined in a general dictionary similar to that referred to earlier, although it is probably more useful to draw up lists function by function. Here is an extract from an international beverage company's list for its marketing function:

❏ *Advertising development and execution—Providing creative direction to develop copy strategy that builds brand equity, testing it and ensuring its correct execution*
❏ *Agency management—Effectively managing all aspects of the relationship (including budget and performance) with all third-party agencies*
❏ *Consumer/trade protection—Determining the need, objectives, and actions for both consumer and customer promotions, identifying target groups and developing programs to achieve specific targets*
❏ *Media execution—Determining media objectives and strategies, identifying target groups and managing the execution of media elements*

❏ *Packaging/product development and execution—Identifying packaging and product opportunities across consumers, customers, and channels. Providing direction and insight to package and product developers. Understanding, testing, and leveraging research.*

How does one rate the breadth and depth of these areas of know-how? A helpful and simple approach is to make a judgment on the following five-point scale for a defined field of knowledge or skill:

A = Aware—Can speak the language; knows what is involved
B = Basic—Has a rudimentary knowledge of the field
C = Competent—Is able to discuss and work competently
D = Distinguished—Is one to whom work colleagues turn for advice
E = Expert—Is known within and beyond the organization for his/her expertise

International electronics company Philips uses a variation of this scale. Its four levels are:

I   Foundation
II   Practitioner
III   Expert
IV   Leader

This extends the technical knowledge into the know-how of leading others in the domain that applies the technology.

Managers and employees find these simple scales quite an easy way to make an evaluation of proficiency, and to reach agreement about the results.

A number of options present themselves for tracking measures and ratios. For strategically important skills, for example, we can choose from:

❏   The number of people with D or E levels
❏   The proportion of people with D or E levels
❏   The percentage achievement of a targeted level for D or E levels
❏   The percentage profile of each level.

One particularly valuable analysis of our human asset value is in the strength of our capability in core areas; that is, those that are directly linked to the nature of our organization's business, to strategic business goals, or to the most important added-value areas to stakeholders.

Mapping know-how

We can map the know-how of the whole organization, or of teams and work groups. Each key knowledge and skill area is taken and the entry level (A–E) defined at that needed to be selected for the position. Then we can specify the level that would be expected after completing the learning curve and reaching some maturity in the role. Each person can be plotted at various times to identify where development needs exist, or where specialist expertise can be found. A good database of this kind will enable vital planning to take place.

Figure 5.3 shows a simple way of looking at the profile of each individual and of the team as a whole.

KNOWLEDGE OR SKILL	Entry level	Fully competent level	Person 1	Person 2	Person 3	Person 4
Product knowledge and demonstrations	A	C	D	B	C	C
Operation of discount/promotion schemes	A	C	C	C	C	B
Operation of guarantee and service	A	C	C	C	C	C
Sourcing of items	A	D	C	D	C	B
IT systems	B	C	C	D	C	C
Team cooperation	C	C	B	D	C	C
Personal customer delight skills	B	D	C	D	B	C

Figure 5.3 *Team capability profiles—example for retail shop staff*

Training events can be aimed at one of the levels, so that people can be helped in planning their development.

EDUCATIONAL LEVEL AND PROFESSIONAL QUALIFICATIONS

Qualifications tend to be downplayed in the UK, but they have greater importance in the US and many European countries where studies can be much longer and more focused. They represent a standard that has been reached that gives confidence to an employer or a customer. If I have a Master's degree in a specialist subject, it will be assumed that I know a great deal about that subject unless proved otherwise. A professional qualification may be necessary to give me a license to practice, as well as encouraging people to deal with me. In many countries there are occupational qualifications, such as the vast array of National Vocational Qualifications in the UK. These always include aspects of technical know-how referred to above.

For some organizations, or parts of organizations, qualifications may have special importance. In an R&D environment, the percentage of people with higher degrees may be a critical measure and a benchmark against competition; in finance, the percentage who are fully qualified is a measure of departmental strength.

Measurement

Measurement here is simple. It will be based on the number with—as opposed to the number without—a certain level of qualification. This can be expressed as an absolute number or as a percentage of a population.

Thus, we might have measures such as the percentage of employees with postgraduate degrees or those with a professional qualification in accountancy. Organization-wide measures may be useful. It depends on their nature and size, but measures that concentrate on subgroups of the total are likely to be the most useful for monitoring.

Targets may be set to change the figures if they are deemed too low, as may be the case through benchmarking against competitors. Finding out, for example, that a rival is using graduates as salespeople raises questions about our policies and consequent ability to compete.

36) EXPERIENCE

Even though some organizations still cheerfully find ways to say goodbye to people above a certain age to "make way for new blood," experience is generally valued and respected. While broadly having a maturing effect and increasing personal capability, experience can also have a negative aspect, in the sense that people rely on a past that has become irrelevant. Nevertheless, experience generates much of our know-how (particularly that which is industry and company specific) and has value in itself. Thus, the context in which we learn our knowledge and skills can be important as the know-how gained. Experience gives us both breadth and depth.

Measurement

Different kinds of experience would include:

- ❑ Time spent in a certain field
- ❑ Having been in certain kinds of organization
- ❑ Having had certain responsibilities or accountabilities
- ❑ Having been in particular situations.

Experience may not result in any spectacular achievement yet still have value in itself. Obviously successful experiences are good news, but sometimes unsuccessful ones can still have much value for learning. One company gives advice to young ambitious graduates as follows: "Make sure you spend one to two years in a role that directly involves customers; it does not matter so much whether you are particularly successful, but everyone needs to know how customers think and act."

Experience is obtained in the following ways:

- ❑ Being accountable in a function for some results or value added
- ❑ Being in a particular type of situation
- ❑ A type of project
- ❑ A type of problem or opportunity.

The extent of experience is described by:

- Time spent
- Scope and stretch
- Parameters of size.

An experience "dictionary" would have sections based on the way the organization is structured. For example, in a manufacturing organization we might have the following: General management, sales, marketing, customer service, manufacturing, logistics, quality, procurement, finance, HR, and IT.

Table 5.1 gives an example of how an experience dictionary can be built up, in this case for generic management experience. For technical and professional areas, it might be helpful to link this directly with a know-how dictionary.

This provides a basis for assessing experience. We can do this for individuals in a team using a similar format to that used above for know-how (see Figure 5.4). The first column lists the key areas of experience relevant to the team. In this case it is a marketing team, and we have assumed for the purposes of illustration that the jobs in the team are

AREA OF EXPERIENCE	Entry			When experienced			Person A			Person B			Person C		
	Time	SC	SZ	Time	SC	SZ	Time	SC	SZ	Time	SC	SZ	Time	SC	SZ
International management	–	–	–	2+	2	1	3	3	2	2	2	2	4	3	3
Product marketing	2	1	1	3+	3+	3	2	3	3	2	1	1	4	4	3
Distribution channels	1	1	1	3+	3+	3	3	2	2	1	2	1	3	3	3
Pricing	1	1	1	3+	3+	3	2	3	3	1	2	1	4	3	3
Etc.															

SC = scope, SZ = size

Figure 5.4 *The experience profile of a team*

Table 5.1 *Example of a generic management experience dictionary*

Experience area	Level	Time spent	Scope/stretch	Size
Team management *(Being responsible for the people management of others)*	1	< 1 year	Same job, same place	2–5 people
	2	1–2 years	Varied roles, same place	6–10 people
	3	2–5 years	Varied roles, two sites	11–20 people
	4	> 5 years	Varied roles, distributed	> 20 people
Managing through managers *(Bring responsible for the people management of other managers)*	1	< 1 year	Same roles, same place	2–5 people
	2	1–2 years	Varied roles, same place	6–10 people
	3	2–5 years	Varied roles, two sites	11–20 people
	4	> 5 years	Multifunctional, distributed	> 20 people
Functional management *(Leading a function as a member of the business management team)*	1	< 1 year	Serving one business unit	Functional support/advice
	2	1–2 years	Serving several business units	+ complex problem solving
	3	2–5 years	Country wide	Functional leadership
	4	> 5 years	Company wide	Functional strategy development
Project management *(Delivering discrete results using resources "owned" by others)*	1	< 1 year	Internal, own department	Budget < £10K, length < 3 months
	2	1–2 years	External, own department	10–100K, 3–6 months
	3	2–5 years	Internal, cross-department	100–500K, 6–12 months
	4	> 5 years	External, multifunctional	> 500K, > 12 months
International role *(Working in contact with or located in other countries)*	1	< 1 year	Regular liaison with people from other countries	1–5 countries involved, or technical/professional secondment
	2	1–2 years	Responsiblity for resources abroad, frequent visits	6–12 countries or management secondment (developed world)
	3	2–5 years	One international secondment	13–30 countries or management secondment (less developed world)
	4	> 5 years	Several international secondments	Globally or country leadership
Matrix functional role *(Ongoing functional role, achieving success through others without own resources)*	1	< 1 year	Within a business area	Technical/support advice
	2	1–2 years	In one country	+ complex problem solving
	3	2–5 years	In one area/region	Functional leadership
	4	> 5 years	Global	Functional strategy development

similar and have the same entry criteria and learning opportunities. The figures refer to the levels derived from a dictionary similar to that above. Each person is evaluated against it. In this example we can conclude that A is a relative newcomer and C is very experienced.

Our database of experience can then be used to give any analysis necessary and, more importantly, to track changes. Thus we might want to know or monitor:

- The total number of years' experience in a particular field
- The average number of years' experience for a relevant group
- The proportion of people with more than x years' experience
- The proportion of people with a certain kind of experience
- The "rookie ratio" = percentage of employees with fewer than two years' experience.

4) PERSONAL NETWORK—"KNOW-WHO"

Everyone has to interface with other people to a greater or lesser degree. People can be significantly more effective if they have good relationships—with people who have specialized

> WHO YOU KNOW CAN BE AS IMPORTANT—IF NOT MORE SO—THAN WHAT YOU KNOW.

knowledge, influence to make things happen, and a network of their own to call on, both internally and externally. Beyond the natural internal circles, each of us builds up a network of contacts that grows with experience. Sources include previous classmates or colleagues, professional bodies, leisure clubs, industry organizations, and so on.

There are some roles where this aspect is absolutely critical to success, in public relations, for example. When interviewing prospective new investment bankers, one CEO of an investment banking firm was known to spend most of his time on the question "Who is in your Roladex?"—it was relationships that brought most of the business. A person's network and range of personal contacts has additional value in that they can make it accessible to others.

Measurement

Depending on the nature of the organization's activities, we might have useful measures such as:

- Proportion of customers known personally
- Number of prospects based on a personal relationship
- Number of competitors with which we have a personal link

❑   Number of relevant officials known
❑   Number of relevant experts known outside the organization
❑   Range of contacts in other divisions, departments, countries
❑   Number of employees known with management potential (a measure for a management development manager).

This aspect of capability can be defined in the following ways:

Extent of network
❑   Level of contacts (upwards, downwards, sideways)
❑   Internal/external balance
❑   National/international.

Variety of contacts
❑   E.g. business, political, government, professional, academic.

Quality and relevance of relationships
❑   Business acquaintance, business provider, social acquaintance, etc.
❑   Anticipated speed of response
❑   Degree of influence.

These three components can be rated for both ideal and actual on a scale of one to five, where one represents a very low level and five a very high level. Figure 5.5 overleaf illustrates how this might be mapped.

We can also create a database of the key relationships held by individuals, as in Table 5.2.

Table 5.2 *Individual relationship map*

Name	Internal group loyalties	Important external relationships
Bill Jones	Ex Middlesoft Ltd Successful Marks & Spencer account team, 1995 Harrow office	Woolworths account since 1997 Debenhams account since 1996 Retail Society Golf Club
etc.		

NATURE OF CONTACTS	Entry level	Fully competent level	Person 1	Person 2	Person 3	Person 4
Customers known personally—general —at a senior level	1 1	4 3	3 2	5 3	4 4	3 3
Prospects based on personal relationships	2	4	3	4	3	2
Relationships within the organization down the supply chain	1	3	2	3	2	2
Relationships with other sale groups	1	4	3	3	4	3
Relationships within product development	1	3	3	4	2	2

Figure 5.5 *Mapping the networks available to a sales team*

When people leave an organization their internal relationships may give us warning signs that others may go with them; when restructuring, care must be taken to avoid damaging external relationships.

PERSONAL VALUES AND ATTITUDES

Values and attitudes shape many of the ways a person behaves. *Values* reflect a person's ethos about their work and their interaction with the people connected with it. They rarely change.

Attitudes are closely related to values, and are about how people view their world, what some call mindsets or mental maps. They are shaped by education (including business schools), by the environment and its demands, and by the culture to which people belong. The initial six years in my first organization, for example, have influenced my views about good management all my life: my attitudes to business ethics, people management, industrial relations, process improvement, and so on.

Attitudes can be changed where people see that this is necessary. For example, people who had expectations of a lifelong career may adjust to the need for "employability"; exposure to other cultures changes tolerance levels, and previously held beliefs about work, management, and norms of behavior can all be changed.

Measurement

Values and attitudes should not be measured separately, because it is their *outcome* that matters. They will be reflected in a person's behaviors. The degree of alignment with company values is a suggested component of the Individual Asset Multiplier. Assessment of this alignment has to be based on the strength of those behaviors that specifically support the organization's written and unwritten values.

PROCESSES FOR EVALUATING CAPABILITY

The process of measurement of capability has varying degrees of difficulty. Qualifications, experience, and a person's network are factual and present no problem. "Know-how" can be assessed reasonably objectively within a good framework; the simple A–E system mentioned above works remarkably well. Tests can be applied to both knowledge and skill areas.

Assessing personal behaviors and attitudes is judgmental, however, and need to be based on perceptions. They can vary with circumstances, with motivation, with different types of work and so on.

Appraisal systems

Systems for appraising performance are being continually redesigned. This is because changing cultures and values alter the priorities of what we look for in performance.

❏   In assessing results, we want to focus on value added. We should have set targets in this way, and we want to discuss how they were or were not met.

❏   We want to discuss the value added to the employee, as a stake-holder. How have the person's capability, motivation, job challenge, and so on changed?

❏ We want to review the range of capabilities the person has and how they could be developed.

❏ We want to discuss their potential to deepen or broaden these in the future.

❏ We want to discuss their alignment with company values.

This is an opportunity to reassess the components of the Individual Asset Multiplier. The overall "value contribution factor" should be judged against the targets for adding value to stakeholders. It should be validated by others: a more senior manager, or peer manager, or a trained HR practitioner. There are thus three outputs of an appraisal discussion:

❏ A narrative summary of performance

❏ A revision of the IAM factor ratings

❏ A personal development plan.

There are alternatives to hierarchical appraisal that reflect the reality of many modern project-based organizations, where people do different things in different teams during a year, and no one person is "boss." An IT consultancy in the City of London developed an approach as follows:

❏ Each individual chose a mentor for the year, who could be a peer or any more senior person.

❏ When the person was assigned to a project, the project manager completed a one-page summary of their contribution and gave it to the individual and their mentor.

❏ They also belonged to a technical group with a technical leader, who commented on their technical capability.

❏ Finally, they belonged to an administrative group, and their line manager also had an input to their appraisal.

The role of the mentor was the key one here, in pulling together the various components and guiding the development plan.

360° feedback

For many years, the person's manager was the only judge—and in many organizations still is. This is generally fine for "know-how," which can be assessed more objectively, although even here, the individual and their peers are probably the best judges of how good they are. However, when looking at personal behaviors one has to ask who has the best information. Who is the best judge of leadership capability? Surely those being led. Of teamworking? The other members of the team. Of customer focus? The customers themselves.

This has led to the extensive use of multi-input feedback systems or 360° approaches, where views are obtained from people both above and below the individual concerned. HR departments have tended to offer this first to leaders and managers, but the principle applies to all. Any person concerned for their own growth would want the best possible feedback they can get on their capability.

It has become accepted that feedback should be anonymous. Nevertheless, the most valuable part of feedback is the narrative comments obtained, and openness should at least be considered. In my last managerial role we instituted a simple, employee-owned approach where each individual chose some of those they had worked with and asked three simple questions:

❑ What do you think I have done particularly well this period, and why?
❑ What do you think I could have done better and why?
❑ What advice would you give me for improving the value from my contribution?

The answers were discussed with their mentor, a person they also chose themselves.

Self-assessment would be part of a 360° feedback exercise, but need not be so formal. A good dictionary allows people to make their own self-evaluation. Many organizations have sophisticated software enabling this, and leading to options for development from which people can choose.

Assessment centers

Since the 1970s, assessment centers and, latterly, development centers have been used extensively in the US and the UK, less so elsewhere. These work traditionally to a formula of multiple competences to be assessed (typically 8–12); multiple situations (simulations, tests, discussions); and multiple observer assessors (one per two participants). By careful design to bring out competences in as varied a way as possible, evaluations of strengths and weaknesses are made.

This format is particularly valuable if a person is not known well, or if there are varied opinions about capability. It has several dangers, however: untrained assessors, the use of weak evidence to give the semblance of an evaluation, and the artificiality of the simulations.

Assessing real-life performance will generally be a better guide, unless we are testing a person against quite new demands through using the center.

THE PERSONAL CAPABILITY PROFILE

A CV or resumé is a chronological and biographical summary of where a person has been. A personal capability profile is about where a person *is*. It is a summary of their particular strengths under each area of capability. In our A–E scale for know-how, it would list those areas where a proficiency of C or above exists. It is a statement of an individual's own human capital. As such, it forms a basis of comparison with prospective, current, and future roles, and for individual development planning. For most people it should change each year.

> EVERYONE SHOULD HAVE A PERSONAL CAPABILITY PROFILE, A STATEMENT OF THEIR PERSONAL CAPITAL THAT COVERS THEIR RANGE OF CAPABILITIES.

A format is given in Figure 5.6. The column "Strategic importance" is optional but can be used to relate to core capabilities—either in relation to the overall business itself or to a major strategy.

Name:	Current role:	Last updated	
Capabilities		Level indicator	Strategic importance
Education/qualifications: *What qualifications do you have? When were they acquired?*			
Personal behaviors: *What are your 6–8 significant personal strengths?*			
Technical, professional, and business know-how *In what areas of know-how do you have real expertise, either knowledge or skill?*			
Experience: *In which areas have you had significant experience? What special situations or problems have you experienced?*			
Network: *What particularly useful networks of people or personal contacts do you have?*			
Personal attitudes/values: *What major values and attitudes are important to you?*			

Figure 5.6 *Personal capability profile*

CAPABILITIES AND THEIR VALUE TO THE ORGANIZATION

When we look at capability as a component of value, we are not just interested in what a person brings to their current job role. They may bring knowledge and skills from previous experiences, and the greater the variety of roles they can fulfill, the more valuable they are to us.

Table 5.3 shows a hierarchy of value to an organization of different levels of skills. All of the levels can contribute to value, but to varying degrees. The loss of people with company-specific experience is the most painful of all because of the longer time needed to rebuild the loss.

Table 5.3 *Transferability of skills*

Commodity skills	Those that are required by most organizations or work situations. Examples are basic IT skills, dealing with the telephone, and working with others.
Professional skills	Arising from specific qualifications or training, which are again transferable across various types of organization and will be the core of the self-employment option.
Industry-specific skills	Knowledge about how a particular industry or business sector operates; skills unique to the industry.
Company-specific skills	Understanding the culture, the politics of getting things done, and about particular processes and ways of doing things; sharing in values and goals.

Is it possible to combine the multiple complexities of personal capability into one measure for each person? The Individual Asset Multiplier is aimed at doing this. Our judgment will be based on the following:

❏ How does a person's capability relate to the role they currently have and its demands?

❏ What range of capabilities do they have that provide flexibility to fulfill a number of roles?

❏ What strategically important components do they possess? For example, a highly developed profile of the personal competences we want; expertise in core knowledge and skills; uniquely relevant experience or networks; or highly aligned personal values.

POTENTIAL

We have what we have today, but what of the future? Existing capabilities and strengths can be enhanced, but we are also concerned to develop the latent potential of individuals and at the same time provide continuity in the organization. This implies that we:

❏ Know what the potential of people is, or is currently perceived to be
❏ Will ensure that a dialog takes place matching the views of potential with the aspirations of individuals
❏ Will actively help that potential to be realized.

THE HUMAN CAPITAL MONITOR

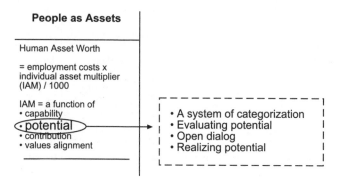

Figure 5.7 *Potential*

"Potential" is a transient and subjective concept, and we can only realistically talk of *current perceptions*. We have also to ask: "Potential for what?"

Many organizations put all their attention on those aimed at senior management, so-called high flyers or high potentials. Who is in a position seriously to influence future value? Some examples might be:

❏ Senior customer representatives
❏ Talent scouts
❏ Capable coaches
❏ Technical experts
❏ Skilled people developers
❏ Business-oriented IT systems people.

The development of depth of expertise in a core competence may be an equally important form of potential and deserves as much attention as building future management—who in any case are not likely to represent more than 10 percent of the organization.

Development and growth have both direction and speed. This component of the Individual Asset Multiplier could be looked at as in Table 5.4.

Table 5.4 *Evaluating potential*

Direction	Speed	Goal	Valuation
Upwards hierarchically	Fast	2–3 levels higher	1.6–2.0
Upwards hierarchically	Slower	1–2 levels higher	1.1–1.5
Toward technical or professional expert	Fast	International expert	1.6–2.0
Toward technical or professional expert	Slower	Company/local expert	1.1–1.5
Available for lateral movement	As needed	Flexible, multiple skills	1.0–1.3
In the right job at the right level, but with a special skill such as coaching	Static	Expand role; develop to superior role competence plus growing special skill to expert level	0.5–1.2
In the right job at the right level	Static	Expand role; develop to superior role competence	0.5–0.9
Operating at a level beyond capability	Action—manage problem	Position that fits the person's level	0.1–0.4

THE LANGUAGE OF POTENTIAL

Language gives powerful messages. Since developing our human assets is one of the most important things we do in a value-creating organization, we need to use language with care. A set of descriptions of potential that reinforce hierarchy and grades will not be consistent with the need to develop all our capabilities.

It is strongly recommended that the language used always includes the term "current perception," such as "CPP—Current Perception of Potential." People change in their aspirations, as a result of development, and in how they are seen to have performed.

Systems in use include:

❏ Expected timescale for next promotion—now/+1/+2/+5 years, for example
❏ Anticipated ultimate grade level
❏ Number of levels expected to rise and the speed of doing so.

The third option has been adopted in assessing the potential part of the Individual Asset Multiplier. The first is too pragmatic and short term; the second looks too far ahead.

For example, Consignia (the UK Post Office), in an effort to avoid the implied connection between potential and hierarchy, talks about levels of "stretch." Unisys has a seven-point classification that recognizes the importance of the nonpromotable key player, as well as different speeds of anticipated progression. Sainsbury's categorizes its managers as:

❏ Career manager
❏ Restricted mobility manager
❏ Stable/expert manager
❏ Stable general manager.

HSBC Bank uses a three-dimensional approach to classifying people and their contribution, as in Table 5.5.

Table 5.5 *Three-dimensional approach to classification*

Scope for growth (hierarchical)	Short-term value	Long-term value
1 = ⇑⇑⇑⇑ 2 = ⇑⇑⇑ 3 = ⇑ 4 = ⇔	Key expertise 1–4	Professional/technical and/or management

These examples all recognize and value a range of different kinds of potential.

Many organizations find it difficult to be open and transparent with their people concerning their views on potential. The case both for and against openness is summarized in Table 5.6.

Table 5.6 *Transparency in discussing potential*

For openness	Against openness
• Enables people to be active participants in their development	• Fear of disappointment, conflict, and demotivation in some circumstances
• Encourages openness and honesty on both sides	• Fear that the discussion will be difficult and will require much preparatory work
• Commitments made are more formal and more likely to be honored	• The knowledge that unforeseen changes may ruin commitments and built-up expectations and result in bitterness and disappointment
• Judgments will be made on sounder evidence	• All judgments about the future are subjective and therefore dialog based on them is inherently risky
• Insecurity and suspicion about what is being written about people are removed	• A great deal of effort is required to manage this well and we do not have the resources
• Manages expectations, helps people to make realistic plans	• Managers are not skilled in handling these situations well
• Mitigates frustration with lack of a route forward and hence unwanted attrition	• Managing resulting expectations is too difficult
• Encourages consistency in operating the processes	• The undesirability of distinctive "labels" for individuals
• Provides a motivational opportunity	• Affects the team where one or more members are "set apart" from others
• Consistent with the legal requirements of Data Protection Acts	
• Leads to holistic and future-oriented personal development plans	

(I agree — but notice the "understated" way this opinion is presented)

The case for openness is therefore strong, and the inhibitors can be mitigated. It is a reality that many line managers do find such judgments and discussions difficult, and need training to handle them successfully. More junior managers lack the personal maturity to advise beyond a narrow horizon. A good person to conduct this dialog might perhaps be the "grandparent" in a hierarchy—a much more helpful role than being a cursory signatory on an appraisal. Another option is to use third parties such as designated mentors and coaches, human resource staff, or external coaches and advisers.

The most important element in any classification of potential is to recognize that it occurs at a point in time. It needs to be revisited regularly, as people change and develop. This transience and opportunity for revisiting make an easy platform for being open and transparent with people about the perceptions currently held. Thus, dialogs about the future should begin, "As we see it at the moment with the knowledge available to us…"

Well-designed processes can help in personal planning and the eventual dialog between individual and organization. Such processes might include workshops, personal diagnostics, and career planning workshops. Looking five to seven years ahead to a "career aiming point" helps us to go beyond the opportunism of the next job and focus on "stretch" in a career. A truly useful capability framework that describes people and posts in a matching language is an immense help if one is available.

MAKING JUDGMENTS ABOUT POTENTIAL

The task when assessing potential is to compare the person we see today with an envisaged role in the future. If that role is close to the current one, and we are talking about greater breadth or depth, we want to assess the ability to grow and strengthen current capabilities, which is relatively easy. However, if the role is quite different—such as an executive position—we may be looking for some capabilities that cannot be demonstrated in the current position. We have to come to some judgments about these, based on what we see now.

Psychologists can test and interview people and make a report based on their personality and ambition. Increasingly popular is a form of development center as discussed earlier, using a competency framework as a base and simulating a variety of situations that typify the target job. Care must be taken with the results, however: Any conclusions need to be put alongside other processes that take account of the individual's everyday performance and behavior.

"Live" stretching activities have immense value, for example:

❏ Acting roles—managed and observed
❏ Planned on-the-job development through extra responsibility or accountability
❏ Real-time job performance, targeted and measured against results and capabilities.

Performance in the current role is a guide, but we have to beware the trap of equating it too closely with potential. Many an engineering manager should still be an engineer, but has been promoted because it was the only route forward and because they were the best engineer in the team. Well-defined profiles of the capabilities needed for each role makes it much easier to avoid this problem.

Different levels of judgment can be used:

❏   The person's manager
❏   A consensus of several managers
❏   Peer consensus
❏   Self-assessment
❏   Mentor assessment.

The more of these that are combined, the better.

SUMMARY

The essence of individual human capital is the capability that people bring to the organization. One of the greatest challenges is to be able to define and measure its components. Much effort has been expended in this cause in building competency frameworks, but many of these are heavily biased toward personal behaviors. The evidence is clear that managers look for more than this when making job-matching decisions.

Six components of capability were discussed and how they can be measured. We will find time and again, when using strategic cause-and-effect staircases, that the level of capability of a particular area is crucial to success.

A person also brings potential to grow, and to do so in different ways. Growing in specialist depth can bring as much future value as having the ability to be a senior executive. We need a broad understanding of potential, therefore, and a descriptive language that is inclusive. The continuous reassessment of potential is important, as both perceptions and aspirations change with time. Being open with people about how their potential is perceived is recommended, and the earlier we help people understand what a career means to them, the better.

CHALLENGES FOR ACTION

❏ How is capability defined in your organization? Does it provide a common language that all managers and employees can relate to easily, and does it enable objective matching of people against current or future posts?

❏ Do you have measures that enable assessment of the levels of capability that people have, and help define development objectives?

❏ How inclusive is your approach to description, identification, and assessment of potential? Do you recognize several kinds of potential that bring value?

❏ How frequently is potential reassessed? How is it done?

❏ How often does an individual get the opportunity to discuss their aspirations and with whom?

6

Maximizing Human Capital

S INCE THE HUMAN CAPITAL AT OUR DISPOSAL IS INDEED OUR MOST
valuable asset in terms of what it can contribute, it deserves to be
looked after carefully. This chapter focuses on the ways in which
we can categorize and record assets, and the examination of three
key processes in managing human capital: acquiring new assets, keeping
those we have, and developing their capability and potential. For each of
these we consider how success might be measured and the factors that
can influence it. Planning for human capital investment and reporting on
progress are also covered, as is the effective management of continuity
and careers. The chapter extends the first column of the Human Capital
Monitor as in Figure 6.1.

CATEGORIZING HUMAN CAPITAL

Traditional systems for grouping people are based on grade and functional structures, and often only in terms of headcount or cost. In the
value-creating organization, however, we are not interested in boundaries
of this kind since they may bear little relationship to either stakeholders
or adding value. Categories that would be of interest include:

❑   Those based on the components of "Individual Asset Multipliers"—
    What is the distribution of different kinds of potential? Who are the

THE HUMAN CAPITAL MONITOR

People as Assets		Maximizing Human Capital—Measures	
Human Asset Worth = employment costs x individual asset multiplier (IAM) / 1000 IAM = a function of • capability • potential • contribution • values alignment	*Acquisition* *Success*	Total Human Asset Worth acquired Average IAM of new recruits Increase in strategically important core capabilities	
	Drivers of success	Employer brand League position in 'most admired companies' lists Reasons for leaving Acceptance rates	
	Retention *Success*	Attrition percentages Total loss of HAW Reduction in collective core competency profile Stability of key groups Costs of undesired replacements	
Maximizing Human Capital	Drivers of success	Employee satisfaction Reasons for leaving Pay levels	

• Acquisition   – How
• Retention   successful
• Growth   are we?
           – What drives
           success?
	Growth
	Success
		Increase in strategically critical capabilities
		Increase in average capability element of IAM
		Increase in average values alignment element of IAM
		Increase in average contribution element of IAM
		Rate of internal promotions
		Continuity (succession) ratios	

	Drivers of success	Investment in training Investment in development vs. "remedial" training Percentage of competence-enhancing customers Nature of the learning environment Percentage of personal development plans implemented	

Figure 6.1 *Maximizing human capital*

people most aligned to our values? Who are the most flexible people who can be employed in a variety of roles? Who are the greatest contributors to added value?

❑ Teams dedicated to a stakeholder-based goal

❑ Those people who would be the most difficult to replace.

We can combine the value-adding contribution with ease of replacement. We noted in discussing capabilities in Chapter 5 that there is a range of transferability of skills: from "commodity," through professional, to industry specific and finally company specific. The greater the emphasis on a requirement for company-specific knowledge, the more difficult that knowledge is to replace. Skills in the second or third categories might also be in short supply.

Using "added value" and "ease of replacement" as the parameters, the population can be plotted in four quadrants, either by roles or a combination of roles, and also by key people as individuals or teams. This is shown in Figure 6.2 overleaf.

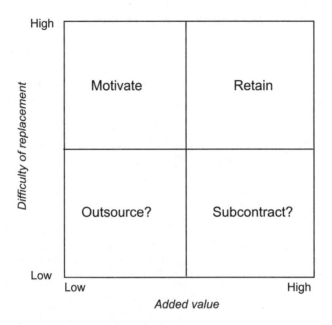

Figure 6.2 *Added value vs. ease of replacement*

Each quadrant has a different priority for management:

❑   *High added value/hard to replace*—The priority here would be retention. These people might come from any level in the hierarchy, but each represents a real asset loss so they are as important as any financial report. This category ought, therefore, to be subject to regular reports regarding any changes in resource. Typically in this category we would expect to find top salespeople, highly experienced managers, product technical specialists, or creative designers, plus a range of individuals who bring specific value.

❑   *Low added value/hard to replace*—This would include those who have special knowledge of the organization and its systems, those responsible for maintenance or housekeeping, and those who are particularly loyal and dedicated, albeit in low-value-adding roles. Management's priority here is to motivate long-term commitment and maintain performance.

❑   *High added value/easy to replace*—Examples here might be professionals whose skills are not industry specific, who can easily cross organizational boundaries and yet bring significant value. Many HR people are in this category, as are finance, PR, and legal professionals. They are often self-directed, and management has the option to subcontract their services, or to use interim resources or consultants.

❑ *Low added value/easy to replace*—this group might comprise people doing routine tasks that are common to many other organizations. Such groups can often provide classic opportunities for outsourcing.

The traditional HR approach of considering all employees in much the same way, often on the grounds of a kind of justice or fairness, might need rethinking once the organization starts to look at them according to the value they contribute. More attention will be paid to the retention or growth of some groups than others. This need not, of course, cut across any equal opportunity policies or programs.

THE HUMAN ASSET REGISTER

Just as we have an "asset register" of more traditional assets, so we want to keep regular track of what is happening to our "stock" of human capital. Modern information systems can organize data in just about any way the organization requires it, but the value-creating organization is primarily interested in grouping people by stakeholder-facing teams. So a register would look like the one in Figure 6.3 overleaf.

A key role for HR management, in partnership with operational colleagues, consists in the maintenance and growth of this stock of human capital. There are three distinct tasks:

❑ Getting the best people
❑ Keeping them
❑ Growing them.

Fortune magazine creates annual league tables of the perceived ability of US firms to attract, develop, and keep talented people. The pharmaceutical

Employee	Employment Cost	Capability Factor	Potential Factor	Contribution Factor	Values Factor	IAM	HAW
A							
B							
C							
D							
Sum for all employees							
Average per employee							

Figure 6.3 *Human asset register*

firm Merck held top position for many years, and many other well-known names consistently held leadership in their own sector. These are always firms known for their positive approach to the use of advanced human resource practices.

ACQUIRING NEW HUMAN ASSETS

Since every individual is a potential asset, as well as a resource, the most important aspect of acquisition is to select and recruit people with Individual Asset Multipliers (IAM) of more than 1.0, and preferably as high as possible—in other words, people who add to our stock of capability, experience, knowledge, and have the potential to grow.

Outcome measures of successful acquisition might therefore include:

❑ Total HAW acquired
❑ Average IAM of new recruits
❑ Increase in strategically important capabilities, both in quantity and average proficiency level.

These calculations might be best made, say, six months after a given recruit has joined. This is because the IAM is best assessed in the working context rather than just during the selection process.

If we are to be successful in attracting the best people, we need to ensure that potential applicants perceive the organization to be worth joining. Success will be influenced by employer attractiveness. How can we understand and monitor this?

Measures of the influences on successful acquisition management include:

❑ Employer brand—regular survey of features seen to be attractive or unattractive
❑ League position in "Most admired companies" lists
❑ Reasons for leaving—information about what frustrates people
❑ Acceptance rates—percentage of offers made that are accepted.

The employer brand

The word "brand" comes from the Norse for "promise." It is what is communicated—consciously or unconsciously—to every employee or prospective employee. How is our organization perceived by prospective recruits, and how do we want to be perceived? What kind of character- istics will attract the people we need? This is more complex than just being seen as a good employer or a reputable and well-known one. Employee perceptions are often based on public image, or on what friends or relatives might say about an employer for which they have worked.

It is essential to establish and develop our own particular brand, which might be rather different from our image in the marketplace. Do we want to attract people who will work many hours, or be especially achievement oriented? Do we want the best technical brains we can find? One of the schemes that has greatly aided employer reputations in the UK—particularly smaller ones—has been the "Investors in People" award for investment in training and development. Companies who have achieved it give a signal that "this is a good place to work."

Once the brand is defined, our success in marketing it effectively needs to be measured. Those potential recruits who declined an interview or rejected a job offer will comprise a useful population in this context. Their perceptions can be invaluable in assessing the brand.

Fortune magazine publishes an annual "America's Most Admired Companies" list, and other similar lists are available in different countries. In the UK, *Management Today* publishes a survey of the best British companies to work for, and in February 2001 the UK *Sunday Times* printed the first of a regular review of the top 50 companies that people enjoyed working for most. League tables like these can have a significant influence on prospective employees. Universum, a Swedish publisher, surveys annually the companies that MBA graduates want to join. Of course, public admiration may be different from the perception of knowledgeable professionals. In the US, "admiration" is closely related to profitability and perhaps the feeling that "share options will grow here."

Each organization needs to choose its own benchmark list, and see where it would like to be. League positions also provide a useful means of target setting and benchmarking with competitors.

One very effective way of influencing the employer brand is to create comprehensive links with schools, universities, and the community. Rolls-Royce, for example, has over 200 UK employees who are school governors, and provides a variety of engineering-related support to educational institutions.

All brands require investment. There are many diverse ways to build this type of brand and it takes time, so regular monitoring is vital to ensure that it is moving in the right direction.

Reasons for leaving analysis

When people leave the organization we can be certain that they will tell many other people why they have made their choice. Dissatisfied leavers are sure to spread the dirt about your company and work against the image you may be trying to create. So we need to take the reasons for leaving very seriously. One way to get a more accurate steer on this is to ask people three months after they have left what their real reasons were. (In the interests of good relations these are often covered up in the face-to-face exit interview).

Thomas Davenport's research suggests that "interesting work" is the main reason people stayed with a company. Most organizations categorize the reasons for people leaving and it is very often the case that the largest category concerns lack of personal growth and career progress. These are precisely the kind of things that a value-creating organization would want to get right.

The numbers of people leaving ought to be analyzed regularly into the relevant categories. These may be expressed as a percentage of all the people leaving. The attrition (labor turnover) analysis, as a whole, should then be conducted according to those groups who are critical to value-creating staircases.

Acceptance rates

The rate of acceptance of job offers is a measure of recruitment effectiveness and also has an impact on the associated costs. But it can also be an important sign of comfort with what people conclude about the organization and the people they have met—their reaction to an offer is a vote of confidence and vice versa. It makes sense to analyze these by particular kinds of potential recruit. One key area, for example, is the intake of young entrants—typically graduates and postgraduates—since this kind of recruitment, at least in boom times, is characterized by intense competition.

The measurement can be calculated, in each category, as the percentage of offers accepted over, say, the last six months. The particular methodology will depend to some extent on the frequency and scale of recruitment activities overall.

New assets are also acquired through takeovers and alliances. Managing this effectively is discussed in Chapter 10.

What the value-creating organization looks for in recruiting

The objective in choosing recruits is to increase all of the components of the Individual Asset Monitor. So acquiring specific know-how, experience, and know-who capabilities will add to the current stock. Nevertheless, there are some particular skills and attributes that the value-creating organization would seek in any recruit:

❏   Commitment to continuous learning and the ability to learn effectively

❏   Commitment to continuous innovation—always looking for new and better ways

❏   Commitment to personal knowledge management—giving and receiving knowledge through deliberate sharing

❏   Commitment to continuous change—adaptable, flexible, improvement seeking.

There will be evidence of these behaviors both inside and outside the work situation.

In the value-creating organization we focus on much more than merely the demands of the current job vacancy. We will be interested in the potential for other jobs in the future, plus responsibilities that can be taken outside of the job itself, plus bringing knowledge from outside to share with others. We want to see our new human asset as a long-term investment. The current vacancy may be relatively short term in comparison to the cumulative service that we may hope for from a new colleague in the organization.

RETAINING HUMAN ASSETS

Human capital is mobile, but once we have acquired it and maybe invested in it, we want to hang on to it. In the 1990s in particular, organizations became very laissez-faire about letting people go, accepting that increased mobility would be the norm. As the value of human capital has come to be more appreciated, strategies for retention are now high on most organizations' agendas.

People will leave, of course. In markets that are competitive for scarce skills, people and teams will be courted and tempted. In a commercial firm, losing a key asset to a competitor is a double loss—not only do we not have the benefit, but it might actively work against us. Some say that the more competitors are tempted to hire your people, the higher the external view of your human capital worth. This may be true, but it can also be a signal of other negative factors like your inability to provide attractive opportunities. Some companies, even in sectors that employ highly marketable skills, are noticeably more successful than others in keeping their people. Money, in itself, might well be an insufficient reason to cause people to move. Loyalty, relationships, a particular type of work, or feeling generally comfortable about the organization's culture, can be enough to keep people. The more people move from job to job, the more they get used to it, however. It is always the first change that is the hardest to make.

Having said that, why do people choose to stay or leave? It is critical for an organization to understand the causes of voluntary resignation, which can be split into three categories:

❑ Personal reasons (spouse moving; pregnancy, etc.)
❑ Dissatisfaction with a "hygiene factor"—pay, supervision, resources, flexibility of working
❑ Dissatisfaction with in an inadequate "motivator"—opportunities, training, recognition.

The most common reason for people leaving is feeling they aren't making progress or have no opportunity. In other words, people are saying: "This organization is ceasing to add value to me; I will take my human capital and offer it elsewhere."

In Chapter 2 we discussed the value an organization adds to people in exchange for loaning their human capital. If they feel that value is inadequate, inevitably it raises the question: "Will I get more elsewhere?" They weigh up the value of any new opportunity relative to the current one, and offset any psychological, financial, or other costs incurred in making a move.

Organizations can often lack imagination and creativity when it comes to creating appropriate opportunities. Returning expatriates are an obvious example. Headcount constraints, and devolved profit responsibilities, can mitigate against what is self-evidently right for the company; namely, keeping the person. The organization can so easily fail to consider the good sense in this despite having, at the same time, veritable armies of consultants and contractors.

The key outcome measure in this area would be attrition itself (labor turnover), which perhaps in the future will be known as asset losses. All losses are expensive if they require replacement, but some are clearly more so than others—especially if they are in the upper right-hand quadrant of Figure 6.2. The cost of unwanted losses is certainly worth tracking in its own right. They include recruitment and selection—typically 20–35 percent of a year's remuneration; the lost opportunity cost of the value that the person was adding; and the cost of the learning curve bringing the new recruit up to speed. Best expressed as a percentage of salary, a table can be drawn up (from experience in our own organization) for different types of job and the appropriate percentage applied. For most managers and skilled technical staff this figure will be close to 100 percent of a year's remuneration. However, it is not just a question of the cost of replacement, but also the *value* that is lost.

HR departments report attrition as the number of people who have left divided by the average headcount for a period. Such figures reflect headcount thinking. Our emphasis should be much about who has left us and their value to us. If we are using a measure of value such as Human Asset Worth, we have an ongoing measure of "absolute" loss that can be tracked. This can be compared with the acquisition of new HAW referred to above. In a similar way, we should track the loss of key capabilities using the same categorization as for acquisition.

In addition to retaining the individual assets themselves, there is value in stability and this would be an additional outcome measure. The service–profit chain described by Heskett, Sasser, and Schlesinger, which has proved its validity in a number of organizations, links customer retention and employee retention directly, and this is all to do with the stability of relationships between customers and staff. The measure might be expressed as the proportion of a particular staff group with more than x years' service, or service in a particular field. This would be valuable in looking at customer service teams, and others where stable relationships have particular value.

The factors that influence our success in retention are many and varied, but particularly reflect the levels of motivation and satisfaction that people are experiencing within the organization. It seems extraordinary that many companies still do not do any kind of employee surveys, or do them so infrequently that they are unable to show any trends or connections with changes put in place. Cost is often given as a reason. However, the costs involved in compiling financial information are accepted as essential to the business; again, it is a question of balance. Questions in a survey that particularly affect retention will be as follows:

❏   How important to you are … (list here elements of potential added value to employees such as those listed on page 21: pay, benefits, development, the right tools for the job, etc.)?
❏   How satisfied do you feel with what is provided (for each element)?
❏   What is your overall satisfaction with the company?

And the nub of them all:

❏   If you had a better opportunity to go elsewhere tomorrow, what would be the likelihood of your taking it?

The percentage of people responding positively to these questions should be regularly tracked, and analyzed appropriately according to group.

We cannot ignore the fact that perceptions of poor pay will also cause people to leave, even though it is rarely a major reason. So we will certainly want to track our position in the market, especially for the key skills that are strategically important.

To summarize, outcome measures of successful retention management are:

❏   Attrition percentages of key groups derived from cause-and-effect staircases
❏   Total loss of Human Asset Worth, both as an absolute amount and as a percentage of the current stock
❏   Changes in the collective proficiency level of core capabilities
❏   Stability—percentage of key groups with more than x years' service
❏   Cost of undesired replacements.

Measures of the influences on successful retention management include:

❏   Employee satisfaction—regular survey of levels of satisfaction, particularly areas of frustration relative to the areas of adding value to people

❏　Reasons for leaving—further information about what frustrates people

❏　Pay levels—position in the market for key skills.

Practical approaches to retention

Retaining the best human assets is an absolute priority in the value-creating organization. When retention is managed effectively, the organization is never taken by surprise. There are some fundamental means of ensuring that this is done well.

Understanding what drives and motivates each individual

There are various instruments available to assess this, such as the Work Interests Schedule developed by John Hunt of the London Business School, and the well known Myers-Briggs Type Indicator. However, the most important practice is regular and continuing dialog with people about how they feel about their work and the organization.

Every decision to leave is a combination of "push" and "pull" factors. Pull factors come from opportunities for new pastures that are brought to someone's attention. With the continual extension of the headhunter's reach, one does not have to be an executive to "get the call." If the would-be seducer strikes fertile ground where there are already push factors—various elements of dissatisfaction—it is a slippery slope to the employee leaving.

Dialog with key individuals needs to be very regular, and much more frequent than the once-a-year exercise of the typical appraisal discussion. When people are identified having a number of single days off, or seen scanning the appointments pages and websites, it may be too late!

At the World Economic Forum in Davos, Switzerland in 2001, Dr. David Finegold of the University of Southern California presented a paper on employee retention in high-tech companies. He argued that what employees *say* is important to them (in surveys and focus groups) does not necessarily match the way they behave. He particularly pinpointed the fact that employees tend to say that work–life balance is important, but he showed statistically that there was no correlation between working excessive hours and people leaving. Nor was pay a great influence (other than for the very youngest employees), except for stock options. These mattered considerably to people, along with career advancement and the opportunity for innovation and risk.

Having a flexible approach to employment conditions
The value-creating organization will make available to all employees the same processes of performance review, career planning, application for promotion, and so on. This does not mean that it will treat everyone in the same way as a result. What motivates individuals is so variable that we need a great deal of flexibility to meet people's needs. There are many options for working time and place, flexible benefit policies, and a variety of reward strategies, for example.

In large companies, this kind of flexibility can sometimes be achieved by spinning off various units into separate entities, each with its own rules. For example, IPC, a large UK publisher, created a reduction in turnover of vital IT staff from 20 to 2 percent in 1999 by moving 50 e-commerce staff into a discrete company called IPC Electric. The new organization created its own approach to remuneration, and effectively a quite different culture: informal dress code, office layouts suiting the staff, flexible hours, and so on. This initiative included a share scheme in the new company that was an incentive to all employees to stay.

Providing an environment that minimizes dissatisfaction factors and maximizes satisfiers
This is such a significant influence that the next chapter is devoted to it in detail. Surveys show that the most common source of stress is the relationship with the boss, although many other factors can cause people to look elsewhere. This is one argument for reducing the sanctity of the boss–subordinate relationship, and involving third parties such as coaches and mentors.

Creating an attractive future
One increasingly common strategy for retention is providing employees with equity, or another form of long-term reward, to tie them into the

longer term or some more specific point in the future. This future can be rolled forward through new awards each year. It is not always easy to radically change the salary base of those whom we particularly want to keep. Nevertheless, rewarding contribution to added value through long-term incentives can be both discriminating, based on the different levels of contribution, and attractive to the individual.

There are other kinds of future that provide incentives to stay. These include the anticipation of promotion or greater responsibility; planned expansion and diversification that will bring new opportunities; involvement in some special aspect of the organization outside the current job that might hold particular appeal; the opportunity for an international assignment; or the promise of early retirement.

Do employees return?

Few companies today would take the view that once a valued employee has left they should not be allowed to return. When I failed to save the high-potential graduates in ICL who wanted a new and different experience, I would say: "I am happy for you to take an 'external secondment,' it will make you much more valuable when you return!" If they went off to another organization I kept track of them, even inviting them to company graduate events, recognizing the importance of maintaining the network. We invited some of them to tell us what they were doing—a significant number were now suppliers or customers of ICL. They were still stakeholders, but in a different category.

Consultancy McKinsey trains its people well, even in the knowledge that it might lose a large proportion of them. What is important is that it wants to ensure that every leaver feels positively about the firm. There is a good chance these ex-employees, in any new role, might well be looking for the kinds of services that McKinsey provides. Effectively, the firm is protecting and growing potential revenue. It would be hard to track, but what a great measure of intellectual capital: Ex-employees who now bring revenue into the company!

Growing Human Assets

Human assets do not normally depreciate, although without proper nurture and direction they can certainly reduce their level of contribution. They can also find themselves with redundant capability, or fail to keep up to date in their field. There are also estimates of the *unfulfilled potential* of people in organizations that state as high as 60–80 percent being unutilized.

> EVERYONE'S CAPABILITY SHOULD INCREASE OVER TIME.

Experience itself provides new knowledge every day.

In practice, the learning process can be stunted through personal apathy, or because the organization itself does not encourage it. A value-creating organization would look for processes enabling growth to take place in a planned way, both within and beyond the workplace, in addition to unplanned experiences that will always arise.

We should see this reflected in the expansion of an individual's personal capability profile (see Figure 5.6) and in the capability component of their Individual Asset Multiplier.

Development is a longer-term outcome, which can be defined as the ability to grow people's potential and create continuity. Measures include succession capability and the rate of internal promotions. Sometimes it is necessary to buy in capability that we do not possess, but external recruitment, particularly at more senior levels, can suggest a failure to develop people, and sometimes a failure to select them effectively in the first place.

Measures of growth

The following are the kind of measures that enable the organization to analyze growth (or otherwise) in human capital:

❑ Increases in strategically critical capabilities
❑ Increase in the average capability element of Individual Asset Multipliers
❑ Increase in the average values alignment element of Individual Asset Multipliers

❏ Increase in the average contribution element of Individual Asset Multipliers
❏ Rate of internal promotions
❏ Continuity (succession) ratios.

Success will be influenced by factors such as those that follow.

Investment levels

Much of the investment in training and development programs is an act of faith (as illustrated by the frequent vagueness of objectives), or a consequence of budgetary allocation (related to a previous year), or both. It should, of course, be based on the needs of the organization at the time.

Accounting for the costs of training and development rarely distinguishes between that which is needed for *maintenance* and that which is an investment for the *future*. The former is about creating a higher current contribution through better knowledge and skills. The latter is concerned with growing individuals (or teams) to enable them to contribute more or differently in the future. In Siemens' annual report, for example, expenditure on training is positioned alongside that on R&D and capital expenditure, giving the clear message that these are all seen as investments.

One budgetary allocation might cover all the following elements. The first of these is a genuine expense; the others are investments aimed at a return through more effective future contributions:

❏ Training new recruits in the essentials of their jobs and the business
❏ Increasing the personal effectiveness of employees in order to improve current value contribution
❏ Increasing current added value (such as in the use of new systems and better methodologies)
❏ Developing expertise and potential so that people can contribute at a higher level of value in the future.

The overall investment in this area can be quoted in various ways, for example:

❏   A percentage of the pay costs of the organization or group (typi-
     cally between 3 and 8 percent)
❏   A percentage of revenues (typically 1–3 percent)
❏   Training days per person per year (between 2 and 10).

So much learning happens through real work experiences that the normal measurement of what takes place off the job is a limited indicator. It
is an easy one, nevertheless, and a reasonable measure of commitment to
people development. It also has the advantage of being a standard benchmarking measure.

Competence-enhancing customers

Celemi, a Swedish learning and change consultancy, uses an interesting
concept. Recognizing that some of its customers provide unique learning
opportunities to its business, it introduced the measure of "percentage of
customers who are competence enhancing." Its particular interest is the
extent to which a given customer can bring new knowledge to the firm
as a whole. Individuals who benefit from customer knowledge pass it
around to ensure that it is shared.

The learning environment

The underlying culture and climate of the organization are discussed in
Chapter 8. A key part of this is the focus on learning and development.
One factor is how supportive people find the culture in terms of their
own learning. The existence and successful implementation of personal
development plans form a way of measuring this.

To summarize, measures of the influences on success in growth management include:

❏   Investment in training—increasing current capability—as a per-
     centage of payroll costs
❏   Investment in development, compared with expenditure that is
     remedial or training aimed at maintaining current value
❏   Percentage of customers who are competence enhancing
❏   The nature of the learning environment, measured by surveys

❏ Percentage of personal development plans implemented over a year.

One example of a company with a measurement system for human asset management is British American Tobacco. It uses four headings in the form of a car dashboard, or cockpit, which looks like Figure 6.4. The headings are each supported by a set of indicators, as in Figure 6.5. (The term "lister" indicates someone with potential.)

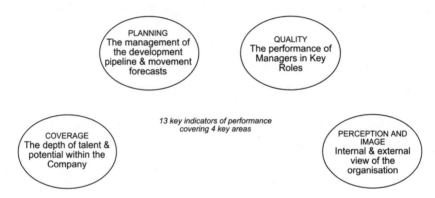

Figure 6.4 *BAT's HR dashboard*

A BALANCE SHEET AND PROFIT AND LOSS REPORT FOR HUMAN CAPITAL?

It is helpful to see the management of the stock of human capital in balance sheet terms. A balance sheet implies that we can balance items in the same dimension—money, in business terms. The Canadian Institute of Chartered Accountants has made an impressive study through its Corporate Reporting Initiative (the address for its website is given in the references). It concluded that it is not possible to mix the indicators of intellectual capital with the transactions of accounting.

Fitz-Enz, in his *ROI of Human Capital*, suggests a Human Capital Income Statement, which incorporates the costs of the processes for managing human capital and relates them to the financial value added for the organization. He also takes account of the "hidden costs" of lost time and

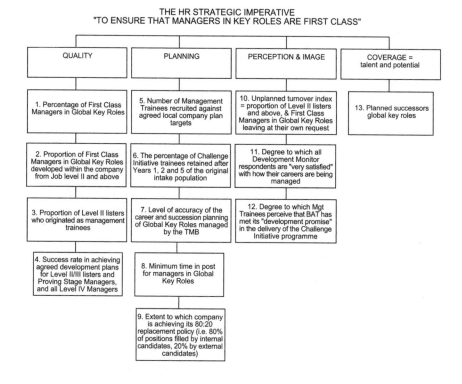

Figure 6.5 *The detailed measures of BAT's HR dashboard*

money through attrition, unwanted learning curves and other waste, as in Figure 6.6 overleaf.

The cost lines in this statement will never be entirely accurate, and are unlikely to fit with traditional cost accounting systems. However, this approach has considerable merit, because it helps us to understand the financial cost of maintaining human capital in relation to the financial value added it produces. We measure the cost of maintaining other forms of capital, and we should know what we are spending on our human capital.

REVENUE
Human capital value added	$2665	*Revenue less nonhuman expenses*

DIRECT EXPENSES
Acquiring	15	*Cost of hiring*
Maintaining	1128	*Pay and benefit cost*
Developing	12	*Cost of training*

GROSS INCOME	1510

INDIRECT EXPENSES
Vacancy costs	126	*Revenue lost for, say, jobs unfilled*
Learning curve	438	*Revenue lost for partial productivity during first year of employment*

NET INCOME	946

Figure 6.6 *A Human Capital Income Statement (from Fitz-Enz)*

MONITORING MOVEMENTS IN HUMAN CAPITAL

Chief executives need to know the state of play of their human capital, both the good and the bad news. A good management information system provides levels of data. The top level summarizes the main parameters by which progress is judged, plus ratios and trends. If it is dynamic, i.e., continually fed real-time data, it will highlight key events such as new survey data and key resignations. Good management decisions depend on understanding trends and comparisons as well as absolute figures, so these must be built in. In terms of our stock of human capital, we need to know the following:

❑ Major events in acquisition, losses, or growth as they happen. Who has been hired this week and what is special about them? Has anyone from our critical high-value groups resigned? Is it too late to take action? What major events aimed at growing capability have happened?

❑ Trends of attrition in key groups and how the figures compare with our targets or benchmarks. This would be calculated monthly

❏ How the overall HAW is moving, both at a corporate level and especially for critical groups. A report such as those in Figure 6.7 would provide the basis for this.

HUMAN ASSET REGISTER REPORT (1)

Employee groups	HAW—end last period	HAW lost	HAW gained	HAW—end this period	% change	% change on year

HUMAN ASSET REGISTER REPORT (2)

Employee groups	Mean IAM	% change on year	Mean for potential	% change on year	Mean for capability	% change on year	Mean for contribution	% change on year	Mean for values	% change on year

Figure 6.7 *Changes in Human Asset Worth*

These reports would be established from records that are being continuously updated. Although individuals can and should update many of their own records, and can self-assess themselves on the value components, clearly other judgments must be taken into account and the update should be performed by a designated person.

DESCRIBING ROLES IN THE ORGANIZATION

A value-creating culture will want wherever possible to give people space for innovation and expansion in their roles. Except for those jobs that have stringent safety or regulatory requirements, traditional job descriptions that define in detail the tasks that have to be done can be inappropriate.

> ROLE DESCRIPTIONS SHOULD SPECIFY THE ENTRY REQUIREMENTS, WHICH ARE THE MINIMAL LEVELS OF CAPABILITY NEEDED FOR SOMEONE TO TAKE ON THE ROLE, AND THE LEARNING OPPORTUNITIES AVAILABLE TO JOB HOLDERS.

A *role description* exists to enable a match with possible candidates and to provide guidance for the incumbent regarding what is expected. A good format is shown in Figure 6.8. This focuses on the link to stakeholders (in most cases it will be just one) and the appropriate measures of added value. We should distinguish between the entry requirements for a role and what is involved in a fully competent contribution. This is not the same as matching with the best possible candidate. The focus in the role description is to recognize the importance of workplace learning in developing capability.

For each role, we should always be asking the question: "Could it add more value than it does?" With some additional expertise, for instance, could the service engineer sell on additional services, or issue real-time invoices?

RESTRUCTURING

Restructuring seems to be the order of the day in most organizations. It may result from mergers and alliances, or from internal realignment. Inevitably, organizations on some occasions find themselves with too many people: because a market has collapsed, or the level of profitability cannot sustain the cost base, or there is duplication. Restructuring for whatever reason should be aimed at increasing value, for example:

❑ Increasing contact with customers
❑ Having fewer hierarchical levels, to encourage empowerment and innovation

ROLE: Product development manager		Last updated: 10/01
KEY PURPOSE: To develop new product lines for the automotive industry and enhance existing ones in ways that respond to the expressed needs of customers		
ADDS VALUE TO THESE STAKEHOLDERS	Accountability	Measure(s) of added value
Automotive industry customers	Provide a stream of new and enhanced products	% sales coming in from products introduced in last three years
Development engineers and staff	Create high levels of motivation and commitment	Satisfaction surveys Retention rate Absenteeism rate
	Stimulate innovation	Volume of ideas produced
Shareholders	Achieve competitive product to market times	Time for new product to be established
LEVELS OF CAPABILITY REQUIRED FOR ENTRY:	• First degree in science or engineering • 3 years' experience in product development environment • Strong concern for customer's needs first	• Strong skills in teamwork, project leadership and control, analysis • Knowledge of automotive industry's use of firm's products (at least "competent" level) • Knowledge of product development process teachniques (at least "competent")
LEARNING OPPORTUNITIES:	• Team management • Joining international "community of practice" for knowledge sharing • Joining product development committee	• Enhancing all above areas • Prioritizing resources and projects • Project budgeting • Customer research techniques

Figure 6.8 *Sample role description*

❏   Eliminating non-added-value work
❏   Eliminating duplication.

Some reductions are over such a long term that natural wastage takes care of the reduction. We are happy to lose people who have low IAM factors. However, there will be times when a job is not available for a valuable person. Do we let them negotiate a package? Or should we send them unwillingly to the outplacement firm? Do we in fact provide incentives for people to leave, such as beneficial early retirement, enhanced redundancy terms, funded retraining, part-time opportunities, and so on? When IBM underwent a massive staff reduction in the early 1990s it could claim that it never forced any individual to take redundancy. However, it offered such a high level of incentive in some countries that departure became impossible to refuse.

Indiscriminately allowing every person who puts up their hand to take advantage of these benefits is clearly not in the interests of a value-creating organization. Losing significant amounts of human asset worth has happened many times, only for the organization to find that unique knowledge and capabilities have to be bought back from the individuals under a completely different type of contract, both written and psychological. By then the apparent cost saving has gone on the record.

Computer services company ICL has for many years had a unit called Linkwise. This is a pool of people whose jobs have disappeared and who are available for new assignments. They are used as a resource to top up projects or do temporary assignments, until they find a new post. This is an approach clearly compatible with valuing human capital.

MANAGING CONTINUITY

Providing the organization with continuity—a better term than "succession planning"—is of undoubted value in itself. Porras and Collins (1994), in their well-known study of visionary companies, found continuity of management to be a major factor in success, together with the maintenance of a distinctive culture to which all employees were aligned. Successful visionary companies carefully developed, promoted, and selected managerial talent from inside the company. Across a total of 1,700 years of company history studied, there were only four individual cases of an outsider coming directly into the role of chief executive.

Although there is always the attraction of bringing in new blood and capability, the evidence is that a primary policy of growing our own assets is a better strategy for long-term value. There is no doubt that an organization that seeks to promote internally wherever possible, and makes everyone aware of this, encourages retention of its talent. Continuity planning becomes a key process. The ideal is to have people in the right place with the right capabilities at the right time. We need continuity in all the key added-value areas in the business, not just management, particularly where the knowledge of the organization, its culture, and its people is a major contributor to performance.

In the dynamic environment, building a continuity plan on the basis of existing organizational "boxes" (which so often deploys the same names in several boxes) is unlikely to be the best approach. Linked with business development, our concern is whether we have enough "pools" of specific potential to meet our future requirements. Looking for clones of existing leaders can be a dangerous, but easy, trap to fall into. However, there will be certain roles for which we will want to know if we have succession: the CEO, for example, and some critical posts that would be particularly difficult or undesirable to fill from outside.

Regular auditing of talent and continuity is a feature of the value-creating organization. We would like to know:

❏ The proportion of a population with "high" and "some" potential in each of the areas we believe are critical to success
❏ The availability of specified pools of succession capability
❏ The percentage of promotions resourced from inside
❏ The cost of recruitment due to inadequate succession.

Human capital reviews

Discussions of talent and how we manage it are a fundamental process in the value-creating organization. Some have annual rituals, where senior managers gather to discuss their management resources and their high flyers, sharing judgments on performance and potential, reviewing succession, and making plans for some people. This is most likely to be done function by function and department by department. However, in addition there should be a focus on those core capabilities that add the key areas of value to stakeholders, and that will take us beyond the often limited population that is normally reviewed.

At the other extreme, people movement and development are a monthly item on the executive agenda. In this case, the topic is often rushed, however. No business is static and decisions are continually being made on people movement, so the annual discussion is soon out of date.

The optimum is a regular meeting of a dedicated and representative group of executives, suitably empowered by the board. They should meet as frequently as the pace of change demands—probably every one to four months—and be involved in reviewing each unit of organization and each individual in the defined target population, as follows:

❑   Reviewing the role requirements and capabilities needed to meet the demands of the future
❑   Setting measures and targets for people development and monitoring achievement
❑   Reviewing the state of continuity in key areas
❑   Continual monitoring of the positions and people who are key in adding value
❑   Making recommendations on plans for individuals and filling vacancies that arise
❑   Maintaining functional capability, through recommending specific training and development programs as needs dictate
❑   Ensuring that the necessary data maintenance is adequately resourced.

We would expect this group to have a continuing interest in the Human Asset Worth registers.

Part of managing talent is to be aware of the special opportunities that the organization has to offer. There are always some positions that offer unique learning opportunities. For example, many headquarters jobs provide a helicopter view of the organization and give external contacts. Roles involving business planning, international operations, or managing alliances are other examples. There are positions in every function that do not require in-depth previous knowledge or experience, but where personal capabilities provide a sufficient platform for transfer. These enable a person to change function and quickly be effective. Such positions need to be identified and kept unblocked and available for individuals' career progression.

Career management

Dialog with employees about their ambitions is an important part of the value-creating organization. Personal aspirations and corporate judgments must be matched and modified as needed. Not only do we know that many people leave because they are frustrated at not knowing what might be planned for them, all discussions about personal growth are fundamental to human capital management. Yet many organizations shy away from an open discussion, for the same reasons that we listed in Chapter 5 in respect of potential. They mostly do so out of fear: of confrontation, of creating expectations that might not be realized, of exposing what might be an unsubstantiated judgment, of demotivating someone at the wrong time. They also do so out of a feeling of inadequacy, that maybe there is no plan for the individual, or that discussions about potential have been merely cursory.

Despite most employees' suspicions of behind-the-scenes career plotting, many organizations do not have plans for career development for the majority of people. Arguably, such plans are a poor use of time anyway, since life brings so much uncertainty and turbulence. At least there should be a view of direction and speed and, depending on the direction, some critical kinds of experience that are required as a guide to next steps.

It is part of the popular rhetoric to tell people that they are responsible for their careers. Certainly, they should feel ownership. Most organizations advertise jobs openly, at least up to the level below the defined senior management group. Many now have web-based systems, with intranet application. However, there are limits to an individual's ability to make things happen. Self-development, unchanneled and unadvised, can be wrongly directed and counter-productive. If people have to rely solely on keeping their eyes open for the right opportunity and applying for it, they may well find it very hard to get through the doors of a new function and cross a boundary. Disappointment and demotivation can set in.

The benefit of dialog is that with a common agreement between individual and organization, help can be provided where it is needed. Sometimes it is in the longer-term interest of the organization not to take the best-qualified person for the job, since that implies the person with the least to learn. A good network of mentors can help significantly here, opening the doors that an individual may find it hard to do on their own.

Should the organization manage careers behind the scenes? Some continue to do so, such as ExxonMobil, which believes that this enables it to develop people in a systematic way to meet its future needs. In the value-creating organisation we just want to make sure that we are developing potential, providing continuity, and retaining our best people. At the very least, we are going to plan together with those people, and then see what can be coordinated as we merge the individual plans. Inevitably, we will take more interest in those who are seen to be future senior managers. They need to cross organizational boundaries (such as functions and countries) to broaden their experience and may require some assistance in doing so.

HUMAN CAPITAL BUDGETING AND PLANNING

A human capital investment plan will be built around the strategic and stakeholder value staircases discussed on page 16. The organization's requirements—for example, for increased capability or accelerating the readiness of people with potential—will be compared with what is in the Human Asset Worth register.

A VALUE-CREATING ORGANIZATION WILL PLAN FOR CHANGES IN ITS HUMAN CAPITAL BUDGET ALONGSIDE ITS BUDGET FOR PEOPLE-RELATED EXPENSES.

Capital investments are typically subject to tests of rate of return. Where the value added is going to be financial, we can develop formulae based on the net present value of expected returns. If it is nonfinancial, we have to make a judgment as to the impact of the investment on the strategic staircase. Take investment in a business school program for executives. This will have capability objectives (in knowledge and networking), and perhaps expectations of greater leadership effectiveness, or cultural change. Each of these may be linked through to a specific strategic goal, and we assume a logic that says that a percentage improvement in these parameters feeds up the system, influencing the desired result in due course.

Resources are always limited. Not every category of stakeholder value has the same merit, and it is a matter of careful judgment as to who gets the priority for investment. Our desired outcome is long-term shareholder return, and first priority goes to investments aimed at future earnings streams. Some investments are directed to avoiding value subtraction, such as in image or employee retention. Therefore, each investment needs to be rated against:

❑ Impact on strategic business goals
❑ Impact on future income streams
❑ Impact on critical increases in stakeholder value measures
❑ Avoidance of unwanted value loss or expense.

SUMMARY

Managing the stock of human capital, as reflected in a register of Human Asset Worth, is arguably the most critical activity of management. First, we need to categorize people according to their capacity to deliver value—a function of their role and personal application. This gives us some direction about who the vital human assets are in the organization, and the extent of attention that should be given to them. A human asset register will help us make intelligent decisions when restructuring, so that high-value people are retained if at all possible.

The key processes for managing our human capital are acquisition, retention, and growth. In the value-creating organization these need always to be approached with value in mind, which means thinking of stakeholders and the long term in addition to any immediate needs. Each of these areas deserves its own measures of success and indicators for the factors that influence that success the most.

Growing and developing people are fundamental activities for an organization dedicated to future value. They require a range of roles, skills, and processes that demand disciplined involvement throughout. A characteristic of the value-creating organization lies in the prevalence and importance given to individual development plans.

The major part of learning comes from experience, and the way we manage the provision of new job opportunities is a vital activity. Traditional role specifications tend to describe the capability required of a fully competent person. The learning opportunities that are provided by each role should be carefully identified, and the requirements to enter a job should be as low as possible.

Managing continuity has the dual goals of developing individuals and meeting the human capital needs of the organization in the future. Processes for both are needed.

Finally, just as we budget for the expenses related to people, so we should make a plan for human capital investment that is clearly linked to our strategic and stakeholder value goals.

CHALLENGES FOR ACTION

❏ How do you classify people in your organization? Does the method have any relation to value added?

❏ What would be needed for you to be able to understand the value that is added by individuals and teams?

❏ Do you have any kind of register of the overall value that people contribute?

❏ Looking at who left the organization in the last year, who do you regard as a major asset loss and why?

❏ How do you measure your attractiveness as an employer?

❏ What is your data on retention/attrition telling you? Is it giving you the real information needed for retention management?

❏ Do you have measures for employee growth and continuity?

❏ Do you know the costs of managing human capital processes?

❏ How is talent managed in your organization? When and how is it discussed?

How often are there surprises?

❑ What is your investment in training and development compared to that of competitors?

❑ Do your people have personal development plans? Do you know the extent to which these are implemented? Do people feel that the environment encourages continuous learning, sharing, and innovation? When and how did you last check?

❑ What is your process for continuity management and the movement of people?

❑ How does the movement of people between jobs take place? Is there a sensible balance between personal responsibility and corporate assistance?

❑ How are roles described? Do they distinguish between entry criteria and learning opportunities?

❑ Do you make a human capital investment plan alongside budgeting for the costs of employing people?

7 (second column)

Motivation and Commitment

P EOPLE BRING THEIR PERSONAL HUMAN CAPITAL, IN ALL ITS DIVERSITY, to our organization and we may nurture and develop it. But what is it that influences and enables them to give superior performance? We can have people with enormous capability, yet who fail to realize the contribution that they could make. They may lack commitment or motivation. Perhaps their efforts are misdirected, or they are pursuing their own personal agenda. People in organizations operate in an environment, which we may think of as a *soil*—the basic underlying culture—and a *climate*, which is more transient and local. Together they affect, as with plants, the output and growth of people.

In this chapter we will look at motivation itself and the indicators of whether it is high or low. We then examine aspects of organizational culture and local climate that influence motivation, and how these can also be measured.

In other words, we come to the second column of the Human Capital Monitor (Figure 7.1). First, we need indicators of the evidence of motivation and commitment, and secondly, measures for the contributing influences. We have five of these, listed in Table 7.1.

THE HUMAN CAPITAL MONITOR

People Motivation and Commitment	How successful are we?
Measures – How successful are we?	• Attrition percentages • Absenteeism levels • Quality levels, scrap and rework levels • Volume of suggestions for improvement • Customer service satisfaction levels • Employee satisfaction and morale surveys • Why people choose to leave/stay

Figure 7.1 *People motivation and commitment*

Table 7.1 *People motivation and commitment—the influencing factors*

Factor	Indicators of success	Contributors
Leadership effectiveness	• Productivity or added-value measures • Multi-rater feedback on capabilities • Values rating in Individual Asset Multiplier • Absenteeism for the group • Attrition and transfers from the group • Stability index—average service by choice • Empowerment index	• Selection critiria—% success rate • Leadership development—investment p.a.
Practical support	• Opinion survey questions	• Investment in workplace equipment per head
The workgroup	• Team assessment of working practices • Team stability index	
Learning and development	• % with personal development plans • % completion of development plan activities • Increase in critical capabilities • % people promoted in a year • % leaving due to lack of growth • Opinion survey questions	• Investment in training and development per head • Cultural match to a learning organization template
Rewards and recognition	• Opinion survey questions • % leaving due to reward dissatisfaction	• Benchmarking market position

INDIVIDUAL MOTIVATION AND COMMITMENT

Thomas Davenport, in *Human Capital* (1999), views workers as investors of their own human capital and uses a formula for Human Capital Investment, defined as follows:

$$\text{HUMAN CAPITAL INVESTMENT} = (\text{ABILITY} + \text{BEHAVIOR}) \times \text{EFFORT} \times \text{TIME}$$

It is this combination that leads to performance, and much of his book examines the conditions that will lead to maximum effort through commitment.

"Effort" is described as "the conscious application of mental and physical resources towards a particular end ... by applying or withholding it, we control the when, where and how of human capital contribution."

Who plays the main part in determining commitment and motivation: the organization or the employee? Sometimes personal, non-work-related problems can weigh on people's minds and affect commitment. Often these are temporary situations and demand managerial sensitivity.

Frederick Herzberg followed on from the Theory X and Theory Y thinking of Douglas McGregor with his famous article in 1966, "One More Time—How do You Motivate Employees?". He distinguished between "hygiene factors"—those that, if not addressed, lead to dissatisfaction—and "motivation factors"—those that contribute to positive job satisfaction. At the time he was protesting against an approach he characterized as KITA ("Kick in the Ass"). Negative KITA is about pushing and subtly threatening employees; positive KITA is exemplified by incentives, offering more benefits and communicating well. Herzberg demonstrated that significantly important motivators were achievement, recognition, work itself, and responsibility. Personal growth and advancement were also important. On the other hand, demotivators were primarily to do with supervision and the working environment. His solution was to focus on enriching people's jobs.

In 1987 the *Harvard Business Review* republished the article as a classic. Herzberg commented that 20 years on KITA was alive and well, particularly in the context of a preoccupation with the bottom line. He felt that his analysis had stood the test of time, and most managers would probably agree with him.

Despite these more general observations, motivation can vary according to temperament and also to career stage—the particular point a given individual has reached. For example, desire for high earnings might dominate in the early years, where, for others, the opportunity to travel or to be in leading-edge work might be what is most important. Everyone has their own aspirations. Generation X—younger people brought up in the IT economy—are characterized by not expecting to stay in the same career or with the same organization, as their parents perhaps did. Instead, opportunities to gain valuable qualifications, or to have the freedom to try new ideas are important. And they are usually keen to have a financial stake in their organization's success.

There are many visible effects of high commitment and motivation: People working particularly hard, prepared to take on extra tasks, wanting to be involved in many aspects of the organization. But how can we quantify levels of motivation? We can see its effect in both business outputs and in the way people behave. It is much easier to make a collective assessment than to track individual by individual.

Output indicators particularly affected by employee motivation

Customer satisfaction
The service–profit chain, mentioned on page 128, argues that customer satisfaction is directly linked to employee satisfaction, particularly for those employees involved directly with customers. These may include a wide variety in practice, for example:

- Salespeople
- Call center operators
- Customer service people
- Service deliverers such as shop assistants, airline cabin crews, garage mechanics
- Invoice departments
- Supply chain specialists
- Telephonists and receptionists.

The method used for customer evaluation is critical. Increasingly, firms ask for immediate feedback from a customer to the individual representative of the service. This may put the customer in a tricky position, however—feedback tends to be more honest if it is given anonymously.

Measures of customer service are also affected by systems and resources. Comparing the measures over time must be accompanied by looking at any system changes that have taken place before conclusions are drawn regarding employee commitment. For example, a new call center system that schedules engineer visits may cause a deterioration in service that is nothing to do with the engineers themselves.

Quality and rework levels

Whatever employees are working with, products or services, the level of the quality of their work is a measure of their commitment. If they care about their work and their customers, whether internal or external, they will be concerned to do things right first time.

Suggestions and improvements

The quantity and quality of suggestions and improvements made, especially voluntarily, can be an indicator of people's involvement in their work. There will always be suggestions for improving hygiene factors, and these should be distinguished from those that relate to the work itself or to customer benefits, for example. We would judge whether the number received is a positive or negative indicator by reference to previous history, or to internal or external benchmarking. Quality can be reflected in the percentage of suggestions that are adopted, and the value added to stakeholders (including cost savings) that accrue from them.

Surveys

Employee surveys can give us clear signals and create "morale indices" for tracking over time, can allow us to measure progress against cultural goals, and enable us to benchmark key indicators with other organizations.

How often should they be done? This depends on the pace of change in the organization. Employees can get fed up with filling in questionnaires, and excess quantity reduces quality. Once a year would be normal, but for a specific culture change program surveys might be done before the change, during, and after.

One company example is the Individual Dignity Entitlement survey used by Motorola. This produces an index, which affects managers' bonuses. Six questions are tracked every quarter:

❏ Do you have a substantive meaningful job that contributes to the success of Motorola?
❏ Do you have on-the-job behaviors and the knowledge base to be successful?
❏ Has training been identified and made available to continuously upgrade your skills?

❏ Do you have a career plan and is it exciting, achievable, and being acted on?

❏ Have you received candid positive or negative feedback within the last 30 days that has been helpful in improving your performance or achieving your career plan?

❏ Is there appropriate sensitivity to your personal circumstances, gender, and cultural heritage so that such issues do not distract from your success?

Organizations exist to coordinate the exchange of survey results between companies, and firms also create their own clubs for this purpose. Ideally, the questions we would want to benchmark would be those that we see as fundamental to our value-management strategy. They will be about innovation, learning, knowledge and information sharing, personal development, and overall satisfaction.

One organization that collates and disseminates such data is ISR (International Survey Research), which has monitored certain key questions in a variety of countries for over ten years. In 2000, for example, ISR reported that in the 1990s in eight European countries, the overall employee satisfaction level varied between 55 percent for Italy and the UK and 69 percent for Switzerland. There are definite cultural factors in how people respond to such surveys, so that comparisons within countries and against time have more validity than those between countries. Relatively little change had happened over 10 years, Switzerland showing the greatest increase (+6 percent), and the UK declining by 2 percent. The subsidiary questions showed the highest satisfaction overall with "the work itself" and the least with "pay." "Performance and development" was also one of the lowest figures.

In terms of testing commitment and motivation, we will want to ask questions such as:

❏ To what extent do you look forward to coming to work on Monday mornings?

❏ How positive do you feel about the goals and objectives of your group?

❏ How satisfied do you feel with the nature and challenges of your work?

Excessive absenteeism and staff losses

"Excessive" is a judgmental word. Here we mean "beyond the industry norm, or beyond a target level we believe is achievable." The Saratoga Institute, collecting information worldwide, shows median, 25th percentile, and 75th percentile absenteeism rates for different countries. In Europe, Germany has the highest overall rate with a median of 4.6 percent of days lost, compared to 3.1 percent for the UK. (Despite this, Germany has substantially higher productivity than the UK.)

People who are highly motivated by their work have less time off than those who find their work unfulfilling or where there is a general malaise concerning morale. Similar organizations or units can vary significantly in their absentee rates. We should set a target that we believe we should be able to expect from a highly motivated workforce, and regard the difference between this and our actual rate as a gap to be closed.

We can measure absenteeism as a percentage, and also as a real cost. No added value is created by a person who is absent, and absence may incur extra costs through overtime, temporary staff, and loss of output.

As we saw in Chapter 6, attrition or labor turnover rates are perhaps the most potent indicator of poor morale—people voting with their feet. Again, we need to judge whether the level is beyond a reasonable target. Internal benchmarking can be a helpful guide. For example, in the do-it-yourself and hardware chain B&Q, a study in 1999 found that the best store had an attrition rate of 20 percent and the worst 220 percent. Even allowing for some factors of geography, this helped set a general target.

Whenever we look at collective data, we need to be careful that averaging and consolidating are not hiding what we really want to know. Some groups of people are much more strategically important than others, and we might want to make the attrition target zero for them.

To summarize, indicators of the levels of motivation are:

❑ Attrition percentages, especially against industry norms
❑ Absenteeism levels compared to industry norms
❑ Quality levels, scrap and rework levels
❐ Quantity of suggestions for improvement, and value added as a result

❏ Customer service satisfaction levels
❏ Employee satisfaction and morale surveys
❏ Analysis of the reasons that people choose to leave.

CONDITIONS TO MAXIMIZE MOTIVATION

Davenport suggests that a focus on the value of an employer to an individual may be more important than concern about the value of the individual to the employer. He defines four factors that matter to an employee:

❏ Intrinsic fulfillment—what excites people about the work itself and the culture and life of the organization
❏ Financial rewards—a combination of base salary and other benefits
❏ Growth opportunities—for development and promotion
❏ Recognition—nonmonetary rewards.

He quotes a survey done with a firm called Cypress Consulting looking at what made people stay in the organization. Cypress knew that there were two peak periods for people to leave: in the first and fifth years. It surveyed all those with more than six years' service. The top and middle-level performers rated the factors in the order above, with "interesting work" scoring 8 out of 10 on average and the next factor, rewards, 6.5.

Davenport argues effectively that such knowledge is important because organizations have options about the distribution of spend per person between these areas. Statistical data about people's preferences leads to "efficiency curves"—the loyalty and productivity obtained for a given spend—for particular types of investment in people. From this come conclusions about the redistribution of the amount spent on employees in order to optimize the potential return. Davenport acknowledges that individual preferences differ from grouped averages, and concludes that the provision of as much choice to an individual, on top of a core available to all, is the most desirable answer.

Buckingham and Coffman went through over a million pieces of data collected by survey firm Gallup to determine what employees regarded as a positive working environment. One of their standard questions concerns whether employees feel "engaged," "disengaged," or "actively disengaged." Their extensive studies in the US showed 26 percent in the first category and 19 percent in the last. A similar study in the UK in 2001 showed figures of 17 and 20 percent. In researching what it is that makes the difference, Buckingham and Coffman came up with 12 questions to which people wanted positive answers:

1   Do I know what is expected of me at work?
2   Do I have the materials and equipment I need to do my work right?
3   At work, do I have the opportunity to do what I do best every day?
4   In the last seven days have I received recognition or praise for good work?
5   Does my supervisor, or someone at work, seem to care about me as a person?
6   Is there someone at work who encourages my development?
7   At work, do my opinions count?
8   Does the mission/purpose of my company make me feel that my work is important?
9   Are my co-workers committed to doing quality work?
10   Do I have a best friend at work?
11   In the last six months have I talked to someone about my progress?
12   At work, have I had opportunities to learn and grow?

If we can create a workplace where these answers to these questions will be "yes," we are likely to maximize motivation and commitment. There is no doubt that, as Herzberg, Davenport, and others have emphasized, the nature of work itself—in terms of interest, challenge, and learning opportunities—comes top of the motivation league.

CULTURE AND CLIMATE

Culture refers to the systems, processes, and behavioral expectations—built up over time—that affect all parts of the organization. Examples would be the structure of rewards, corporate values, or standardized

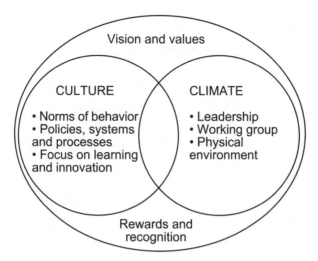

Figure 7.2 *Culture and climate*

processes. Every organization and subgroup within it has developed its own culture, which is not easily changed. It can be a significant barrier to any aspirations, blocking vital change or causing mergers to fail. It can also be a company's powering strength.

Climate includes all the local influences that coexist with the wider culture; and there may be many variations. It is particularly affected by the people—their geography and history—and by local leadership.

The enormous difference that a culture can make to productivity can be seen by comparisons within an industry. Southwest Airlines is a famous example of a very people-centered culture, full of fun and care for employees. In 1993 the number of passengers carried per employee was 2,318, comparing with an average of 848 for all American airlines. Lufthansa flew 470 passengers per employee. The famous German airline was not short of competence or other intellectual capital, but its ways of working were radically different, and its ability to harness and leverage its human capital was constrained, although it has now changed considerably.

The combination of culture and climate includes the following kinds of characteristics:

❑   Norms of behavior—what is expected, what is OK and not OK
❑   The amount of "fun" that goes along with the work

❏   What gets rewarded
❏   Degrees of freedom and empowerment as opposed to bureaucracy
     and restraint
❏   The match between authority and responsibility
❏   The extent and effectiveness of communication
❏   The amount of trust in the organization
❏   The level of respect and flexibility regarding the individual.

These are not fixed for ever, although most can be affected by changes in management and direction. If the organization is taken over or merged, it can experience a revolution—which is usually acutely uncomfortable. Merging two organizations with polarized approaches to some of the dimensions above is a recipe for disaster.

Five factors that influence successful motivation

The following factors have been chosen as those that make the most difference, for which we need indicators of our degree of success:

❏   Leadership direction and management style
❏   Physical environment
❏   Working group
❏   Opportunities to learn and develop
❏   Rewards and recognition.

How these relate to culture and climate is summarized in Table 7.2 opposite.

THE EFFECTIVENESS OF LEADERSHIP

Those who study the rise and fall of firms have no doubt that high-quality leadership is an organization's major asset. Poor leadership not only affects things like low morale, absenteeism, and attrition, but might also give rise to complacency, failure to respond to markets and customers, poor strategic choices, and many other undesired effects. Share values

(doesn't make sense)

Table 7.2 *The effect of culture and climate on motivational factors*

INFLUENCING FACTORS	MAINLY CULTURAL	MAINLY CLIMATE RELATED
Leadership and management style	Relatively low—influenced by espoused leadership vision and values	High
Physical environment	Medium—subject to corporate policies and funds allocation	High—mostly shaped by team leaders and the teams
The working group	Very low	High
Opportunities to learn and develop	High—influenced by organizational emphasis on learning, investment in growth and potential, and corporate processes	High—on-the-job and action learning, plus money, time, and recommendations given for personal development
Rewards and recognition	High—corporate schemes and processes likely to be significant	Medium—mainly in scope for recognition

usually respond noticeably when key leaders leave or join organizations, so this is measurable in real shareholder value.

If the organization has strong values, and this component is given considerable weight in the Individual Asset Multiplier, leaders will be expected to be role models for those values. Therefore, one measure of leadership would be the average value of this component, either company wide or in a given unit.

The US-based Conference Board published a study in 1998 called "The Leadership Gap," where it surveyed the Fortune 1,000 companies, and found that only 8 percent rated their leadership as excellent and almost half as fair or poor. These sad figures come from a national culture that is famous for its positivism!

Leadership comes at different levels. In many organizations the chief executive has a pivotal place as the final decision maker and model of behavior. But in organizations and cultures where hierarchy has less influence, *collective* leadership and decision taking are common. Evaluating individual leadership styles in such teams may be unhelpful, since it is the combination of individuals that comprises the real leadership.

When it comes to local climate, an individual team leader of a remote part of the organization will probably have a greater effect on the output of that particular team than will senior management decisions. However, they are not always their own masters in their freedom to manage. I am continually amazed at the constraints placed on many affiliate (as US companies call their overseas operations) company managers by headquarters back home in America, and this is often also true of Germany or Japan and others. The local people may have some simple solutions to a morale problem, such as pay adjustments, bonus changes, new office layouts, but they are not allowed to implement them as they are not consistent with "policy."

The role of leadership in maximizing the effectiveness of human capital is spoken and written about continuously. In a value-creating organization these are the behaviors we want to see:

❑ Providing clear direction and vision, enabling people to take decisions themselves
❑ Ensuring that people are clearly accountable
❑ Being a visible role model for the organization's values
❑ Showing an overriding and balanced concern for stakeholder value
❑ Supporting the growth of people's capability through coaching and work assignments
❑ Building and maintaining a learning and sharing environment
❑ Providing recognition for achievement
❑ Empowering people to innovate and take decisions
❑ Outlawing a "blame" culture
❑ Continually being open to feedback
❑ Keeping people fully informed of what is happening and regularly listening to their input.

How can we track leadership capability and understand whether the balance of its impact is positive or negative? First of all, it is leadership's job to produce *results*. The productivity or added value of the unit is the ultimate output measure and this is a fair reflection of a leader's ability to gain results through people.

The best people to judge how effectively a leader is leading are the followers, hence the strong emphasis on behavioral assessments, based on capability frameworks and 360° feedback. The resulting summary of perceptions is also an output measure of leadership effectiveness, since the style and behavior of leaders will affect morale and motivation. Good systems of multi-input feedback will give more than a mere numeric evaluation, but through open comments offer examples that enable individuals to relate to the reality of how they are seen. However, some of the instruments in use are extremely complex, and delve into such detail of perfection that they risk being demotivating to the leader concerned.

One other sign of good leadership is that people want to join the team and are reluctant to leave. So a stability index may be useful here: the average time people have been with the particular leader by choice.

Are there any inputs to leadership effectiveness other than the leaders themselves? Clearly, one is our ability to select—and promote—the right people, and the criteria and processes we use have a significant influence. A measure would be the percentage of appointments made that are successful. We adapt our criteria based on experience and in order to increase the success rate. Another input is the extent to which we invest in leadership development, programs aimed at self-awareness, personal change, and people management skill improvement. Not all such programs achieve very much in terms of the outcomes we have mentioned, however, and this is often due a lack of clarity on the desired outcome.

Leif Edvinsson introduced to Skandia a human capital measure called the empowerment index. This is constructed from an independently conducted survey of how people feel about control over their daily work. It is about being provided with the necessary time, training, resources, and authority to do what you feel your accountability requires. This requires considerable trust and security on the part of the leader. Given the knowledge and skills, and hence personal confidence, much evidence shows that people perform and grow more successfully under these conditions. It seems a worthwhile output of effective leadership.

To summarize, measures of effective leadership include:

❑ Productivity or added-value measures for the group being led
❑ Multi-rater feedback on leadership capabilities
❑ Values rating in Individual Asset Multiplier
❑ Absenteeism for the group
❑ Losses from the group through attrition and transfers

❑   Empowerment index—perception of self-determination of the working environment

❑   Stability index—average service in the team by choice.

Measures of influences on effective leadership are:

❑   Selection criteria—percentage success rate of appointments made

❑   Leadership development—days' investment per year per leader.

THE PRACTICAL ENVIRONMENT

In my first management job as a production manager with Procter and Gamble, my six months' training period included Friday afternoon sessions with the plant manager. In these meetings we would discuss various people management topics. Soon after my appointment, I remember putting into practice a simple lesson from his session on motivation. I went around the operators asking what frustrated them most. As a result of this, three simple purchases of long-awaited equipment got me off to a good start as their manager! Small things can be very influential on morale and motivation—office temperature, some privacy, a printer that works, a coffee machine, and so on.

British Airways designed its new headquarters with the goal of maximizing the opportunity for people to meet and exchange. A central "street" provides refreshments, places to sit with colleagues, and information booths. Flexibility of time and place for many roles has led to "hotdesking," where it is assumed that desks are only required for part of the time and you take the nearest desk available. Some people value the freedom inherent in the arrangement; others become very demotivated by an absence of personal space and having their established environment turned upset down. Personal productivity is reduced until a person feels stabilized. We need to avoid general rules for all without taking the trouble to understand the needs and concerns of each person individually.

Space is one thing, but equipment and facilities are another. The "brain drain" of doctors and scientists from the UK to the US in the 1970s and 1980s was largely due to the prospect of being able to work with the latest equipment. Today, for example, information systems hardware and software are such essential tools that their availability can be a major motivating or demotivating factor.

All too often, company policy determines what is "good for you" in the work environment. Standardization of where and how people work comes from seeing people as cost-based human resources. Case studies of highly innovative companies show how freedom for people to define their own working space, facilities, and equipment can be very significant. So one input measure here would be the degree of freedom that people have to "do their own thing."

These are the kinds of questions worth asking:

❏ How satisfied are you with the tools and equipment provided for your work?

❏ What changes in your working environment would you find motivating, or would remove irritations and dissatisfaction for you?

⏵ THE WORKING GROUP

For most people, the group they work with can be a powerful influence on their level of satisfaction. Many people want to make and enjoy friendships at work, and like the social side of it as much as anything else. The rise in voluntary working from home and self-employment is much publicised, but this section of the population is still very much a minority.

A workgroup is often unjustifiably called a "team," which should be defined as a group with one common goal and yet interdependence. Good leaders seek to maximize team spirit, on the assumption that this is a positive input to motivation in its own right. But many work on their own personal accountabilities, with some dependence, either psychologically or workflow-wise, on other colleagues. Sometimes the dependence is critical, and an input or output from other group members determines the person's effectiveness.

It might be worth asking a particular group to define its own desired "character." Their resultant picture of themselves can then comprise a useful benchmark for them to periodically check against. For example, the group might say:

We want to be a group where:
- ❑   We all have special skills and knowledge that is known and respected
- ❑   We share new learning from any source
- ❑   We put the team needs above personal preferences
- ❑   We celebrate success and work to learn from our mistakes
- ❑   We always talk positively about the group to others
- ❑   We face up to interpersonal difficulties honestly and constructively.

At some agreed interval, group members can rate how far the group is from achieving its goal, in their view. If teamwork is one of the espoused values of the organisation, data from such surveys might be collected and monitored.

There are many openly available tools for members of a team to enable mutual assessment and team development. One of the better known is by Dr. Meredith Belbin, who identified nine different contributory roles, and his questionnaire identifies the primary and secondary roles of each person. Another is the Team Management Index developed by Margerison McCann. This groups team members under Explorers, Organizers, Controllers, and Advisers, and has a 15-minute questionnaire for individuals to complete.

Relationships with other workgroups—either internal or external—may also be very important, and this can be built into the measurement instrument, such as "We cooperate fully with the X or Y team."

There is evidence that stability of teams and workgroups who share common goals is related to continuing performance. People learn how to work (and play) effectively together; they come to share similar values and processes and trust one another; they plan and strive for common purposes—celebrating or commiserating about their achievements together.

In summary, examples of measures here are:

- ❑   Team assessment against an ideal template of working practices
- ❑   Inter-team cooperation indices

❑ A team stability index, by taking the average time that team members have spent with the team (this index can be averaged for units or departments).

LEARNING AND DEVELOPMENT

In exchange for the loan of human capital, learning and development form a major part of the added value that people expect in return. This does not necessarily mean progressing continually onwards and upwards, as that is for relatively few. But people want to see investment in their capability, and opportunities to use their potential.

> A SENSE OF MAKING CONTINUAL PERSONAL PROGRESS IS WHAT CONSTITUTES A CAREER FOR MANY PEOPLE.

There are some fundamental aspects of the organizational culture that foster learning, innovation, and change. These are so critical to the value-creating organization that the next chapter is devoted to understanding them. Here we will focus on the individual's perspective, and how we add value to everyone.

Supporting individual learning

We want to enable all employees, at all levels, to be consciously competent as regards the processes of learning. They should see improving their own value as closely linked to building their capability—not in a vague general sense, but in a planned and targeted way. Table 7.3 outlines the steps that they should be able to undertake and the skills needed to do so.

All of this requires considerable knowledge of how learning can be made effective. Ian Cunningham, in *The Wisdom of Strategic Learning*, provides excellent advice on self-managed learning, and how it can be made a way of life within an organization. One effective mechanism is learning sets, where individuals come together from diverse backgrounds, but at approximately the same level in the organization. They explore concepts and ideas, share experiences and knowledge, and help each other with their own learning plans.

Table 7.3 *Process for effective self-management of learning*

STEP	KNOWLEDGE AND SKILLS
1 Diagnosing learning needs	• Understanding the components of capability • Using any capability dictionaries, either hard copy or electronic • Using self-assessment tools • Receiving feedback constructively • Creating a personal career plan and knowing the capability requirements of a target job
2 Defining learning objectives	• Setting priorities • Defining end goals in SMART (Specific, Measurable, Achievable, Relevant, Time-based) terms • Understanding the value of on-the-job experience and action learning
3 Choosing learning solutions	• Understanding the process of learning • Understanding personal learning style • Awareness of learning opportunities from the people and situations in the workplace • Knowing what courses are available • Balancing time and money
4 Negotiating time, money, and other resources	• Negotiating skills
5 Implementing the plan	• Time management • Disciplines of monitoring learning
6 Reviewing success	• Did it happen? • Self-assessment • Seeking and receiving feedback

Good learners will also understand their preferred learning style. Figure 7.3 shows the cycle of learning. Each of the four stages matches with a learning style and each of us has a preference. There is a questionnaire published by Peter Honey, written with Alan Mumford, that is a standard in this area. Briefly, it links four styles—theorist, pragmatist, activist, and reflector—to the four stages of the learning cycle, and the associated guide (see References) explains how one can be more effective in using the whole cycle. Training courses rarely take people around this cycle effectively on their own; effective learners know how to complement them to complete the cycle. *(seems underdeveloped)*

Personal development plans

Feedback on performance is the main source of personal development needs, especially when it is multi-input, i.e., a balance of self, peer, boss, and subordinate views. We need also to know something about how the business is changing and whether the requirements of the role will demand new knowledge and skills, or a greater depth of existing ones.

cf Lewin + Kolb

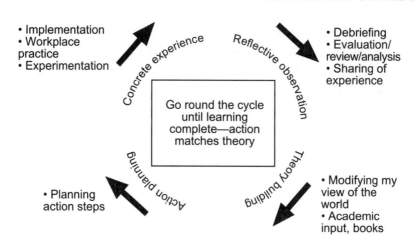

Figure 7.3 *The learning cycle*

These may arise from business change, from technology developments, or from changed responsibilities.

Then, from a personal point of view, there is the question of how I intend to grow my potential. If I have a target job in mind, do I understand what is required of it and what gaps I need to fill, either in skills, knowledge, or experience? Many organizations also invest in a person's employability as part of a *quid pro quo* for employee flexibility. This is investing in aspects of the individual's human capital that may not be of benefit to the business itself. The focus here is on transferable skills—such as an MBA or learning a language—which may not have a current direct business link. This can be looked at as more of an employee benefit than specifically for the benefit of the organization; an expense rather than an investment. Development actions taken under this heading should be distinguished separately.

Most people do not have very clear career goals, other than the desire to make progress. But we start from a belief that everyone has some capacity for growth in their capability and, for some, into more demanding roles. The value-creating organization will be concerned about the following:

❑   Every person has the opportunity to explore their potential and ambitions

❏   The organization has a systematic approach to judging potential, and a common language to describe it
❏   A dialog takes place between the individual and the organization
❏   Where needed, assistance is given to help people realize their potential.

For the first point, we can use structured workshops, with some specialist questionnaires, helping people to explore:

❏   What they are particularly good at
❏   What they know they enjoy
❏   What drives them
❏   The nature of their aspirations and the level of their ambitions.

Unisys has an online Career Fitness Center. This enables people to assess themselves at their own desk—their capabilities, their ambitions, career paths available, training and development options—leading to a personal career plan. In Sun Microsystems, career exploration workshops are offered to people to enable them to explore their capabilities and their "fantasy job," and the options—both internal and external—that might suit them best. They can choose a career mentor, who might or might not be their boss, and develop an agreed development plan. All jobs (other than a few very senior ones) in Sun are openly advertised and anyone can apply. The emphasis is very much on personal ownership, but with heavy underlying support.

     The earlier in a person's career this exploration of motivations and ambition can be done, the better. It enables the person to orient themselves to the line of progress that is best for them, discovering what Ed Schein calls their "career anchor," or preferred kind of work. They will need to revisit this exploration later; typically one might do this two years into work, seven years, fifteen years, and twenty-five years. The latter is important, as ambition gives way to other kinds of personal fulfillment. Many older employees can give value in new ways, such as coaching others, maintaining key customer relationships, and so on.

     I am indebted to Chris Smith of Cable and Wireless Global for Figure 7.4, which summarizes the inputs to a personal development plan.

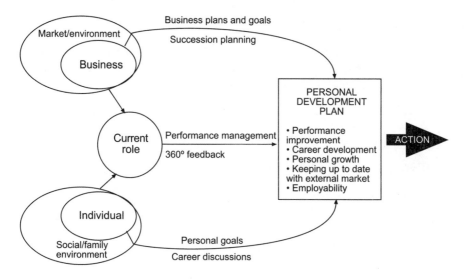

Figure 7.4 *Inputs to a personal development plan*

The choice of learning objectives in the plan is critical. People make progress by concentrating on a few things at a time, so prioritization is necessary. Many personal development plans have very vague generalized objectives (such as "improve communication skills"). A good capability framework helps to create SMART—Specific, Measurable, Achievable, Relevant, and Time-based—objectives that will help us define the right learning solution and evaluate its success.

Building blocks of experience

By far the largest part of capability development comes from experience. Development plans should therefore feature not just action learning, but specific blocks of experience to be gained. Figure 7.5 overleaf is an example of a format designed for the finance function of a large retail company, aimed at assessment and planning for professionals.

Other players in developing individuals

The obvious person to pinpoint as helping individuals develop is their team leader or manager. Such a person holds unique opportunities, as

CAREER BUILDING BLOCKS IN A FINANCE FUNCTION

For the individual concerned, shade the box where the experience exists already (write in the number of years of exposure), and use a yellow marker pen to indicate where experience is needed in the next 5–7 years.

AM Cash/asset management	CC Credit control	EC Electronic commerce	ER External representation
FA Financial accounting	FM Financial modeling	FOM Finance operations management	FSD Finance systems development
IA Internal audit/control	II International involvement	IL International location	INV Investment analysis
MM Managing managers	MT Managing a team	OT Member of operational team	PC Pricing and commercial
PM Project management	PF Planning and forecasting	HQ HQ coordinating/ development	RM Risk management
SP Strategic/ business planning	TX Taxation	TY Treasury	VN Valuation

Note: If the aiming point is a finance director or managing director, experience outside the finance function may be specified, e.g., logistics, distribution, purchasing, IT systems, retail operations, commercial, marketing, property management, company secretarial, personnel.

Figure 7.5 *Career building blocks in a finance function*

they determine who does which tasks, sits on which committees, or takes on new challenges. They control the management of experience.

Many organizations say how much they want their managers to be coaches, and this is clearly desirable. But some will never be good at coaching and it is unrealistic to cajole them or hope that they will get better. We gain more from helping individuals learn how to detect the people around them who can help them: developing "coachee" skills, asking for coaching help, and being clear about what is needed. For example, making requests such as: "I need to improve my relationships with the accounts department. Could I just go over with you what is happening periodically and perhaps you can suggest ways in which I could approach them differently?"

We could summarize the manager's role in developing staff as including:

❑ Stimulating individuals to help themselves
❑ Involving others in the learning process
❑ Delegating responsibilities
❑ Looking for opportunities for new learning
❑ Showing by example, role modeling
❑ Systematic coaching
❑ Organizing job sharing/rotation
❑ Allowing risk taking
❑ Encouraging experimentation
❑ Giving (and receiving) feedback
❑ Ensuring the transfer of off-the-job learning to others
❑ Assisting with the implementation of new learning
❑ Budgeting sufficient funds
❑ Arranging experience/knowledge sharing.

The manager is not the only partner in the learning process. Individuals can learn from all the people around them, and receive coaching as well. Indeed, it is not unknown for a manager to seek coaching from an experienced subordinate. In my first job as a production manager, Arthur was a senior operative who had seen young graduate managers come and go for years. Arthur advised and coached me through both technical and personnel problems just as much as my formal manager did. Many of the roles outlined for the manager can also be taken by team members, or by external coaches and mentors.

Mentors are people who have a long-term offline relationship with an individual, helping them with decisions about career moves or various problems they are facing. If organizations provide them at all, it tends to be for certain populations such as new graduates or "high potentials." Many people develop informal mentors of their own.

Measures for success in learning and development

We want to see processes working effectively, evidence of personal growth, and individuals who can answer "yes" to questions such as the twelve summarized by Buckingham on page 158. These enable us to define some key measures:

❏ The percentage of people with personal development plans
❏ The percentage completion of development plan actions (measured annually)
❏ The increase in the capability component of the Individual Asset Multiplier (measured individually or collectively)
❏ The number of people leaving because of perceived lack of opportunities for growth
❏ Opinion survey questions relating to how people see investment in their growth, opportunities for career development, availability of feedback, manager support for learning, availability of training for their needs.

These output measures will be most influenced by the prevailing culture and an appropriate level of investment in training and development.

REWARDS AND RECOGNITION

In reward management there are four fundamental questions:

❏   How should we determine an individual's base salary?
❏   When and why should we increase it?
❏   How would we want to utilize bonuses and incentives?
❏   What would we want to recognize in a nonmonetary way, and how
      should we do it?

In the value-creating organization, it is logical that remuneration in total should reflect a person's Human Asset Worth. However, we suffer from a chicken-and-egg syndrome, since we have decided that salary should be the basis of calculating HAW. It is the Individual Asset Multiplier part of this that should give us clues about the relative value of people. Fortunately, we do not have to rely on base salary alone.

Job evaluation and grading

Evaluating jobs for their size and responsibility is primarily aimed at internal fairness, since it is possible to agree more easily about the nature of a job than it is that of a person, and this helps avoid accusations of discrimination as well. Nevertheless, fixing a grade for a given job has increasing difficulties in a value-creating organization.

❏   It assumes that jobs and organizations are static when they are usu-
      ally not
❏   It perpetuates hierarchy as an organizational model, and size of
      responsibility as a major source of "points"
❏   It assumes that the boundaries of the job will be the same for each
      individual holder
❏   It takes no account of the prior knowledge and experience of an
      individual, nor their potential
❏   It searches for internal relativity in a world where often pay rates
      are determined by external market factors
❏   It causes political games to be played to secure desired results.

Because of this, the principle of paying for the job must be questioned. Clearly it is not totally irrelevant, but at best it should provide only a base framework for salary banding. There is an inherent lack of logic in the assumption that the value of an employee relates primarily to their current job. Jobs are not static and their boundaries are increasingly determined by the individual involved, especially in the case of knowledge workers.

There are good arguments for not having grades at all (for example, to encourage lateral career moves), and some broadbanding approaches have largely eliminated them. However, people often need to have some visible sense of progress other than salary increases. One practical solution is to maintain a framework of salary banding based on job responsibility, but to have different grades available for a particular job. For example, if the evaluated level for a role is X, then the range of people undertaking the role could be from $X - 1$ to $X + 3$. Another way is through the use of progressive job titles within the same broad band.

In the British Civil Service—and, indeed, in other large bureaucracies—a person's grade defines their cumulative value, at least as perceived by superiors. The Service values you for your experience and consistency of performance, and grades you accordingly. Whereas jobs are also graded, the system of promotion is based on the person and you are available for jobs requiring a person of your grade.

Many organizations in the UK have multiple career ladders where people can rise to higher levels because of expertise alone, without becoming managers. This approach is consistent with rewarding personal value, but is not a common practice in many other cultures where hierarchy predominates and it is unacceptable to have subordinates with a higher salary.

Base salary and its increase

What should base salary reflect? In the past it mostly reflected the current job size, and people moved within the band allocated by either time served (as in the public sector in many countries, and in Japan generally), or by annual performance, or a combination. HR departments conducted salary surveys of the market, against job groups and particular individual jobs, to decide the range of increase desirable. Some organizations have policies about positioning in the market; for example: "We aim to pay in the upper quartile," or some similar statement.

External salary benchmarking is nearly always job based, and elaborate analysis is done to take account of company size. Data relating to individual incumbents is rarely included, and this means that a rough guide is all that is achieved. The salary an individual actually holds within a company, especially at a senior or specialist level, is often the result of recruitment bargaining or of the way salaries and promotions have progressed internally over time.

Competency-based pay is a move toward individual valuation and away from the job focus. It is often firmly within the job evaluation framework and may be a substitute for performance-based pay, or an additional factor. More commonly, the assessed competency level is positioned within broad salary bands. The issue is what constitutes "competency" and whether the factors are holistically related to contribution, rather than mere behavior.

What would a value-creating approach look like?

The *amount* of value added is not consistent from period to period, and rewards based on it should be in variable pay (on which there is more detail below). The *basic* value of a person must be related to the factors that comprise our Individual Asset Multiplier, namely:

❑ The range of relevant capabilities
❑ Potential for growth
❑ General contribution level to value added
❑ Alignment with values.

We would expect salary to increase with any positive movement in these factors. Capability should grow with experience—new experiences that are relevant and valuable, not just time served. If we cannot see any change over a year, it would make sense to question whether the person should remain in the role. Getting new knowledge through a course or qualification *per se* is not enough; "capability" implies that a person can apply what they have learnt within their role.

Promotion also tends to be associated with a salary increase. This is to some extent a legacy of job evaluation and hierarchical thinking. If the promotion is an upgrading on a professional "ladder" resulting from demonstrating a new level of knowledge and experience, it is a retrospective reward for increasing capability. If, however, it is a promotion to a higher level of responsibility, a token rise may be given in anticipation of the extra value expected from the new role, with the opportunity for further increase as increased value is demonstrated.

It is probably a good idea to move away from a fixed date of increase for everybody. A flexible approach can help emphasize the focus on the individual. Computer company ICL gave every manager a "pot" of money each year, and planned how it could be used throughout the year to recognize individual promotions or other changes in value contribution. Such increases would take into account any general rise in salaries through cost of living. When a person moved departments, they took their planned increase with them.

Performance

The basis of salary increases, other than on promotion, has moved strongly toward performance. HR departments agonize about the number and wording of performance levels to reflect accurately what people have achieved and how they have done so. Elaborate procedures are developed around the objective setting and performance reviews, aimed at finalizing an annual rating that feeds into the pay increase, even though in times of low inflation the differential reward may be minimal between one level and another. Performance in recent years frequently reflects assessed levels of behavioral competence as well as achievement of job-based objectives.

There are many difficulties with this approach.

❏ The assumption that a person's value increases—either internally or externally—because of a year's performance has little logic. That does not mean that we would not appreciate their performance and want to reward it, but it brings us back to the fundamental question of what base salary should reflect.

❏ Even with preset objectives, there are a number of factors that influence performance other than the person's efforts and capability. It is rare that one can control one's organizational destiny over a year, and objectives themselves become out of date often shortly after being set. Readers may have experienced, as I have, objectives not being set till well past the second half of the year!

❑ The process of setting objectives is far from perfect in most organizations. Often it is through negotiation, but sometimes objectives are submitted by the individual and approved without much discussion. One person's tough objectives may be another's piece of cake—and yet when it comes to performance ratings achievement is the goal rather than the value added from the achievement.

❑ The rating process itself is fraught with what are often emotional difficulties. To give a rating lower than last year might be objectively justified but can ruin self-esteem, especially if that rating influences promotion discussions. Consequently, managers tend to minimize conflict. One UK public-sector organization's experience was that after two years 95 percent of the people were good or very good—effectively a two-point scale. The original purpose of scales had been lost.

❑ Ratings are usually individual. For people whose main goal is a shared team objective, they would be inappropriate unless we can isolate their own contribution.

❑ A rating is an average—and averages are the enemies of truth. What matters is the detail of what went well and what did not, and why. In the end, a narrative summary has to be communicated to be of any value; why go beyond this?

In conclusion, ratings are not to be recommended. The performance that really matters is the achievement of targets for adding value to stakeholders. It is much more logical to reward results achieved through variable pay systems than through base salary. Of course, *consistently* good results will be reflected in the added-value factor of the IAM. This is why companies like Exxon-Mobil and Enron use a ranking system for pay awards based on perceptions of the individual's worth.

Variable pay

Variable pay comprises incentives and bonuses: money-based rewards that depend on results achieved. *Incentives* are designed to motivate people toward specific kinds or levels of achievement. To be effective there has to be a close and (as perceived) worthwhile relationship between the effort and the reward. *Bonuses* reward achievement after an event, and the anticipation may be an incentive in itself even if the final amount is initially unknown. The trend in recent years has been to move to a higher ratio of variable to base, and to extend the principle of variable pay to more and more people. Nevertheless, many organizations are still rather conservative in this respect, and the public sector particularly is constrained by government policies from implementing a reward strategy that reflects its organizational goals.

Variable pay should reflect what is delivered. It can be done at three levels:

❑ The individual's personal contribution
❑ The contribution of the team
❑ The contribution of the organization (or unit) as a whole. This is often included to demonstrate the "one family" concept and to counter parochialism. Also it is the results of the whole organization that influence investor confidence.

Many schemes at the enterprise level have been created on the basis of Economic Value Added (EVA), enabling employees to share in the overall results of the company and encouraging them to understand how they can contribute to the value-adding process. Hewitt Associates, one of the leading consultancies in this area, calls such schemes VBM, or Value-Based Management. "The over-arching goal of any genuine VBM system," they say, "is to create a company culture pervaded with value-creating behaviors like improved productivity, eliminating waste and reducing inventory."

EVA-based schemes have been spreading for managers' incentive plans, although outside the US it is rare to take them to all employees. One interesting exception is the US Postal Service, which has more than

70,000 people in its scheme. In 3M and Eli Lilly, where EVA (or an equivalent) is the main base of performance management, schemes are being progressively taken further and further down the organization. These examples are all financially driven, and are appropriate for long-term incentive plans. When used on an annual basis (or less), they may well seem to focus on cost cutting and process engineering under another name. Incentive plans that balance value creation for all stakeholders are to be recommended in order to be consistent with the logic of short- and long-term value creation.

The other powerful way of sharing in the value goals of the company is to enable employees to be shareholders, thereby doubling their stakeholder role. In a concept pioneered in the US and taken up extensively in the UK, more slowly in Europe, increasing numbers of employees are becoming part owners of their company.

In the value-creating organization everyone should share in wealth creation, with a mixture of individual and/or team-based targeted incentives plus enterprise-wide rewards. The timing of payments needs to be carefully considered. When a bonus is only annual, some extraordinary behavior can be seen toward the end of the year as people become more and more focused on their bonus plan. What we want is consistent contribution.

The value-creating organization will be very open with people about the measures in use, explaining where necessary, and ensuring that they are understood and that the way in which they can be influenced is fully comprehended.

Many of the quantified indicators that are commonly used may not have a clear relationship to value. Salespeople can still be bonused on "orders received," for example; the result can be orders at any level of profitability. Staff managers may be bonused on project milestones, activities that are part of their job in any case. An example would be: "To put in place a new leadership development program by July 1st." This is a task objective without any real measure other than a time milestone. At the very least, it should be accompanied by a measure of the value added that results from the activity. Such a program should be linked to both increased leadership capability, as perceived by those led, and to improved results from the leader's team. This may require going beyond the financial year in question to get the measurement—a clear case of a long-term component. If such a program is running regularly, then a target for increase in the parameters of success (e.g., changed 360° perceptions, productivity) can form an ongoing performance measure for the individual concerned.

Restructuring and job changes can make longer-term rewards difficult to manage. And frequent rounds of "musical chairs" also make achievement of sustainable added value difficult. A good guideline to follow might be that a person stays in a role long enough to achieve both the current and sustainable longer-term added value that the role is designed to produce.

Benefits

In some countries many benefits have come to be accepted as normal additions to salaries, and these comprise a significant part of the value added to individuals. Benefits have been built on the top of job evaluation/grading systems and sometimes may be serious aspirations. Employees may be desperate to reach the grade that brings the company car, or entry to the stock option executive group.

These kinds of incentive, if built on the grading structure, encourage people to think that their value is increasing solely through hierarchical progression. In fact, this is a very undesirable philosophy for the organization. People who are unsuitable for management may feel that this is their only way to reach their aspirations; careers are forced upwards in silos when we may need people to grow laterally and build breadth across several functions. Particularly in the UK, where some 40 percent of new cars are corporately owned, the company car is a real symbol of status and often defines the level of a person in the organization.

All this is slowly changing for the better, toward fully or partially flexible benefit frameworks. Providing a menu of benefits, which can add up to a percentage of salary, enables individuals to tailor this part of their remuneration to their individual circumstances. Best of all, it removes the internal pressures for people to manage their careers in a way that may not be in either their or their organization's interest.

Nonmonetary recognition

Nonmonetary recognition can provide an equally strong opportunity to reinforce key messages and reward desired behaviors. For example, the recognition that comes from delivering seminar papers may be highly prized by research people. Some enjoy travel opportunities; others having time to contribute to their local communities. Being celebrated in the newsletter may be appreciated, but a sincere "thank you" can make someone feel good. As with all recognition, a range of available options that appeal to the individual is a better strategy than a general fixed approach.

The value-creating organization particularly recognizes the following:

❑ Customer delight—occasions when a customer is so pleased that they become an "evangelist" for the organization as a supplier
❑ Suggestions and innovations, better ways to do things—the cost of awards here is almost certain to be very much less than the benefits that result
❑ Knowledge creation and sharing—role models should be celebrated
❑ Innovative learning—examples of creative initiatives
❑ Recruitment of valuable staff—what more value-adding contribution than increasing the human asset value of the organization?
❑ Enhancement of the organization's image—through public presentations or involvement in the community.

Measures of the effectiveness of rewards and recognition on motivation

It is interesting that Davenport, in studying what mattered most to high and low performers, found that remuneration on its own had the lowest priority for both groups. However, there are limits and we need to be regularly checking how people feel about their levels and makeup of financial reward. Dissatisfaction with salary can result from a perceived unfair increase, from matching oneself against the market, or from feeling that others are doing better without good cause. It can also be due to the way the system for administering rewards is managed. All of these need to be checked. People will leave quoting salary as their reason—we should try to distinguish between those who were genuinely dissatisfied and those who were attracted by the "offer they could not refuse."

With regard to recognition, we need to check whether people feel it is enough, and what they think of the approaches we use. We might also track the numbers of people who are recognized in certain schemes—for example, excellence awards, idea contributors, or external honors granted.

Thus we have:

❑ Opinion survey questions built around the fairness of remuneration levels and systems
❑ Opinion survey questions concerning levels of recognition
❑ Numbers of people receiving different kinds of recognition
❑ Reasons for leaving related to reward dissatisfaction.

HR policies and practices determine these areas and need continual review. Whereas we want to benchmark against other companies and the market, there are some dangers in changing to what is seen as best practice in order to be fashionable without being very sure that the change will enhance our value-creating environment.

How Do We Measure Culture?

Almost certainly, we shall need to track culture on a number of critical dimensions. We cannot measure culture in any absolute way, but we can characterize it and plan changes.

It is very unlikely that we will achieve any cultural change unless we know where we are going. We need more precision than mere one-line statements such as "being more customer focused" or "being lean and mean." People need a set of behaviors with which to identify, and these must be supported with processes that require those behaviors to happen. In tracking progress, we have two options:

❑ Utilizing an established cultural change instrument

❏ Creating our own template, a set of statements describing where we want to be.

The diagnostic marketplace offers a number of instruments. One such is the Organization Culture Inventory (OCI). This uses 12 interacting dimensions that are scored from one to six, as follows:

❏ Humanistic-encouraging—*participative, involving*
❏ Affiliative—*priority on good relationships*
❏ Approval—*conflict avoiding*
❏ Conventional—*rule based, risk averse*
❏ Dependent—*hierarchical and centralized*
❏ Avoidance—*blame placing, cautious*
❏ Oppositional—*confrontational*
❏ Power—*based on authority levels*
❏ Competitive—*win-lose; me first*
❏ Perfectionistic—*100% solution, no mistakes, highly detailed*
❏ Achievement—*goal-oriented, problem solving*
❏ Self-actualizing—*creative, fun, innovative*

The main advantages of these openly available tools are that many (like this one) are well researched and enable comparisons with other organizations to be made.

Creating your own template

There are benefits in building our own instrument, especially if it is done by the senior management team defining the culture for which they want to aim. It will then be clearly owned by its creators. As they identify gaps between the current situation and the desired state, they will set their own priorities for cultural change programs and drive them. It will also focus on the key areas that they feel are important, rather than attempting to describe every aspect of a culture. They need to be careful that they do not commit themselves to values and behaviors that they are unable to demonstrate personally, however.

The recommended process for creating a template is as follows:

❏ The senior management team should come together to define the culture that will best support their goals for delivering value

❏ Before they start they may want to look at the values—here in the sense of "ethos"—that they want to be the basis of working together

❏ Identify the stakeholders and take each in turn, asking the question: "If we were delivering maximum value to this stakeholder, what would they say about our organization and its people?"

❏ Take the resulting statements and group them in logical categories

❏ Rate how close the organization is toward each statement on a scale of 0–10

❏ Analyse the resulting gaps for priority planning

❏ Repeat the rating exercise every four to six months and reset the change priorities if necessary.

Figure 7.6 illustrates how this process would be used. The template would probably contain 20–30 statements.

Category	Statement of desired culture	Current rating of this statement	Target rating for next survey	Priority for action

Figure 7.6 *Creating a cultural template*

This template can be turned into a survey document and used with a sample of employees, or (preferably) with all of them. The desired behaviors may occur sometimes but not consistently, so ratings should be based on the scale of "always the case" (10) to "never the case" (0). This may be subsumed within a more general employee satisfaction survey, but it is better separated in order to provide the appropriate emphasis.

The aspirational end state has to be communicated in meaningful ways and continually illustrated with examples of it in action. Changing culture is a long process and top teams and chief executives are often not around long enough to see the fruits of their labors. This may be one reason that employees constantly feel that they are in the midst of culture change. The desired state does need to be revisited, so that current management feels ownership. It is all too natural at least to give little priority to the passions of one's predecessors, if not to reject them out of hand.

SUMMARY

People lend their human capital to an organization, but their actual contribution depends on their motivation and commitment. Motivated people give of their best. Although personal drive, values, and circumstances come into play, motivation is mostly influenced by the environment in which people work. The environment is a combination of the underlying culture—the values, rituals, processes, and systems of the organization—and the local climate that is created by leaders and managers.

Levels of motivation and satisfaction can be seen explicitly through indicators such as attrition and absenteeism, and measures of perception such as employee opinions. But we need to understand and track the factors that influence these. The significant factors are quality of leadership, the physical working environment, the work groups to which people belong, the extent to which people are developed, and the rewards and recognition that they receive.

It matters considerably to most people that they have opportunities for training and development. Personal development plans require inputs from four sources: performance feedback, the changing needs of the business, the person's career plan, and additional aspirations for solely personal development. People need help in owning and managing their plans.

In the reward area, systems that enable base salaries to be linked to the value of the individual rather than the current job they are doing are better. Incentive and bonus schemes play a key part, but should be linked to value added to one or more stakeholders, both short and long term. Benefits are an important aspect of this and a flexible approach is worthwhile, including nonfinancial rewards to recognize the diversity of individuals.

CHALLENGES FOR ACTION

❏ How and when are motivation and commitment assessed in your organization?

❏ Do you measure the effectiveness of leadership?

❏ Do you measure the attractiveness of the working environment?

❏ Do you have measures of effective teamwork?

❏ To what extent are people skilled in building and managing personal development plans? Do these go beyond the output from appraisal discussions and embrace longer-term development? What measures do you have to check their effectiveness?

❏ How does your reward system recognize individual value?

❏ To what extent are bonus and incentive schemes firmly linked to both short-term and long-term stakeholder value measures?

❏ How flexible and varied are your benefits and recognition policies?

❏ Do you have a template for the organization's culture that matches the business aspirations? Is it understood by all and at the heart of organizational change programs? Do you track it?

8

(building a supportive environment)

Innovation and Learning

I N THE LAST CHAPTER WE EXAMINED MOTIVATION AND COMMITMENT, AND the specific aspects of culture and climate that affect them. An organization dedicated to future value growth is one that places a premium on innovation, flexibility, responsiveness, continuous learning, knowledge sharing, and adaptability to change. Many organizations readily espouse these aspirations, but find it difficult to make them a reality.

In this chapter the characteristics of an innovative environment are discussed, and creativity is examined as a capability. The concept of a learning organization is assessed, particularly at the level of the organization as a whole. We look at how knowledge is managed and shared, and setting up a system to do this effectively. This is all fundamentally dependent on the expectations, norms, and processes that make up the culture of the organization. The mindset of the human resource professional in the value-creating organization is considered, as is how an organization's HQ might be restructured to put the right focus on intellectual capital management.

INNOVATION

When investment analysts look at a company, they are heavily influenced by news about new products and services that are potential revenue streams. But innovation means much more than designing new products or services. Innovation includes:

❑   Acceptance of and readiness for change in every person, and throughout the organization

❑   Dedication to continuous improvement of processes

❑   Willingness to experiment and explore new ways of working, new suppliers, new technology

❑   Eagerness to learn from others

❑   Creating new markets and customers

❑   Building new relationships and alliances

❑   Establishing new approaches to markets: channels and pricing strategies

❑   New and varied approaches to organization, management, and performance measurement.

On the first day's induction of new graduates in my first job, this maxim was given to us and has stayed with me ever since: "There is always a better way, and it is the job of all of us here to find it." In the manufacturing department, bonus schemes for all employees were based partly on measures of innovation and change. One was about new methods, defined as any change that achieved the same quality of output but required less resource. An annual target was set for a cost savings percentage (approximately equivalent to the rate of inflation), and teams around the factory worked toward their particular part of the target. Another measure was revisions, which was the shortening of standard times for operational tasks as better ways of working emerged. Everyone was involved in the processes of looking for improvement and was rewarded for it.

The process of innovation is itself a key business process. Some of the fundamental issues include: How are customer needs identified? How are these translated into something customers want to buy? How are new products and services introduced and delivered? The measures here are about fitness for purpose, speed to market, and rapidity of takeup by the market. Another important issue is the number of times a product might have to be modified in the light of customer reaction. This factor can be critical, especially if the media pick up early bad signals about a new introduction.

What characteristics do we expect of an environment that encourages innovation? It would include the following:

❑   There are formal and informal systems for encouraging suggestions for improvement

❑   Suggestions are analyzed quickly and evaluated with an open mind

❑   Suggestors are involved in implementation of successful ideas

❑   Everyone is expected to contribute to change and improvement

❑   Mistakes made from experimentation are in no way penalized (in some companies "glorious failures" are celebrated)

❑   Money and time are made available for experimentation

❑   Exceptional new ideas are widely publicised

❑   People are generally empowered to make change without seeking prior authority.

In addition to these creativity-encouraging behaviors, disciplines within working practices must exist. The aim of product/service innovation is to generate future profitability, not merely to have a volume of new product ideas. Each market introduction requires manufacturing, marketing, training, selling, and servicing—all of which are costs that may not have a return. Those involved in design and development need constant close liaison with frontline people, preferably with customers themselves. They also need business knowledge, to enable them to understand the dynamics of product introduction costs and subsequent returns.

Peter Drucker argues that innovation is to do with hard systematic work rather than genius or inspiration. He recommends the zero-based audit, taking a cold look at every process and aspect of the organization every three years or so, putting them on "trial for their lives." Drucker recognizes how important external stimuli are to innovation and puts a great deal of emphasis on continuous listening, benchmarking, and receiving feedback—all key aspects of the learning organization.

In *Thriving on Chaos* Tom Peters gives equally good advice. He emphasizes the importance of multitudes of "small starts" and gives ten preconditions for this to work well:

❑   Let everyone talk to customers and listen

❑   Get customers into the organization

❑   Establish a "do-a-pilot" mentality rather than "write a proposal"

❑   Use small teams for almost any task

❏   View suppliers as co-innovators rather than adversaries
❏   Remove bureaucracy to let small teams get on with it
❏   Flatten the structure and work across functional boundaries
❏   Develop a market-creation rather than market-sharing mentality
❏   Treat products as experiments meriting constant improvement
❏   Management must live the message of rapid innovation.

Companies frequently have innovation as one of their espoused values. 3M has one of the best-known reputations in this area, and it features "3M Innovation" as a company strapline. It puts great emphasis on the freedom to fail, and in R&D has built the priority of innovating into its ways of working. Here are some examples:

❏   The 25 percent rule: 25 percent of sales must come from products developed within the previous five years
❏   The 15 percent rule: people may spend up to 15 percent of the working week at their discretion, provided it is product related
❏   Genesis grants: up to $50,000 for researchers to develop projects past the idea stage
❏   Golden Step Awards: for projects achieving $2 million profitable sales within three years of launch.

Another company with a very successful innovation culture is IDEO, a contract R&D firm based in California. This was established in 1978 and has won more than 30 Industrial Design Excellence Awards. "We believe in a prototype-driven culture, not specification-driven," says founder David Kelley. "That means learning from experience and expecting to make mistakes."

Some interesting aspects of IDEO's culture are:

❏   No recruitment plans, but if someone is seen or approaches the company "who we must have," they are hired
❏   Any potential hire is lunched by 10 employees who rate the prospect, who needs to be at 9 or 10 on all the selection criteria
❏   No hierarchy or organization charts, and therefore no opportunity for promotion; employees do have mentors, however

❏ Motivation comes from internal trophies presented at project competitions
❏ There is no HR department
❏ A great deal of effort goes into cross-fertilization of ideas and people.

Resources

In many organizations there are surprisingly few people dedicated to building the future. There are many who are supposed to worry about it along with dealing with the present—and, not surprisingly, it is usually the future that gets squeezed out. In a sense, we want *everyone* to be thinking about the future in terms of continual improvement, whatever their role. But we also want people whose prime concerns are:

❏ Understanding what products and services people will want to buy in the future
❏ Designing and developing those products and services
❏ Understanding the trends in the competitive marketplace
❏ Seeking and evaluating potential partners
❏ Identifying new areas of competitive advantage
❏ Building the future capability of people
❏ Culture and processes to be aligned with business goals.

Innovation/creativity as a personal capability

Individuals vary enormously in their ability to "think out of the box," create new concepts, or develop new working methods. But truly creative people are rare, and do not always fit in easily with the bureaucracy associated with large organizations. However, we are after an attitude of mind, both in individuals and in the culture of which they are part, that is totally oriented to improvement. This is surely within everybody's scope; all it requires is motivation and a supportive environment.

Innovative people are renowned for the following:

❏ Constantly challenging their own assumptions and those of others
❏ Seeing problems as learning and innovation possibilities

❏ Understanding and regularly using basic techniques for challenging the status quo, like brainstorming
❏ Always being curious.

The implications for managers are about providing time for thinking and experimentation, allowing mistakes, always being open minded, and encouraging ideas.

Fiona Patterson, together with Oxford Psychologists Press, has developed a specific tool for assessing innovation potential based on five years' research. Called the Innovation Potential Indicator, it focuses on key behaviors that enhance or impede change and improvement. It measures four scales:

❏ Motivation to change—the extent to which an individual is open to change
❏ Challenging behavior—the questioning of the status quo
❏ Consistency of work styles—an individual's preferred approach to work
❏ Adaptation—the preference for doing things differently as opposed to using tried-and-tested ways of working.

This instrument assesses natural inclinations and has value as such, but, as we have seen, how well they flourish is very much influenced by the environment in which people work.

Appropriate measures of innovation

We summarise the *output* measures of successful innovation in the next chapter, which is focused on the contribution of people. From a cultural point of view, however, here are some indicators that are inputs to effective innovation:

❏ Investment levels in intellectual capital—in people development, product/service development, market growth, systems that will bring better quality and delivery, etc.—as a percentage of revenues (or, for people, of employment cost)

❏ Full-time equivalents (FTEs) of people spending time on future value as a percentage of all FTEs

❏ Percentage of people rated high on creativity

❏ Appropriate cultural measures and opinion survey questions that support openness, experimentation, and empowerment.

A LEARNING ENVIRONMENT

Innovation and change come from learning. Learning in some people's minds is associated primarily with study leading to qualifications. To others it is predominantly about training. The truth is that the majority of adult learning comes from experience and experimentation.

> THE MAJORITY OF ADULT LEARNING COMES FROM EXPERIENCE AND EXPERIMENTATION

The term "learning organization" dates from around 1989, and is frequently adopted as an aspiration, although many organizations struggle to realize its potential in practice. It is fundamental to growing future stakeholder value. The subject continues to preoccupy management debate, but the essential point is that a learning organization manages learning in a deliberate and systematic way. In other words, learning is not something that simply happens, but rather something that is *managed*.

The best-known description of a learning organization is found in Peter Senge's *The Fifth Discipline*. He sees it as maximizing five disciplines:

❏ Personal mastery—individual capability

❏ Team learning—groups of people learning together

❏ Shared mental models—a common view of how we should operate together

❏ A shared vision—a common aspiration that all individuals embrace

and the most powerful of all:

❏ Systems thinking—seeing the connectivity and synergy of the different parts of the organization working together.

In an effort to break the concept down to the practical details of everyday working life, Elizabeth Lank (who became director of knowledge management for ICL) and I developed a model that is described in *The Power of Learning*. We defined a learning organization as one that:

> *harnesses all the brainpower, knowledge and experience available to it, in order to evolve for the benefit of all its stakeholders.*

An organization needs a culture that maximizes learning at three levels: the organization as a whole, the team or workgroup, and the individual. There are four key enablers to its achievement: a clear committed policy, supporting leadership behaviors, people management processes, and effective use of IT. We produced a Learning Organization Index, a template of some 70 practices that typified an organization wanting to manage learning effectively.

Something like this can provide a good starting point. Nevertheless, it can be more beneficial to create a template that is specific to a given organization, not least so that particular and familiar ways of saying things can be adopted.

Managing learning

A good learning organization looks beyond training and off-the-job programs. It takes a much broader view and considers the learning environment as encompassing a wide range of activities. These four modes of learning illustrate the principle.

❏   *Education*—this is about knowledge and insights, changing people's "mental map." It is not confined to studying for qualifications, valuable as these can be, but includes any form of learning aimed primarily at the mind. This includes many business school programs, e-learning offerings, and self-study through books and research. In terms of our approach to capability, it influences (in addition to qualifications) the knowledge part of know-how, and also may change attitudes and build networks.

❏   *Training*—aimed at skills, in business and professional know-how, and personal behaviors.

❏   *Experience*—here we mean learning from one's current job, plus through planned workplace assignments, projects, secondments, career moves, job rotation, special responsibilities, and so on. Experience also affects the other areas of capability: growing knowledge, skills, and networks.

❏   *Learning from others*—this includes coaching, mentoring, shared experiences, belonging to communities of practice, seminars and conferences. Coaching relates more to specific problem areas needing help; mentoring is more a longer-term advisory role, often taken by someone other than a person's manager. Organizations may have formal mentoring processes for certain groups of people (such as new graduates), but a network of informal mentoring will almost certainly exist as well.

Any identified area of capability growth needs clear, SMART objectives, with the desired level of proficiency clearly stated. The learning solution chosen might well involve a combination of the modes above. Table 8.1 shows, for example, a menu of learning options for developing change management capability:

Table 8.1 *Example of learning options for change management capability*

EDUCATION	TRAINING	LEARNING FROM OTHERS	EXPERIENCE
• Understanding when change is necessary and when not • Doing cost–benefit analyses on change proposals • Models of organizational and individual change: – Books (Kotter, Eccles, Bridges) – E-modules – Workshops – Kotter video – Techniques of analysis	• Workshops in self-awareness in change, communication, and involvement • Problem and potential problem analysis • Project management • Learning from experience	• Coaching from an experienced manager of change • Exchange of experiences—successes and failures • Research of a change project against a chosen model—what worked and what didn't	• Managing a real-life change project through a disciplined process; review with colleagues or coaches • Self-analysis of personal experience as a recipient of change

There is a wealth of literature about the evaluation of training, ways to show that training has been successful and influenced the bottom line. There are many other factors that may influence the final goal, but if we can show that relevant capabilities themselves were enhanced, the training will have an eventual effect on a key outcome. Much training may in fact be *subtracting* value by taking people away from their workplace and engaging them in activities that do not increase their capability for providing value.

ORGANIZATIONAL LEARNING AND KNOWLEDGE MANAGEMENT

Learning at the organizational level is about a mindset: of openness, listening, constant iteration and adaptability. It is also about benchmarking with the best, to see what can be learned from outside. This includes setting up listening mechanisms with stakeholders: surveys, focus groups, meetings with management, and so on.

Lew Platt, former CEO of Hewlett-Packard, is quoted as saying, "Our problem is we don't know what we know." What he meant was that each individual did not have access to all the knowledge and experience available in the company, and consequently was missing out on an immense potential advantage to their work effectiveness. Mistakes are repeated, projects are duplicated, successful new ideas kept quiet about, time wasted searching for information already there. The acquisition, exchange, and application of knowledge throughout the organization form what is often called knowledge management. This is an essential part of a learning organization culture, and therefore vital to human capital growth.

> AN ENORMOUS AMOUNT OF VALUE IS LOST THROUGH INEFFICIENT USE OF WHAT IS ALREADY KNOWN IN AN ORGANIZATION.

The sharing of knowledge in itself builds innovation, as ideas are sparked through interaction. Systematic management of knowledge therefore helps both profitability and the creation of new intellectual capital.

What should be shared?

What kind of knowledge will be useful to others? We do not need to be inundated with the new knowledge acquired by every individual every day, even if that were feasible. We need some kind of architecture for what really needs to be shared. Individuals find their own way of recording or remembering what is important to them, and each group needs to do the same. At the level of the organization as a whole, there may be relatively little that is of interest to every employee, beyond shared information about the infrastructure and news of the company. Nevertheless, the core strategies, competences, and processes of the organization will be supported by what might be called "strategic knowledge assets." Such assets should be owned and maintained by designated persons. They are the people who make sure that all who are involved in using them know what should be shared for general benefit.

An example of a core strategy might be "To focus on customer service and become the best"; and a core competence could be "Our supply chain." A core process might be the methodology for managing mergers and acquisitions. All of these would be supported by our accumulated knowledge in the area concerned.

Elizabeth Lank, writing in *Long Range Planning*, listed three categories of knowledge for sharing.

❏ *Repositories of reference material*—This includes documents that can be shared or reused, such as proposals, market research, product uses, and so on. It also includes basic information about the infrastructure of the organization: sites, procedures, policies, etc.

❏ *Expertise maps*—These enable the sharing of tacit knowledge to take place, making available the knowledge, expertise, and experience of each individual in a way that enables easy access. It is more than a job title and phone number, more than a CV. What we need is people's personal profiles, but including past experience and areas outside of the workplace. The experience needs to be specific—e.g., not just "Five years of project management experience," but "Project management of a £5 million software installation for local government." People should also include specialized knowledge outside of work itself, which may be useful in some specific customer situations. So if a customer has a passionate interest in flying, the salesperson might want to find out more about it from a colleague, or even use that colleague in the selling process. This enables employees to quickly find the experts who can help them. NatWest Markets, an investment bank, created a "Green Pages" with the slogan "Two calls to find out anything you need." BP Amoco has been immensely successful with a directory called Connect, where people have individual web pages on the company intranet.

❏   Just-in-time knowledge—Here we are bringing news, both internal and external, to people as it happens, enabling live discussion about problems, and providing training or formalized knowledge available as and when it is wanted.

How will sharing take place?

Many knowledge management initiatives have been driven by IT departments, and some powerful tools have been developed. Individuals can profile their interests and special search software will comb the internet daily to find items of interest, which then appear in their mailbox. The ability to find information and to query or discuss with colleagues has grown very fast. Technology is not the problem! However, it can only work with what it is given, and is only useful so long as it is used. Many have found that the practicalities of input of, and access to, knowledge systems are frustrating and time consuming. Surfers of the internet are aware of how long it can take to find out quite simple things despite the ever increasing sophistication of search engines, because they are coping with a mounting volume of available information and knowledge.

Organizations with experience in knowledge management have realized the importance of facilitating face-to-face exchange and online electronic discussions, rather than relying solely on complex electronic databases of text and reports and inputs of variable quality. Web and groupware-based tools are becoming more and more sophisticated (and easier to use) all the time, but harnessing them is always subject to the motivation of people to engage with them.

Why should people participate?

Why should an individual give their knowledge freely to others, or find out what others have done? There may be many excuses for not doing so. A very real problem is time: some of the more sophisticated knowledge management environments provide too much for people to access, even with the best will in the world. Accessing all the information available and keeping up to date with it can consume many hours each week, as does taking the time to record and share knowledge and experience as it is acquired.

There are also deeper barriers. People see their knowledge as their personal human capital, their power, and giving it to others might be an unacceptable loss of security. Programs to capture people's knowledge do not often work well. Much better is to let the organization know who has expertise and how to get in touch with the right person. Helping a colleague is likely to be more amenable than giving to a system, and many people enjoy others coming to hear about what they know. It builds rather than threatens their self-esteem. They can also control how much they give.

There may also be a natural obstinacy about accessing what others have found, a desire to learn from your own mistakes or do it your way. These attitudes may be embedded in groups as much as in any individual. The question to be answered always is: "What's in it for me?" Perhaps it will make the job easier by providing easy access to knowledge that will help, or there may be some positive recognition for acquiring and sharing new knowledge.

One way to encourage people to take some ownership for knowledge sharing is to foster communities of practice. McKinsey defines a community of practice as "a group of professionals informally bound to one another through exposure to a common class of problems, common pursuit of solutions, and thereby themselves embodying a store of knowledge." Such communities can emerge naturally, but boundaries encourage isolation in the devolution and decentralization of many large organizations.

National Semiconductor set up a Communities of Practice Council, with a community for each of the critical technologies for its business. The Council helps the communities deal with the technical side of communications, and provides funds for meetings and travel. The company found that building these communities helped staff retention at a time when this was a major problem. However, it avoided trying to manage the communities. Some of the most valuable experience has been in errors and mistakes from which people have learned a great deal, but they may not be too keen to publicise them for all to see. They *will* share them with people they trust, and that is what communities of practice foster.

The supporting culture

Expectations in the working environment condition much of our behavior. What is acceptable and what is not acceptable? What is encouraged and what is discouraged? Admonitions and exhortations to be good sharers of knowledge are unlikely to achieve very much. Leaders are responsible for setting expectations and role modeling them. Unlike some eastern cultures, most western ones do not naturally encourage sharing.

Some of the characteristics we want to see in a value-creating organization that is focused on knowledge management are these:

❏　Positive encouragement for sharing through setting up opportunities and recognizing those that do this

❏　Outlawing personal blame when things do not go as anticipated; open learning from mistakes

❏　Having "managing knowledge" as an established and expected capability for everyone

❏　Building knowledge-recording disciplines into everyday processes

❏　Giving time for storytelling

❏　Providing an emphasis on coaching and knowledge transfer from experienced people to the less experienced

❏　Systematic induction into new positions, including internal transfers

❏　Publicising (on a database system) each person's special knowledge and experience

❏　Using performance discussions to emphasize what is expected.

Building a knowledge-managing organization

Elizabeth Lank listed five practical suggestions gleaned from her experience of trying to make knowledge management more effective in a large computer systems company.

❑ *Ensure that individual performance measurement and reward do not get in the way of sharing.* This means not only care in the design of individual schemes, but providing incentives for people to contribute. In British Telecom, small financial inducements are given for people to both share and access information that is considered strategically vital. It is not difficult to track individual contributions and reward them accordingly.

❑ *Provide public recognition of the desired behaviors*: encouraging publication and speaking, and making knowledge sharers "heroes."

❑ *Integration with key business processes.* Processes form the everyday life of an organization, and some simple disciplines can make all the difference. In the UK, a unit of the Post Office called Post Office Consulting has made this aspect a priority. Its project management procedures, for example, not only have mandatory project reviews with lessons learned to be posted on the database, but right at the start a "knowledge plan" must be prepared. This is designed to force teams to think of the knowledge they should access before they start, how they will manage ongoing knowledge during the project, and what they will do at the end.

❑ *The role of IT.* This is not only having sophisticated systems, but also making sure that people know how to use them effectively. There are a surprising number of managers who are relatively illiterate on basic IT applications; they can just about manage email. IT skills are essential for everyone if we want to maximize knowledge sharing.

❑ *Make it easy.* There are many demands on time, and people quickly become impatient. Systems must be as user friendly as possible. It helps to have some knowledge specialists who assist with the transfer of tacit knowledge, that in individuals' minds and memories, into explicit knowledge, available to everyone. In Post Office Consulting, there are knowledge champions who take accountability for knowledge management in their area and help colleagues to participate. General Motors in the US instituted a process of decision tracking, where trained people interviewed executives after key decisions had been made to understand what led to their judgments. In ICL's service business a knowledge engineer has the job of managing the answers to technical queries and making sure that all technicians have the best answers readily available.

Colin Armistead, Professor at the Centre for Organisational Effectiveness at Bournemouth University in the UK, has researched the approach of many companies to knowledge management. He quotes one of them:

> *For the first six months of our knowledge programme ... we ended up making it as complex as we could, because we thought it was a complex area. Confused the hell out of the organisation ... What helped— stories. Stories from the operators, particularly where by not having access to the right knowledge it cost many months, that sort of thing.*

How do you get started in this critical area? The chances are that you have already begun. A great variety of knowledge will exist explicitly in some form. There will be meetings set up to exchange knowledge. Most companies will have intranets of some kind. But it is quite likely that there is scope for greater coordination, and much knowledge rests in isolated pockets.

Table 8.2 summarizes some of the key measures we might use as a supplement to our Human Capital Monitor. Table 8.3 summarizes the steps involved in building a systematic knowledge management environment.

Table 8.2 *Measures of success for knowledge management*

KNOWLEDGE MANAGEMENT	
OUTCOME MEASURES	INPUT MEASURES
• Reduction in costs of mistakes due to duplication and lack of access to existing knowledge	• Number of functioning communities of practice
	• Number of common databases
• Customer perceptions regarding meeting their needs	• Number of FTEs with a responsibility for managing knowledge
• Access hit rates to key knowledge databases	
• Percentage of new ideas adopted elsewhere	• Number of best practice seminars per annum
• Increase in critical knowledge capabilities	• Investment in IT tools and techniques
	• Match against a desired cultural template

Table 8.3 *Building a knowledge management environment*

STEP	ACTION	COMMENT
1	Make a deliberate decision at the top level that knowledge needs to be managed in a coordinated way	This top-team commitment is essential, so that everyone can see that it is seen to be important and not just the latest fashion from IT or HR
2	Appoint an individual with dedicated responsibility, and a small team	Exhortations alone do not go far. Investing in resources indicates real commitment. Ideally this group would be part of a larger intellectual capital department. If free standing, it should report to the board and not to any one function. The group should be small, and its role coordinating and facilitating; it should not decide what people "should" want. The team needs a balance of skills: influencing, systems thinking, business knowledge, business process development, project management, consultancy, IT expertise, change catalyst
3	Conduct a mapping exercise of what knowledge is being managed already, and how this is being done	Departments will vary. R&D may be well advanced. Look particularly at how knowledge is—or is not—crossing the boundaries in the organization
4	Define a "yellow pages" directory to enable people to have access to others' knowledge and expertise	This is an essential component: putting human capital in touch with others, and publicising their capability
5	Identify strategic areas of knowledge assets	Work down from key strategies and the top areas of added value to stakeholders, looking at the influences on each. What areas of knowledge are critical to support them?
6	Assign ownership to each area of strategic assets	Ownership will mean that the person is responsible for new knowledge, and for capture, exchange, and utilization in their area
7	Identify communities of practice and ensure that they are communicating effectively, both live and virtually	Provide enabling budget money for them, and ensure that they have a champion or coordinator. In some cases this ownership will overlap with the previous step
8	Define the cultural characteristics that are needed for effective knowledge sharing, and measure against them	This should be done by the senior team and provide a template for ongoing monitoring and progress measurement
9	Design a program of cultural and process change as necessary to move toward the required state	This may involve education for attitude change, but mostly it is building the demands of knowledge management into processes and reward systems
10	Equip staff with the necessary capabilities to take full advantage of the knowledge management framework	IT skills, but also those of sharing and learning from other individuals and teams
11	Develop shared knowledge bases and the provision of just-in-time information applicable to all	Include matters of interest to all employees
12	Provide software tools that encourage virtual transfer and exchange	Each "knowledge owner" should choose their own tools—the central role is to ensure that they know what is available
13	Provide a forum for the exchange of practical and useful knowledge management approaches	Learning from others about knowledge management itself
14	Develop metrics that track success in knowledge management	These include the reality of desired behaviors, increases in innovation measures, peer assessments about sharing, cost and time savings as a result of better knowledge sharing, improved employee and customer satisfaction

CORPORATE UNIVERSITIES

Corporate universities are on the increase. In the 1990s the number rose from 400 to over 1,000, and it continues to grow apace. The term covers a multitude of different realities.

For some it is a rebranding of their training department, with a heavy element of e-learning. The virtual university, which brings corporate and technical knowledge to the desktop, is a feature of Dell and BAE Systems. Ernst and Young has a Virtual Business School.

It can be a vehicle for professional accreditation, and for marketing publicity. Centrefile, a company specializing in outsourced payrolls and HR systems, encourages all employees to take professional courses through its university. It seeks competitive advantage through its qualified staff, and has been very successful.

Frustration with business schools has led some organizations to conclude that they could manage educational programs better themselves, using learning partnerships as appropriate. They achieve tighter control and ownership over the learning process by linking learning to real business goals and strategies. Senior experienced managers are part of the faculty.

This model may be called by another name, such as the BT Academy (British Telecom) or the Lufthansa School of Business. Leading-edge companies are increasingly viewing the company itself as a university, continually stimulating people through an educational and development agenda that is built into the organization's business infrastructure.

Anglian Water, a British utilities company, set up its Aqua Universitas as the center of its knowledge base. With no staff and no products, senior managers acted as deans of faculties, the name given to the owners of strategic knowledge assets.

The ultimate is to see the university as the hub of intellectual capital development. It keeps watch on the outside world, conducts internal and external research of interest to the organization, and advises the board on scenarios. It has a range of partnerships, one of which is with the board itself. There are very few who have this role, a notable one being Motorola, which has always given the highest priority to learning.

Table 8.4 shows the increasing stages of sophistication of the concept.

Table 8.4 *Evolution of the corporate university concept*

ROLE	CONTRIBUTION	RESOURCING
Promotes acquisition and dissemination of new knowledge and insights: • Organization and leadership • Technical/organizational research • Performance improvement and audit • Benchmarking • Surveys	Holistic approach to knowledge creation and diffusion as primary strategic imperative	Works in partnership with: • Top management • Leading-edge R&D • New products and marketing • Business schools • Other companies • Consultants
Virtual center for recording, codifying, and disseminating corporate knowledge as it accumulates through knowledge engineering, action learning, and experience in the workplace	Toward a learning organization culture	Mobilizes and legitimates role of all managers as facilitators of learning and innovation
Promotes sharing of work-based knowledge	Basic functions of any corporate university	Employs selected managers as facilitators of learning
Central hub—integrated coordination and direction of programs and standards	Essential foundations for effective learning	Offers education/training solutions linked to corporately defined needs. Customer/contractor relationship with educational suppliers
Center for cultural dissemination and absorption of corporate values and culture		Closely integrated with corporate employee communications function

Embodies a mission for learning in the organization and a coherent framework for describing capabilities

HRD infrastructure—corporate culture, policies, processes, and practices—support effective functioning

In the value-creating organization, whether with the name of university or not, a model close to the top of this table would be a target. Learning and innovation are the very foundation of growing future intellectual capital. The visibility of the university concept gives a clear internal and external message about what is important.

HUMAN RESOURCES MANAGEMENT FOR INNOVATION AND LEARNING

The contribution of the human resource function in adding value has been admirably covered by Dave Ulrich in his book *Human Resource Champions*. Value is added to the organization through professional expertise and to employees in their capacity as stakeholders.

Once an organization recognizes that its human capital is fundamental to its success, this provides the opportunity for HRM to be a true "business partner" and prioritize activities according to the level of value that will be contributed to the organization. Much of the infrastructure created by the HR function has historically been built around a hierarchical and cost-based approach to valuing people. The overall framework for people management may need to be rethought to ensure that employees develop a mindset based on adding value, particularly in terms of learning and innovation.

Table 8.5 captures some of the characteristics of such a mindset.

Table 8.5 *The value-based approach to people management*

WHAT WE WOULD DO	WHAT WE WOULD *NOT* DO
• Organize by stakeholders	• Organize by functions
• Focus multidisciplinary teams directed at adding value	• Divide and subdivide work for greater efficiency
• Look for complementary capabilities in a boundaryless world	• Look only internally, drawing walls around the organization
• Be flexible and adaptive to local conditions and needs	• Apply the same contractual and compensation conditions to all
• Have a set of key people measures linked to stakeholder added value	• Be limited to measures of the HR function's effectiveness
• Understand who adds most value and how	• Focus on job value, regardless of the person
• Have a priority of retaining high-value people	• Reduce salary costs through uncontrolled voluntary redundancy schemes
• Link rewards to added value	• Build reward systems on hierarchical levels
• Have a clear distinction between work that maintains today's value and that building future value	• Treat all people as heads, equal for accounting purposes
• Strive to eliminate nonadded-value work	• Strive to cut heads
• Ensure that every person's potential is understood and developed	• Believe that only high-potential people need attention
• Work toward a template of a value-adding, learning, innovative culture	• Restrain initiative through heavy bureaucracy and procedures
• Have a comprehensive approach to describing capability	• Have capability frameworks limited to personal behaviors
• Encourage the input of, access to, and sharing of information and knowledge	• Restrict employees' access to information
• Maintain a human asset register	• Produce headcount reports

A DIRECTORATE OF INTELLECTUAL CAPITAL?

Nobody questions the need for the finance function. It is generally a powerful and often large function, with a clear focus that everyone understands. Money is spent all over the organization, and it is coordinated and controlled through a series of rules and processes to which people conform perhaps more than any others. The finance function is also involved in planning and financial engineering (tax and treasury) and often incorporates the IT systems department. Even the HR function may be tucked under the finance director.

Our intellectual capital deserves much more attention, because of its place in the value equation. It too is distributed all over an organization, but rarely is coordinated in any coherent way. It will be managed, if at all, function by function. Each function fights its own battles for money and resources. Intellectual capital is compartmentalized; often the various parts of the organization do not have access to all that is available because boundaries and politics get in the way.

In recent years some companies have set up a central knowledge management unit reporting to the board, but without holding many resources. Its job is to set up the structural capital required, coordinate initiatives, and evangelize the cause of knowledge management. This concept needs to be broadened to incorporate the whole of intellectual capital—including human capital.

Operationally, the value-creating organization would organize around *delivering value to stakeholders*. Cross-functional staff come together to create customer-serving teams, for example. A headquarters should be structured around the *type* of support given to the organization.

Headquarters often has the image of the ultimate overhead with which contact should be avoided as far as possible. If asked what added value is received from it, most operational people would give a wry smile at the irrelevance of such a question. It is with pride that many organizations boast of the leanness of their headquarters, and progressive purges based on empowerment and decentralization, a focus on shareholder value, and a general reaction to overhead costs have brought some HQs of major corporations way below three figures.

Smaller they may be, but rarely have HQs been radically restructured. In almost every case we will find the traditional functions alive and well: finance, legal, corporate affairs, human resources, IT, corporate planning, marketing, and quality. They may not all report to the CEO directly, but they will all be present and have their distinct boundaries.

Each typically protects their territory, and all feel the need to be involved in issues of strategic change. They guard the requirement to approve things because of their controlling role: finance people to spend money, or HR to authorize a salary increase. They will also run their own functional hierarchies through the organization, develop systems and processes in those hierarchies, and hold their own conferences and regular meetings. Functions have professional institutions, entry examinations, networks, and tribal rituals. All of this is human nature, a sense of professional belonging.

Although there are certain to be exceptions, it is generally taken for granted that most of these professional functions are necessary. To have your function represented on the board is a matter of pride and prestige, and to be excluded gives a feeling of "second-class citizenship." One cannot attend any gathering of HR people and not hear someone lament the paucity of board-level HR directors, part of a continuing angst about their own influence and importance.

Everyone involved believes that all the requirements they impose are in the corporate interest. The problem is that the functional silos are driven just as much by their own agendas, led by the functional head. Within their boundaries, each creates initiatives aimed at helping the organization be more effective. Line managers, who are judged primarily by business results, may find themselves juggling operational priorities with requests to participate in the design or implementation of a range of new systems, processes, planning formats, or financial reporting. "Why do we employ all these professionals," they may ask, "when all they do is dream up work to divert me and my people from what we are supposed to do for the customer?"

In their book *Corporate Level Strategy*, Goold, Campbell, and Alexander explore in depth the value provided by corporate parents. The book was the fruit of ten years' consulting and research and is an authoritative work. They conclude that the impact of corporate staff functions is generally negative, and that they destroy value. The reasons they cite include a lack of feel for frontline needs and priorities, and that the parent can become a quasi business in its own right.

We need to "zerobase" headquarters by leaving aside the functional traditions and asking: "What is the added value that a headquarters can provide and how can it be effectively delivered?" This means looking at every activity and what it is doing for the corporation. Starting with each person in each function, classify the nature of their work, and the type of added value (if any) that their activities provide. We then turn the HQ through right angles, so that it is activity based rather than functionally driven.

If we do so, we will probably find the following groupings, illustrated in Figure 8.1.

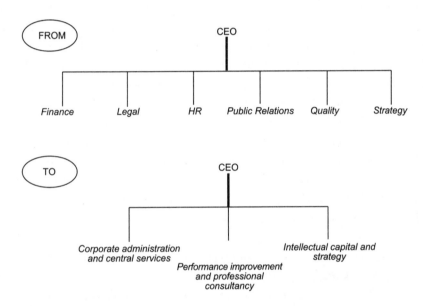

Figure 8.1 *Restructuring functions in the value-creating organization*

Corporate administration and central services (stakeholders: shareholders, parent companies, government)

An HQ has to coordinate and consolidate internally, and has to manage a large part of the organization's external interfaces. Most functions contribute to this in some ways. This group includes, for example, consolidated accounting, internal audit, tax management, treasury management, legal services, pensions, senior management contracts and remuneration, property management, investor relations, public relations and compliance, HR administration, and the "chairman's office."

These all need their specialists, but coordinating them under one director provides both coherence and efficiency in administration. Some activities may be candidates for outsourcing, which is not the case with the other two suggested units.

Performance improvement and professional consultancy (stakeholders: primarily shareholders through improved current performance)

Where appropriate, the best professional experts in, for example, quality management, change management, process engineering, or systems analysis would be made available to the business units as internal consultants. These are the people concerned with how the organization could operate more effectively. This may mean solving today's problems, taking new initiatives, or designing change programs.

Activities such as business unit performance monitoring would come into this category, since this has little value unless it is action oriented. The design of corporate processes (such as are needed) would be here, and with the unit being made up of experts of several functions it would be able to take a truly horizontal view. Some HR consultants would be part of this team, people who understand cultures, reward systems, learning environments, and work analysis.

Intellectual capital and strategy (stakeholders: customers, employees, the public, suppliers, partners)

This is the group that monitors and coordinates the development of intellectual capital, both structural and human. It will not get involved in areas that must be within operational control, such as customer relations or local working environments, although it may well monitor the indicators and share good practices. Like all HQ departments, its prime role should be supportive rather than controlling. Such a unit would bring professionals in from many traditional functions, and its brief may encompass:

❏   Strategic planning—setting directions and major business goals
❏   The performance measurement system—supporting the business goals and the needs of stakeholder value, managing the Human Capital Monitor and similar instruments

❏ Human resource development—increasing capability at the level of organizational core competences, managing potential and career movement

❏ Knowledge management—ensuring availability and flow of strategically important knowledge

❏ Patents management

❏ Research and development

❏ IT systems development

❏ Mergers and acquisitions management; joint ventures and partners if at the corporate level

❏ Community relations, at the corporate level.

For the functional baronies this may sound somewhat like turkeys voting for Christmas, and it will take a brave CEO to restructure in such a way, with clear accountabilities and minimum overlap. But this would focus on value for stakeholders in a much more effective way. Individual professionals would retain their own expertise, but be using it in a different way, and the broadening of their careers will become much easier since functional boundaries and silos are removed.

SUMMARY

Building and maintaining the kind of environment in which people and ideas will flourish is a real challenge. Innovation is much more than creating new products and services: it embraces continual improvement of everything we do. We need a culture of experimentation and openness to new ideas from within and from others. People don't have to have a natural flair for creativity to play their part. It is worth keeping track of the percentage of people and their time that is dedicated to building futures or to improvements, since it is so easy to be dragged continually into the problems of the present.

The foundation of an innovative culture is a focus on learning in every sense and at every level. A learning organization is one where people, teams, and the organization as a whole value learning, especially that which comes from new experience. Managing the knowledge that the organization has for the benefit of all is a vital process, although not at all easy. Deciding what should be made accessible is a challenge in itself, but mobilizing people to give and to take knowledge is an even larger one. Finding ways for people to exchange face to face is more important than all the tools and techniques that IT provides, indispensable though they are.

The kind of culture demanded for innovation and learning needs to be clearly defined, preferably by the senior management team. Having a clear template enables measures of progress to be made, and creating our own is probably preferable to using commercial audit and survey instruments.

People management systems and processes are fundamental, and the part played by human resource professionals has to be a major influence. If they think "value" rather than "costs," it creates a different guiding mindset for their activities. Finally, an organization dedicated to its intellectual capital should organize to manage it effectively, which might mean a rethink of how professionals are grouped in headquarters.

CHALLENGES FOR ACTION

❏ What behaviors would you see in your organization if innovation were alive and flourishing?

❏ What is the ratio of people dedicated to creating the future versus maintaining the present?

❏ How much effort is put into encouraging a comprehensive learning culture as opposed to designing training events and programs?

❏ How is knowledge managed in your organization? How effective is it? Are there people dedicated to it?

❏ Have you considered a corporate university? If so, what role would you like it to play?

❏ Looking at your people management systems and processes, are they built on a foundation of people as assets or primarily as costs?

❏ How could you organize the supporting functions in your organization to focus more coherently on intellectual capital?

9

(third column)

The Value that People Create

T HE NEXT CHALLENGE FOR THE VALUE-CREATING ORGANIZATION IS TO think about the nature of the value that people create and how it can be measured. When we talk about people's performance, we tend to think about achievement in terms of their objectives and targets. Here we want to understand the nature of the value that is added to each stakeholder.

The first contribution that people make to a commercial enterprise is to create financial wealth that can be distributed; this is the "added value" of accountants' calculations. The second is the additional, non-financial value that they add to stakeholders generally, which encourages them to stay working with the organization. This applies to not-for-profit organizations just as well. A third outcome is the result of innovation—new products, processes, and services that benefit customers or the public. We'll look at these in turn.

People's contribution to added value is the third column of our Human Capital Monitor (Figure 9.1 overleaf).

CREATING WEALTH FOR DISTRIBUTION

Wealth is not the same as profit. Employees create wealth that is distributed to various stakeholders, and some is retained in the business and used for further investment. Profitability is important of course, although

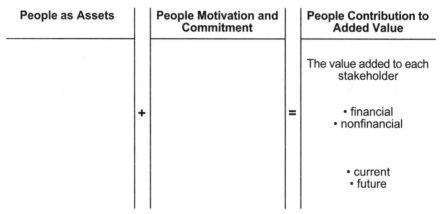

Figure 9.1 *People contribution to added value*

businesses can survive for some years without it provided they have cash. Profits are to some extent a judgment by accountants, and therefore not the best measure of contribution from employees. Revenues are a better measure, as they represent cash into the business.

There is a standard definition of financial value added:

The wealth created through the efforts of the enterprise and its people.

It is simply calculated as the difference between the revenue accruing from goods and services and the costs of bought-in materials and services. Two variations are in use, depending on whether depreciation is subtracted from the resulting figure; if so, it is called the *gross added value*. If not, and depreciation is seen as part of the distribution of the wealth, then the amount is the *net added value*.

Figure 9.2 illustrates how value added is distributed. Financial value added is shared with other stakeholders as follows:

❏ *Customers*: price reductions, promotions, discounts, shared distribution efficiencies
❏ *Suppliers*: volume purchasing, shared supply efficiencies, reduced quality costs
❏ *The public/community*: "free" services, local taxes, sponsorship

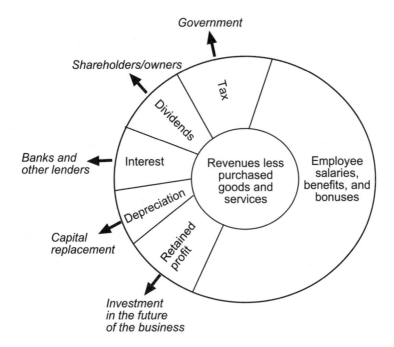

Figure 9.2 *Gross added value: the distribution of wealth*

❏   *The government*: tax collection and other administrative costs carried out on its behalf.

Statutory and conventional reporting in most countries does not include
value-added statements, and consequently says little about the productivity and contribution of the organization's human resource. As far back
as 1977, the UK government recommended that companies should produce such statements (at that time there was a movement to use it as a
source of profit sharing), but this has not materialized. Table 9.1 overleaf
shows the format of an value added statement compared to a more conventional profit statement.

     The message of the value added statement is in the distribution of
wealth, rather than seeing the interests of all stakeholders—other than
shareholders—as expenses that take money from profit.

     Increasing value added per employee does not mean that their
share increases, as this depends on the ratio of bought-in services vs. in-
house production.

Table 9.1 *Example of a value added statement compared to a conventional profit statement*

Conventional income statement	$	$
Sales		**5,000,000**
Less: materials used	*500,000*	
wages	*1,000,000*	
purchased services	*1,500,000*	
depreciation	*300,000*	
interest	*200,000*	
Profit before tax		1,500,000
Less: tax@ 40%		*600,000*
Profit after tax		900,000
Less: dividends		*250,000*
Retained earnings		**650,000**
Value added statement	**$**	**$**
Sales		**5,000,000**
Less: bought in materials/services and depreciation	*2,300,000*	
Net value added for distribution		2,700,000
Applied as follows:		
To employees		1,000,000
To providers of capital		
– dividends		250,000
– interest		200,000
To government		600,000
Retained earnings		**650,000**

Skandia Assurance was able to report in 1998 that it had increased value added per employee from SEK480,000 in 1995 to SEK1,025,000 in 1997, and at the same time reduced the employees' share of value added from 62 to 40 percent. This, the company said, showed a clear transformation of human capital into more sustainable structural capital, i.e., it was using knowledge and system-based assets to generate sales without the need for more people.

Skandia has also worked with an interesting figure called *human capital potential value*. This takes the best-in-class—either internally by unit or externally by benchmark—and calculates what the total added value would be if the whole company returned the same outcome. The company quotes a potential increase in added value of 160 percent if it could emulate the best unit across the whole of Skandia.

Efficiency ratios based on added value

The absolute amount of value added can be divided by the number of people to give a figure per head. This is useful for comparing with other organizations in a similar sector. It should be calculated as far down the organization as revenue breakdown figures permit, enabling us to assess the added value from teams. The further one goes from the "sharp end" (i.e., directly connected to revenue generation), the less easy it is to evaluate the added value of an individual employee.

Some useful ratios for managing through financial value added include:

❑   Value added / costs of labor and capital—a measure of *managerial efficiency*
❑   Value added / sales—a better measure of *productivity* than the conventional profit/sales
❑   Value added / total compensation—perhaps the best overall measure of *productivity*. This is sometimes referred to as the compensation recovery factor.

The proportion of value added to a particular stakeholder/total value added is a measure of the contribution to the particular stakeholder. Thus:

❑   Compensation / net value added is a measure of labor's share in the wealth pool
❑   Net profit / net value added measures the shareholder's share

- ❏ Dividends / net value added measures the shareholder's current return
- ❏ Taxation / net value added is the government's share
- ❏ Interest / net value added is the return to bondholders or banks.

PRODUCTIVITY

Productivity is the output achieved for a certain input. Where employees directly contribute to a quantifiable delivery output, such as sales and production, measuring productivity is easy. It is more difficult when the role is a supporting one, such as an administrative or design function. Sheer volume of output does not indicate that the output is the right output. Productivity in delivering a service—such as IT support—can be measured by the achievement of stated service levels for the resource that is used. In research and development, the volume measure is the number of new products designed, but the real output is their ultimate added value in sales in the marketplace.

Even "hard" productivity measures may not be directly proportional to profitability, cash flow, or added value. For example, a favorite productivity indicator is "revenue per head." This can be growing, and yet profitability and added value can be decreasing because the costs of achieving the revenue are rising faster. In the early stages of a startup this may be fine, since growth is more important than profits. Or we may measure tons or units per head in a factory, encouraging output at the expense of quality.

I once ran a factory making gelatine. The work teams were bonused on tons per week. The scheme was not popular because customer demand was variable; when it was high the teams would produce as much as they could. However, in that market the price of the product depended on a quality index determined for each consignment based on the strength of the gelatine. When we changed the bonus scheme to be based on quality and yield, profitability rose solidly. The obvious output of volume, indicating physical effort, was replaced by an output based on knowledge and skill.

Another example of the dangers of productivity targets is to be found in the UK's educational sector during the 1990s, where the need to meet student quantity targets overrode the quality of teaching and available resources. As a result, students were recruited in numbers far outstripping the capability of many institutions to deliver. The numbers looked good, but most will acknowledge that the marks needed for a standard level of educational achievement have softened. The risk is that success is measured on throughput, rather than outcome.

Another example is found in call centers, where the satisfaction of the call to the caller should be more important than the number of calls handled. People plead for a real person to talk to, and constantly tell stories of endless automated loops and frustrated slamming down of the phone.

Improving productivity by cutting the workforce is what Gary Hamel and C K Prahalad call "denominator management." It focuses on cutting the inputs to the productivity ratios. Much more effective is to focus on growing the outputs—the numerators. Those will be in different forms of added value.

VALUE-ADDED WORK—AND ITS OPPOSITE

Accounting systems treat the work done by people as cost items such as wages and salaries, overtime, bonuses, benefits, pensions, social security, and so on. There is no distinction between the proportion of time spent that is actually adding any value to a stakeholder, and the proportion that isn't.

Tony and Jeremy Hope, in *Transforming the Bottom Line*, argue convincingly for the analysis of work in this way. They suggest a Value-adding Work Index, which is a product of the degree to which work is quality (in the sense of not having to be redone), and the percentage that adds real value to a stakeholder. An enormous amount of time may be consumed by such things as:

- Car travel
- Meetings about internal affairs
- Reviews and updates
- Reading superfluous email

❑   Managing problems that should not have occurred
❑   Redoing work
❑   Reports and information provision
❑   Consultation for its own sake (i.e., it is unlikely to add value to the decision)
❑   Internal negotiation and cross-charging
❑   Arguing for resources
❑   Mistakes, especially when repeated
❑   Duplication
❑   Waiting time
❑   Computer downtime
❑   Regulatory compliance.

You will be able to add to this list from your own experience.

Every organization should have a blacklist of their own, and a notice to place on people's desks or in the meeting room: "Nonvalue-added work going on here!"

There are some roles that can add very little value to stakeholders because they are primarily concerned with "housekeeping," i.e., maintaining the internal workings of the organization. If they did not exist we might well *lose* value. The extent or risk of that potential loss may be a measure of their quasi-value added. Examples are bookkeeping, personnel administration, buildings maintenance, security, legal services, and so on. Each of these is a candidate for outsourcing, rather than letting it take management attention.

There was a time when all tasks were carefully examined and timed. With the growth of knowledge workers, this activity has largely disappeared. No wonder that guru of gurus, Peter Drucker, said as far back as 1991 that "the greatest future challenge is the productivity of knowledge workers." The challenge applies to the vast majority of jobs today. Support functions are adept at creating work (rather than value) for frontline people, whether in private or public-sector organizations. Indeed, the greatest complaint of health and education workers is the volume of paperwork and the need to comply with ever-increasing regulations. These are usually instigated with the interests of the patient or child in mind, but in fact often take time away from looking after their intended beneficiaries.

The degree of value added would be transformed if only a percentage of such work were eliminated. The Hope brothers quote an example from a study by Arthur D Little over a year of a typical engineer in an American automotive company (see Table 9.2).

Table 9.2 *Example of work analysis*

Activity	Value-adding %	Nonvalue-adding %
Solo work:		
Scrap or rework		10
Valuable work	20	
Make work		10
Meetings:		
Useful	5	
Useless		10
Management reviews		5
Preparation for reviews		10
Paperwork:		
Work documentation	5	
Reporting for administrative control and other paperwork		10
Communications:		
Team exchange	5	
Crisis management		5
Miscellaneous		5
TOTALS	35	65

Not good news! Only a third of time spent is value adding, although no doubt the individual engineers are working hard and are relieved when the weekend comes. In another example, Hewlett-Packard surveyed the effectiveness of its UK sales regions. The sales activity was broken down into six key processes and the percentage of nonadded-value work assessed. The data in Table 9.3 were produced.

Table 9.3 *Nonvalue-adding work at Hewlett-Packard*

Process	% Nonvalue-adding work
Planning	0
Product promotion	16
Customer search	28
Selling	35
Postsales operations	62
Control	35
OVERALL TOTAL	**35**

As a result of this study, the vice-president concerned took deliberate action, and half of the wasted 35 percent was eliminated within two years.

There are many consultancy techniques aimed at eliminating non-added-value work, although it seems to be a fact of organizational life that one never arrives at total annihilation.

Automation of processes is aimed at taking out work that is low value added, but process engineering should always precede it. However, Paul Strassmann, who runs his own fascinating website, has shown that there is no evidence that expenditure on information systems over the medium to long term is related to improved financial outcomes. Some firms engaged in installing complex "enterprise-wide systems" may agree with his findings, although Nestlé, as one of the pioneers of the SAP system, reported in 2001 that it would get a payback of its investment in two years. It attributed much of this to eliminating process inefficiencies.

Activity-based management is a way of analyzing the work that is done and the proportion that contributes to adding value. It enables added value to be compared with costs, by proportioning a percentage of the costs. Thus, if the cost of an activity is $100,000, and the proportion of that activity deemed to be added value is 40 percent, the actual value added is $40,000. This is a somewhat crude and purely financial approach, but may be helpful in emphasizing the message of nonadded-value work.

Organizational restructuring goes through fashions, aimed often at cost cutting ("being lean and mean"), or at increasing market responsiveness. Delayering of organizational hierarchies is designed to remove "postbox" intermediaries, and although often reducing career possibilities, it should reduce nonadded-value activity. Reducing the number of headquarters staff is linked to decentralization of decisions and bringing businesses closer to their customers.

Implementing a horizontal information system. Traditional budgets are built department by department and function by function. A horizontal reporting system shows what was

> EVERY INDIVIDUAL AND TEAM CAN HAVE A VERY BASIC PRODUCTIVITY MEASURE, WHICH IS THE RATIO OF ADDED-VALUE WORK TO TOTAL WORK.

spent on key activities. It could show that an underspend against budget might not be great news if we find that very little of the money spent added any value to a stakeholder.

NONFINANCIAL VALUE ADDED TO STAKEHOLDERS

Distributing financial wealth may be the end game, but—apart from those investors with no real interest in the company as an organization—stakeholders have broader interests than monetary returns. People contribute value to the organization's stakeholders in many ways, some of which may have equal or greater weight to any monetary interest. The contribution may be (on average) the same kind of value. But as people learn, innovate, and experiment they are able to contribute more, at a higher and/or different level in the future.

Tables 9.4–9.11 give examples of the nature of nonfinancial added value, some possible measures, and examples of contributing roles. They do not pretend to be comprehensive. There may be subsets of stakeholders that require separate consideration. For example, a local community council may divide its public into different age or income groups.

Employees may be divided according to role (managers, for example, may be a special subgroup) or location. Without making matters over-complex, common sense should be used to identify stakeholders who are particularly important for the organization.

Italics in these tables indicate an area mainly targeted at future value.

Table 9.4 *Stakeholder: Shareholders*

THE HUMAN CAPITAL MONITOR			
Nonfinancial value added to stakeholders—*Shareholders*			
NATURE OF THE VALUE	CONTRIBUTORS	MEASUREMENT EXAMPLES	TARGET
• *Alliances and mergers managed to achieve business goals and maximize retention of intellectual capital*	• Chief executives • Acquisition managers • HR managers	• Achievement against business goals • Unplanned loss of acquired staff • Increase in Human Asset Worth • Increases in strategic capability levels	
• *Investor confidence generated through communications*	• Investor relations • Public relations	• Percentage favorable press references • Share price relative to sector trend	

Table 9.5 *Stakeholder: Parent companies*

THE HUMAN CAPITAL MONITOR			
Nonfinancial value added to stakeholders—*Parent companies*			
NATURE OF THE VALUE	CONTRIBUTORS	MEASUREMENT EXAMPLES	TARGET
• Living the corporate values	• Chief executives • All employees • HR managers	• Employee and leadership surveys • Outcome measures of values such as customer satisfaction and community reputation	
• *Reputation of the parent enhanced*	• Marketing managers • PR staff	• Image surveys	
• *Parent's fulfillment of its strategies*	• Chief executives and senior managers	• Progress indicators that relate to strategy achievement	
• *People and knowledge transfer*	• HR managers • Knowledge managers • IT managers	• Transfers in/out of sister companies and HQ as percentage of all job moves • Participation in cross-organization communities of practice	

Table 9.6 *Stakeholder: Customers*

THE HUMAN CAPITAL MONITOR

Nonfinancial value added to stakeholders—*Customers*

NATURE OF THE VALUE	CONTRIBUTORS	MEASUREMENT EXAMPLES	TARGET
• *New products/services generated*	• Product development • Market research • New product introduction	• Percentage of sales from products/services introduced in last two years	
• Reputation/image enhancement	• Marketing promotion • Public relations	• Percentage of new business coming from referrals • Image perception surveys	
• Quality of service delivery	• Call center staff • Customer service representatives • Trainers	• Customer surveys • Alignment to service delivery agreements • Achievement of set targets	
• Reliability of product delivery	• Logistics managers • Installation staff • Accounting staff • Quality inspectors	• Percentage of deliveries on time • Percentage of deliveries fully complete • Percentage accuracy of invoices	
• Brand definition and recognition	• Marketeers	• Brand perception surveys	
• Satisfaction and *loyalty* created	• Sales staff • Customer service staff • Call center staff • Technical help staff	• Percentage of repeat customers • Customer satisfaction measures	
• Added-value services	• Service sales staff • Service delivery staff	• Proportion of revenue coming from defined added-value services	
• Transfer of information, knowledge, and skill	• Sales staff • Marketing staff • Product development staff • Efficiency engineers • HR staff	• Perception that it happens and examples of it happening	

Table 9.7 *Stakeholder: Employees*

THE HUMAN CAPITAL MONITOR

Nonfinancial value added to stakeholders—*Employees*

NATURE OF THE VALUE	CONTRIBUTORS	MEASUREMENT EXAMPLES	TARGET
• Challenging and interesting work	• Managers	• Percentage of positive opinion survey respones re work	
• Potential discovered	• HRD staff • Managers	• Percentage of people with agreed potential development plan	
• New capabilities developed and potential grown	• HR/HRD managers • Trainers	• Percentage of populations with desired potential categories • Increases in capability profiles for selected groups	
• Provision of feedback on performance	• Managers • HR managers • Trainers	• Percentage of people undergoing feedback process • Percentage of people finding positive value from process	
• Training toward better performance	• HR/HRD managers • Trainers	• Days' training per person • Increases in job-related capabilities	
• Feeling motivated, committed, and recognized	• Managers • HR managers • Trainers	• Percentage of people surveyed indicating high levels of commitment, satisfaction, and recognition • Absenteeism rates • Attrition rates	
• Enjoyment of the working environment	• Buildings managers • HR managers • Managers	• Percentage of people surveyed reporting satisfaction with different aspects of culture and environment • Health and safety statistics	

Table 9.8 *Stakeholder: Suppliers*

THE HUMAN CAPITAL MONITOR

Nonfinancial value added to stakeholders—*Suppliers*

NATURE OF THE VALUE	CONTRIBUTORS	MEASUREMENT EXAMPLES	TARGET
• Enhancement of their reputation/image	• Purchasing managers • Public relations staff	• Number of mentions in favorable publicity • Percentage of new business coming from referrals • Image perception surveys • Percentage of sales from products/services introduced in last two years	
• Onward references	• Purchasing managers	• Percentage of new business for supplier from our recommendation	
• Ideas for innovation	• Knowledge managers • Quality managers • Purchasing managers • Product design staff • Field service staff	• Volume and value of ideas for product change • Volume and value of ideas for forecasting or delivery efficiency • Quality of delivery	

Table 9.9 *Stakeholder: The public*

THE HUMAN CAPITAL MONITOR			
Nonfinancial value added to stakeholders—*Public*			
NATURE OF THE VALUE	CONTRIBUTORS	MEASUREMENT EXAMPLES	TARGET
• Service levels	• Department managers	• Achievement against service level targets	
• Responsiveness	• Department managers	• Satisfaction levels with responsiveness to queries • Time to respond	
• Accessibility	• Public relations	• Availability of "one-stop" information sources • Satisfaction levels with accessibility	
• *Consultation about change*	• Public relations	• Percentage of public consulted on major issues	

Table 9.10 *Stakeholder: Government*

THE HUMAN CAPITAL MONITOR			
Nonfinancial value added to stakeholders—*Government*			
NATURE OF THE VALUE	CONTRIBUTORS	MEASUREMENT EXAMPLES	TARGET
• Support for government programs	• Public affairs • HR managers • Relevant technical staff	• Number of government programs being actively supported	
• *Ideas for change provided*	• Public affairs • Part-time role of various employees	• Number of government bodies on which represented	
• *Resources seconded/exchanged*	• Public affairs • Various managers	• Weeks of exchange time provided in both directions • Number of secondments either way	
• Provision of education and knowledge of private-sector activity	• Public relations • Various support functional managers	• Number of responses to requests	
• Provision of information	• Public affairs • HR, finance, legal managers	• Degree of compliance with requirements • Hours spent providing voluntary information, completing questionnaires, etc.	

Table 9.11 *Stakeholder: Community/environment*

THE HUMAN CAPITAL MONITOR			
Nonfinancial value added to stakeholders—*Community/environment*			
NATURE OF THE VALUE	CONTRIBUTORS	MEASUREMENT EXAMPLES	TARGET
• *Development of young people, providing work experience*	• HR and HRD managers • Managers	• Number of young people given work experience or equivalent • Number of managers involved in development of young people externally	
• *Resource seconded/exchanged*	• Public affairs • Various managers	• Weeks of exchange time provided in both directions • Number of secondees either way	
• Support of ecological balance, enhancement of the visual and aural environment	• Public affairs • Site managers • Environmental managers	• Investment level in improving the environment • External image perception surveys	
• Provision of resource for local programs and committees	• All levels of staff	• Number of staff involved in local programs and committees	

A good example of applying this thinking in the public sector comes from Lewisham Council. In the south east of London, Lewisham has always sought to be a leader in public-sector management. It was one of the first to sign up to the UK government's "Best Value" initiative. Best Value means having services that:

❏ *Local people want and consider provide value for money*
❏ *Constantly improve and innovate*
❏ *Compare well with services provided by other organizations.*

The Council has prepared an annual performance plan and a report on its achievements for its residents. It has put in place measures to achieve continuous improvement in all its areas of responsibility. Some examples of targets for different stakeholders in the community are:

❏ *Saving a minimum of 2 percent per year through ongoing process improvements*
❏ *Increase our lead as the cleanest borough in London as assessed by the Tidy Britain group*

❏ *Enabling at least 55 percent of leavers from care institutions to take up further education or employment*

❏ *Increasing the number of new businesses started as a result of the Council's economic development programs to 50 by 2004*

❏ *Target 38 percent of pupils in schools achieving five or more GCSE grades at above C level.*

Full information of targets and performance is published openly on the internet.

Each organization will have its own table of stakeholder added value. We can decide their relative importance through their place in the cause-and-effect staircases, and everyone should be aware of the three or four most important areas for each stakeholder.

Measures such as in the tables above should be featured in the everyday processes of people management. For example:

> EVERY WORKGROUP AND INDIVIDUAL (AND CONTINGENT CONTRIBUTORS) IN THE ORGANIZATION SHOULD BE ABLE TO RELATE WHAT THEY DO TO SOME MEASURES OF ADDED VALUE TO STAKEHOLDERS.

❏ Each job profile should specify the stakeholders that the role is supporting, and the measures applicable

❏ Measures are used in target setting, and therefore in bonus schemes

❏ Each individual or team is reviewed on their progress against targets as a regular part of performance management.

INNOVATION AS AN OUTPUT

Innovation is a means to an end. However, it is so key to the creation of future value that it should be considered as an output contribution of people in its own right.

The results of successful innovation include:

❏ New services that add value to a stakeholder. Not all new services are *directly* aimed at revenues. For example, not so long ago offering a telephone check-in service to an airline was an innovation aimed at customer convenience, and consequent loyalty—which in the longer term brings continuing revenues.

❑ New products are much more closely linked to revenue streams. Innovation involves not just the production of ideas but turning a sufficient proportion of them into successful ones. A commonly used output measure is:

> *the proportion of sales that come from products or services introduced in the last* x *years where* x *may be 1–3 depending on the sector.*

For example, 3M uses a goal of at least 25 percent of annual sales coming from products less than four years old.

There are risks with measures like this. What constitutes a new product? Japanese electronic companies are adept in introducing almost continual variations and improvements, many of which are testing the market rather than responding to it. So a useful variation of this is to track gross margin rather than sales. We may not know which sales are actually profitable.

Another kind of measure—in, for example, the pharmaceutical industry—is the percentage of sales from proprietary products as opposed to those generically available to all suppliers.

❑ Improved processes and other cost efficiencies, which lead to enhanced profitability. Here we can look at measures such as percentage change in cost per unit; or savings accruing from employee suggestions made.

❑ We might well want to keep track of the production of ideas themselves. We could use measures such as:
—number of new patents registered (patent count)
—number of ideas leading to projects
—citations to patents; these are references by subsequent patent applications, and imply that the original had some usefulness
—number of new suggestions made from employees per head
—number of process changes made in a time period.

Chapter 8 examined the influences on an innovative culture. Combined with the outcomes above, they become part of the Human Capital Monitor as in Table 9.12.

Table 9.12 *Innovation in the Human Capital Monitor*

INNOVATION	
OUTCOME MEASURES	INPUT MEASURES
• Percentage of sales from products or services introduced in the last *x* years	• Number of new products registered
• Percentage of sales from proprietary products	• Number of ideas leading to projects
• Development time for new products	• Citations to patents
• Percentage change in cost per unit produced or customer served	• Number of new suggestions per head
• Cost savings achieved through employee suggestions per year	• Number of process changes made per month
	• Investment levels in intellectual capital
	• Percentage of full-time equivalents spending time on future value
	• Percentage of people rated high on creativity
	• Cultural measures that support openness, experimentation, and empowerment

THE CONTRIBUTION OF THE INDIVIDUAL

Figure 1.3 illustrated the differing levels of contribution to value from the organisation, business unit, team, and the individual employee. At the latter level there are three questions to be asked:

❏ How is the role that people have split between current value contribution, future value contribution, and nonadded-value tasks? We are looking at the ratio of:

(**PVC**   +   **FVC**)   :   **NAV**
present value   future value   nonadded-value
contribution tasks   contribution tasks   tasks

❏ How does the individual manage their time between the three categories of work?

❏ How effective is the individual in generating value using the time that they have available?

If we take a typical week of, say, 40 hours, how much time should be put into present value contribution, how much into future, and how much is required for nonadded-value tasks? For example, a salesperson's main job is to obtain customer revenue (say, 20 hours of the week). They will also be building relationships with potential new customers (measured in the number of new customers over a period), and feeding back a weekly report on how customers are feeling and what their needs are (say, 12 hours a week). Then there is time spent traveling, having meetings, doing routine reports, expense reports, and so on (say, 8 hours). In such a case the ratio of added-value to nonadded-value time in the role available is 32/40 = 80 percent.

This may be the expected norm. However, one person may deviate from this, for two reasons. Their own skills in self-organization plus the demands of their manager and workgroup could mean that the proportions of time spent may differ in their own work environment. For example, the focus on the present may be much stronger (especially if this is driven by a bonus scheme). Secondly, someone may be particularly effective and provide much more contribution from the hours spent.

So some jobs give greater opportunities for adding value, and some individuals produce more value from their job. For each individual, we need to know the information in Table 9.13 (as illustrated in the example of a salesperson).

Imagine if we had this information for everybody. We would really be able to understand the value contribution from people, and also would have valuable data for restructuring how time is spent. Looking at teams in this way can be particularly helpful, not only in evaluating the team's contribution to value added, but in seeing relative individual contributions.

In the example given, the role has a mix of present and future value contributions. Although many have a mix, others are entirely about one or the other. But mixed roles tend often to be dominated by the present and it is a challenge to find the time for the future-oriented work.

One useful tool is to develop a *ranked* order of added-value contribution for roles, and then within a role for the people in them. The ranking could be by percentage of the time available time spent on added-value work. All stakeholders are important, but adding value to customers would generally be considered of a higher priority than others.

Table 9.13 *Added value contribution summary: A salesperson*

The norm for the role

Value-adding %	Present value contribution %	Future value contribution %	Nonadded value %
Role norm	50	30	20
Individual actual	*60*	*10*	*30*

The actual performance in the role

Present value added targets	Present value added achieved	Future value added targets	Future value added achieved
Revenue $500,000	Revenue $700,000	New customer prospects identified—20	New customer prospects identified—8
Delivery accuracy 95%	Delivery accuracy 90%	New customer needs identified—6	New customer needs identified—3
		Loyalty agreements signed—worth $400,000	Loyalty agreements signed—worth $250,000

A table such as Table 9.14 overleaf can be used for roles, teams, and individuals, drawn up separately for both current value and future value contribution.

Table 9.14 *Ranking of value contribution (current or future)*

Role	Incumbents	Contribution value component
A Customer account manager	• • •	• • •
B Supply chain manager	• • •	• • •
C Sales executive	• • •	• • •
D Management accountant	• • •	• • •
etc.	• • •	• • •

SUMMARY

The traditional way to look at the output of people is to employ measures of productivity. These have their uses, but the ultimate measure is the value that is added—the wealth that is available for distribution to the stakeholders. The ongoing assurance of that wealth for the future comes from the confidence that each stakeholder has their own needs for value satisfied. The challenge is to understand the nature of that value, both in financial and nonfinancial terms, and then to quantify it. Every employee should be able to relate their activities to one or more sources of value.

An important area is the way in which people spend their time. Everyone finds themselves involved in nonadded-value work; the important question is, "What is the proportion?" Studies of this are likely to lead to restructuring of work and elimination of nonadded-value activities.

Building future value depends on the capability to innovate and turn results into real value. Measures for the outcomes of innovation are just as important to track as are other outputs of our human capital. They enable us to balance the demands of the present with the constant need to create an attractive future for all who have an interest in the organization.

CHALLENGES FOR ACTION

❏ How is the contribution of people tracked at the level of the overall enterprise in your organization?

❏ What measures do you have of added value to stakeholders other than financial ones? Looking at all stakeholders, are there areas where there are no measures in use?

❏ Do individuals and teams in your organization regularly evaluate how much of the work done is adding value and how much is not?

❏ Do people have work targets directly linked to a measurable added-value indicator?

❏ Do you have measures of innovation in every part of the organization?

❏ Could you rank roles and people according to the value they create?

10

Mergers, Acquisitions, and Alliances

IN CHAPTER 6 WE DISCUSSED HOW TO MAXIMIZE OUR HUMAN CAPITAL. WE focused on the organic areas of acquisition, retention, and growth. However, the quickest way to get new human capital is to acquire, merge with, or make alliances with other organizations. Cisco Systems grew to become one of the world's largest companies by buying numerous startup and research-driven companies—acquiring their people, knowledge, and ideas.

In managing human capital this is therefore a critical area. Unfortunately, it is often not done well, and much of the intellectual capital (including the people) is lost. This chapter looks at some of the questions to be asked and processes to be gone through to make sure that this does not happen.

FAILURE TO ADD VALUE

Substantial new capabilities and technologies can be bought with an acquisition, assets shared and made more productive, and the range of customers rapidly extended. Value is captured through the transaction by transferring it from one economic entity to another. In the longer term, there also may be an opportunity to achieve greater value creation through the synergy arising from the two entities sharing assets and working out a common purpose. A merger or alliance should have such specific goals.

There are several quite different scenarios. A *merger* implies an agreed combination of operations, where two enterprises believe that they will compete better together than on their own. An *acquisition* may be hostile or agreed, but involves purchase of all or part of one organization by another. It is fashionable to refer to many of these by the softer term merger, especially if the parties are of similar size. An *alliance* is normally between organizations or parts of them and is an agreement to help each other in various ways; in product development or certain markets, for example. As the concept of the boundaryless organization takes root, more and more of these are put together based on the benefits of sharing intellectual capital. A *joint venture* is the offspring of two (or more) parents, aimed at a market to which each parent can contribute, but where working together can achieve more. This chapter is confined to mergers and acquisitions, as this is where most of the difficulties lie.

Each year the volume of deals grows. Boston Consulting Group estimated the 1999 value to be $3.3 trillion, or 30 percent of the entire economic output of the EU. All of this creates great wealth for professional advisers; but, sadly, these are the only players in the game guaranteed to win. There are so many stories of failure in mergers, acquisitions, and alliances. Indeed, statistics are regularly quoted showing the percentage that fail to reach their original business goals as being more than half.

One of many such studies, by KPMG in 1999, showed that 53 percent of such deals destroyed value for shareholders. We can be sure that value for other stakeholders was lost along the way too. According to the CSC Index, only 30 percent of mergers leave companies better off financially than previously; J P Morgan found that 44 percent of cross-border mergers in Europe failed to add value after three years—and so the studies roll on with their depressing statistics. In terms of growing shareholder value, it is usually the victim that provides the return and rarely the acquirer.

There are successes, of course. Statistics on percentages always quote the proportion that makes the point! Nevertheless, the failure rate is a major cause of concern, and the reasons are commonly to do with the following:

❑   Cultural dissonance
❑   The battle for control
❑   Loss of key players
❑   Failure to maintain customer relationships.

This is one of the great tragedies of corporate life, as it is such a prevalent occurrence, is so critical to the strategic plans of organizations, and provides so much disruption to people and businesses. And yet, the same mistakes are repeated time and again. Conference programs that I receive in the post featuring "due diligence," the term used for checking out the potential partner, still only focus on the legal and financial routines required. My own experience (as an HR director) of lawyers' demands was that they were entirely concerned with all the liabilities of employment contracts and pensions, and had no interest at all in the richness of intellectual capital that was being purchased.

The HR professional, if involved at the right time, will feel a responsibility to go beyond these requirements. Once the merger or acquisition is happening, however, the pressures of communication, reorganization, and harmonization absorb time, and vital issues of managing the asset nature of human capital can be pushed to the background. How often are HR professionals able to highlight why a deal may not work, when the business logic seems technically sound? Machismo and excitement, plus a great deal of optimism, are barriers to listening.

THE REAL MEANING OF SYNERGY

Many—indeed most—mergers and acquisitions entail restructuring and cost synergies. Synergy is a positive word, meaning that a combination is more than its constituent parts. The financial world has come to see it as the cost savings that result from a merger or acquisition, normally in the loss of jobs. Of course, savings can and should result—but they are surely not about costs alone. The interpretation is that saving costs must be good news for shareholders, but where are the statements of *value* lost?

A substantial premium over and above the financial and physical capital is usually paid for the intellectual capital of an organization being acquired. The proportion of attention given to each element is often totally out of balance, however. IBM paid seven times the book value for Lotus, for example. One could expect that seven times the attention would be paid to securing the intellectual capital that had been purchased (in fact, IBM did put a lot of effort into this). This attention is rarely given, however, partly because of the focus on the figures, and partly because the nature and composition of the intellectual capital value are not well understood. Tools and procedures for safeguarding it may not readily be available.

It is nearly always the case in so-called mergers that one partner is dominant over the other. That dominance is usually by size, but there have been many cases of minnows seeking to swallow whales. Some acquirers leave no one in any doubt about who is in charge: All the old top management is fired immediately and the company name changed overnight. This stance is justified by the need for people to know where they stand as quickly as possible and to avoid any potential opposition or undermining of the new owners. Others move more softly, involve people in the changes, and talk about creating a new company. Nevertheless, despite all the rhetoric that may go on at the time about respecting the new partners and a totally fair distribution of positions, the dominant partner generally absorbs the other into its culture.

Senior executives may often be given high-sounding board positions to start with (such as deputy chairman), as a softening but temporary palliative. It is not long before the majority of influential positions are filled with managers from one partner, and the survivors in the lower ranks feel as if they have joined a completely new company.

Here are some examples.

❑   CityGroup was formed as the result of a merger in 1999 between CitiCorp and Travelers. CityCorp's John Reed stepped down as chairman and co-chief executive in April 2000 and Travelers' Sandy Weill took complete charge. Four months later, five ex-CitiCorp directors had departed and only one remained on the board.

❑   The world's largest pharmaceuticals company was created in 2000 by "merging" Pfizer and Warner. As Pfizer consolidated its effective acquisition, not one of the 60 country managers in the new global organization came from Warner, nor did 13 out of 15 global area managers above them. Henry McKinnell, Pfizer president and chief operating officer, said that "the best person for each job had been selected," but acknowledged that "Pfizer picked the person already running the organization in order to avoid disruption of the business."

❑ The joining together of Daimler and Chrysler in 1998 was hailed as a merger of equals. Yet the dominance of Daimler led to the departure in droves of Chrysler senior executives, thousands of redundancies, and a disastrous fall in profits. The combination of two very different national cultures was a significant additional stress to an already fraught situation, as conflicting approaches to management fought for dominance.

Human capital can make its own decisions about whether it wants to stay. Attractive packages often help them to leave, however. They take with them their relationships, all their tacit knowledge, and their contribution to stakeholder value. Is it any wonder that value is eventually destroyed rather than grown? The speedy firing of the top management team seems particularly crass in this respect. These are the people who probably know the overall business, the key customers, the strengths and weaknesses of their organization better than anyone. They may take with them loyal followers, especially if the acquired company has many long-service people. The incoming management will not be a team by definition, and will set about making their mark by introducing the methods and approaches they know work for them. All of this is a pretty good recipe for losing value.

Laurence Capron at Insead studied 250 mergers to understand synergy and leverage, and compared pre-acquisition motives with post-acquisition behavior. She found that most of the motives related to revenue-driven synergies, such as market share, extended product offerings, and so on. Far fewer were concerned with achieving economies of scale for their own sake. However, life never goes quite according to plan. The highest benefits were reported from extension of product lines and market coverage, but in all other aspects studied, including profitability, approximately half of the companies showed a decline or no improvement. One interesting set of data concerned the rationalization of various kinds of assets. Reductions were three to five times more likely to be from the target's asset base than from those of the acquirer. The study concluded the following:

❏ *More attention should be paid to competence transfer and exploitation of revenue-based synergies.* Rushing to tell the market that something is happening by announcing cost restructuring may not be in the best long-term interest—even though such savings are very likely to be made eventually.

❏ *Rationalizing assets though acquisition does not necessarily lead to cost savings,* particularly where the assets rationalized are those of the target company. This may be because the effect of doing this is less well understood than for the acquirer's own asset base.

❏ *Excessive rationalization of the target's assets may damage the innovation and market capabilities of the merged business.* This is particularly due to the loss of key people. Capron cites the acquisition of First Interstate Bank by Wells Fargo in the US in 1997. Wells chose to close all FI's branch network and 75 percent of the top 500 executives left. FI had focused on relational banking—and as those relationships were steadily severed, so a large part of the customer base defected to competitors.

❏ *Cost savings can be achieved by transfer of competences, particularly to the target but in both directions.* This is the sharing of best practice between the two. Often it actually means "do it our way please," which may cause loss of productivity and confusion for a period.

❏ *Likewise, innovation and market capabilities can and should be improved through mutual transfer.* However, this is dependent on many of the people who hold the key to those competences remaining in the new organization. As above, the transfer of competences of the target to the acquirer is the more difficult to achieve, even though a substantial premium may have been paid for them.

The challenges

The kind of synergy we want is where, for example, our ability to create customer loyalty is enhanced by a greater variety of products and services, by extended distribution capability, or by a larger number of people devoted to innovation. Or our opportunity to develop people is extended through the greater diversity and size of the new organization, and the wider career opportunities available.

We could describe the challenges of the successful merger, acquisition, or alliance as:

❑   The achievement of the strategic goals set out in the plan
❑   The maintenance and enhancement of the value provided to stakeholders by the constituent companies (called "value capture" by Haspelagh and Jemison, 1991)
❑   The enhancement of the combined ability to create future value (termed "value creation" by the above authors).

All of this requires a real understanding of all the elements of intellectual capital. The acquirer that starts with that is at a considerable advantage; if not, it is unlikely to assess and manage its acquired business successfully. So we need to:

❑   Be able to link each strategic goal, through a cause-and-effect chain, with the key elements of intellectual capital that support it
❑   Take each stakeholder in turn, define the key areas of value contribution, and which individuals and teams are critical to that contribution
❑   Compare and contrast the working environment of the two constituents—their cultural norms, processes, values, psychological contracts, and so on—and identify areas of potential dissonance.

THE SIX PHASES OF MERGERS AND ACQUISITIONS

The implementation of mergers and acquisitions follows different patterns, but generally we can separate six phases:

1   Selection
2   Negotiation
3   Announcements
4   Due diligence
5   Integration
6   Review.

The first four stages may vary chronologically depending on different situations, such as:

❑   A hostile bid
❑   An agreed bid
❑   Competing for a company put up for sale
❑   Mutual interest in a merger.

The issue is about the availability of information, which can be in three categories:

❑   Only that which is public
❑   That available through controlled and limited access inside the company
❑   Unrestricted access to people and documentation.

What would the value-creating organization be doing at each of these stages? To look at every aspect of intellectual capital (i.e., including customer and structural capital) would be a book in itself, so we shall confine our discussion to human capital only.

Stage 1: Selection

Selection is a matter of strategy. There are many excellent books that will advise on how selection decisions should be made. As the study by Capron showed, pre-acquisition goals are frequently about growth in intellectual capital, such as customer base, brands, market share, methodologies, acquiring specialized knowledge or competence, products, technology, or research capability. Equally, it may also be aimed at greater efficiency in asset utilization, eliminating duplicated resources, and sharing facilities and systems. Here the argument will be based on cost synergies.

The commonest strategic reason is known as horizontal diversification, extending the reach of existing technology and markets. This frequently means a combination of large organizations that were previously competitors. Cost synergies always prevail in this case. Exxon and Mobil merged to form ExxonMobil during 1999, and in August 2000 Chairman Lee Raymond announced that it expected to save $5 billion annually. Some of this money would go to an increased capital spending program, but a large amount was expected to be given back to shareholders through a buyback. In this case there was a combination of extensive capital assets. However, many smaller acquisitions are almost entirely of intellectual assets in the form of technology and expertise, or a loyal customer base.

Where cost synergies are prime, it is rare, yet important, that the value associated with those costs is taken into account, even as an estimate. A travel company of which I have been a client for many years sold out to a larger company, but assured its clients that they would see no loss of quality or service as a result. In addition, a significant proportion of the substantial savings made in overheads were passed on to the customers, who felt even more positive about the company. Cost savings brought added value to the customers in financial terms, with no loss of non-financial value.

At this stage we may only know what is in the public domain about the target company. This may include a great deal of information about the top management and the culture. The larger the company and the higher the profile, the more will be available. When NatWest Bank in the

UK became a target for takeover in 1999, an enormous amount of information was already in the public domain through studies, articles, presentations, and literature.

Here is a checklist for the selection stage that would be relevant to the organization's human capital:

❑ What do we know about the top management? Their careers— background, seminal experiences, interests, directorships, public involvement?

❑ Are any of them founding members of the company?

❑ If the founder is not still in the company, did they leave a cultural and stylistic legacy?

❑ How many sites does the company have? What is the international distribution of employees? Which are the dominant sites?

❑ Is there any information about the number of people, or expenditure level, in R&D?

❑ If the company is already a competitor, what do our salespeople say about it in the marketplace?

❑ How does the company position itself in employment advertisements? What kind of people does it advertise for? How often?

❑ Has it acquired companies itself? Will it have pockets of people from previous cultures? What do we know about how it handled them?

❑ What can we deduce about its culture (see below for detailed parameters)?

❑ What can we find out about its investment in training and development?

❑ What do the accounts tell us about productivity and added value? How do they compare with industry norms?

There are many public sources of such information, via the internet, media publications, and company literature. Market research can be commissioned, and specialist consultants can produce valuable reports. Employees may have knowledge of the target company that can be (carefully) tapped into. The time will come when intellectual capital indicators are in the public domain. We give some examples of public reporting of this in Chapter 11.

Top management likes to believe that there are no barriers that cannot be overcome, if the merger or acquisition is seen as the right thing for company strategy. And yet there may be factors that come out of the above analysis that would become a major barrier to success. When Glaxo and SmithKline Beecham first started talks, for example, they had to be called off because of "key differences between the two chairmen." Back in the late 1980s, Ford Europe and Fiat called off a merger "because we are both proud companies and each will believe our way is best."

If the acquisition is hostile, there is no opportunity to get the vital detailed information that would provide a better judged decision. The perceived strategic fit, plus the financial figures, may be all that drives us, and our valuation will be based on the current market value plus a premium that advisers estimate might be sufficient to attract the target's major shareholders. Not surprisingly, many acquirers find later that they have overpaid handsomely, and are faced with quite unforeseen problems to tackle.

On page 244, we listed three key requirements in relation to intellectual capital, and in particular human capital:

❏ Linking strategic goals with key elements of intellectual capital
❏ Defining the key areas of value contribution
❏ Comparing and contrasting the working environments in which value is generated.

Tables 10.1–10.3 give some examples of the kind of analysis that is needed, and this will become more comprehensive as access to information extends.

At this stage, the analysis may be incomplete but it should be enough to give warning signals. Risk areas can be explored further, and evaluated as potential hidden costs. For example, we might assess a risk as 25 percent of the employees leaving voluntarily through inability to absorb our culture. There will be a cost associated with this, but also— depending on who the employees are—a risk of total failure of the strategic goal. This is the time to stop, unless we are confident that the challenges of overcoming the risk can be met.

Table 10.1 *Strategic goals—Revenue based*

STRATEGIC GOAL	INTELLECTUAL CAPITAL CONTRIBUTORS	AREAS OF VALUE ADDED TO STAKEHOLDERS
To increase market share in *x* market by 50%	• Range of products (+25%) • High-image brand extension (+20%) • Customer base (+40%) • Major contracts (+50% in revenue) • R&D resource (+25%) • Distribution network (+40%)	• *Customers*: price reductions; broader product range; faster delivery; integrated supplier • *Employees*: broader base for developing technical and professional capabilities and for career development • *Suppliers*: opportunities for larger contracts • *Shareholders*: increased productivity from resources
To rapidly increase our competence in e-commerce	• Technical system designers • Distribution network • State-of-the-art payment systems	• *Customers*: ease of virtual business at reduced prices; continually up-to-date data on products; online technical service • *Employees*: opportunities for new capabilities • *Suppliers*: opportunities for larger contracts • *Shareholders*: increased revenues
Etc.		

Table 10.2 *Strategic goals—Cost based*

STRATEGIC GOAL	AREAS OF POTENTIAL COST SAVINGS	AREAS OF VALUE ASSOCIATED WITH THESE COSTS
To reduce distribution costs by an average of 10%	• Shared warehouses; reduction of 35% of sites • Shared websites and e-distribution networks • Larger contracts with hauliers and price reductions	• Skilled employees and their customer relationships in each site • Image issues linked to website; reputation linked to operational side; effectiveness of networks in delivering customer satisfaction
To reduce advertising costs by 75%	• Shared agency • Reduce marketing staff by 20% • Better media purchasing clout (say = 15% of costs)	• Relationship of each agency and knowledge of products and market • Added value/knowledge of marketing individuals
Etc.		

Table 10.3 *Assessment of the working environment*

AREA OF COMPARISON	CHARACTERISTICS OF ACQUIRER	CHARACTERISTICS OF TARGET	SYNERGY OR OTHERWISE
Values	Explicit, established, internalized	None made explicit	Unless values obviously clash with practices, probably positive
Decision-making processes	Formal, established, written down	Informal, variable, based on managerial judgment	Major risk
Work flexibility	Generally formal, time based, workplace based	Variety of situations based on personal/work need	Major risk
Promotion policy	Internal first, external rare	Expedient	Likely to be seen as positive by employees
Etc.			

Stage 2: Negotiation

This stage involves a very small number of people, but includes the critical decision as to whether to proceed. It is the essential fact-finding stage that will lead to a valuation. Unless the bid is hostile, parties will generally be willing to divulge a great deal of salient information. Knowing the right questions to ask makes the difference. Since it is highly likely that we will pay above the book value, we ought to understand the intellectual capital that justifies the premium.

We are restricted by the number of people to whom we can talk. However, some of the areas to investigate regarding human capital would include the following:

Senior management's general approach to intellectual capital and the long term

❑   The focus of their communications, internal and external
❑   To what extent these feature ideas, people, innovations, growth
❑   Their stated investments in research and development, training and development, and new systems

❏ What they say they are proud of
❏ Their awareness of the external world: competitors, benchmarking, industry involvement
❏ The way knowledge is managed—are there specific individuals who have responsibility for knowledge assets?
❏ Details of customer satisfaction surveys.

Human capital

❏ People-related policies
❏ The principles of the remuneration system
❏ What information is available on productivity and added value?
❏ Does the contribution of human capital feature in the company's performance measurement system?
❏ What do the retention statistics tell us (especially of key technical groups, senior managers, graduates)?
❏ What do the absenteeism statistics tell us?
❏ What is the distribution of higher degrees and professional qualifications?
❏ How are role profiles constructed?
❏ How is the organization structured? How many levels does it have? How are accountability, responsibility, and authority distributed?
❏ What is the distribution of people: functions, managers and specialists, locations?
❏ To what extent have people come from previous mergers and acquisitions?
❏ What data do we have on employee satisfaction?
❏ What is spent on training in relation to the competition?
❏ Does the organization have any management development programs? What are their goals, and do they involve partners such as business schools?
❏ Is there any information on the effectiveness of training investment?
❏ What are the systems for the identification and development of talent?
❏ How many people are identified with potential for significant future growth?
❏ To what extent is there succession in place?

❑   Does the organization work with competency frameworks? What are the competences in use? How acceptable/useful are they to line management?

❑   Do these relate to expectations of leadership? If so, how is leadership assessed? What data is available?

A checklist for cultural comparison

There are cultural assessment tools available, and they could be used for mapping the constituent cultures. However, few of them deal with specific systems and processes, and these can be real sources of future conflict. There are always subcultures and the view from a head office is not necessarily the view from operational locations, so some sensitivity to this is required.

These tools can have value, but creating one's own checklist gives the opportunity to focus on the key areas of synergy or conflict that are anticipated. Culture is not just about the "soft" ways in which people work together, but also about the "hard" processes of business life, and these are often not covered in the available instruments. Table 10.4 offers a checklist to be used when the full information is available.

Table 10.4 *Cultural checklist*

CULTURAL AREA	ITEMS TO CHECK
Values	❑ Are there any defined values? ❑ How are they expressed/communicated? ❑ To what extent are they reinforced through processes and training? ❑ Are they generally known by heart by employees? ❑ What additional or even contrary values exist in tacit form that reflect history and the real culture?
Approach to strategy	❑ Is there a process for strategic planning? Who takes part in it? ❑ How far ahead does it look? ❑ How is it communicated? ❑ To what extent does the strategy "live" through guiding the actions and decisions throughout the organization? ❑ Are the plans reviewed against outcomes and the lessons learned as needed?

CULTURAL AREA	ITEMS TO CHECK
Organization	❑ What principles underlie the structure?
	❑ How many levels of management are there?
	❑ How are global and local needs balanced?
	❑ What are the main roles of HQ?
	❑ When was the company last reorganized and why?
	❑ Are there any pockets that have a special history (e.g., a previous acquisition)?
	❑ What identifiable tribal loyalties exist?
	❑ Which functions have been outsourced? How satisfactory is the resulting service?
Knowledge management and learning	❑ What is explicitly said in company literature about these issues?
	❑ Are they reflected in values or processes?
	❑ How natural is it to share across boundaries?
	❑ What mechanisms exist for this to happen? To what extent are they used?
	❑ Are people able to get the information they need easily?
	❑ Are people able to distinguish between learning and training, and recognize varied forms of learning?
	❑ To what extent do people have written personal development plans, and manage them?
Approach to quality and customer service	❑ To what extent is quality seen to pervade the output of every department?
	❑ What happens when a customer complains?
	❑ What is the status of any service level agreements?
Performance management	❑ What are the measures of performance most frequently discussed?
	❑ Which measures are used as incentives for senior management?
	❑ What process is used for reviewing performance for teams/units?
	❑ What process is used for reviewing performance of individuals?
	❑ Does the concept of added value have any currency? Would individuals be able to relate to it?

CULTURAL AREA	ITEMS TO CHECK
Decision processes	❑ What is the extent of committees, and what areas do they cover?
	❑ What kind of issues are on the top management's agendas as a group?
	❑ How are business proposals decided?
	❑ How much is people-to-people and how much paper-to-people?
	❑ How long does it take for certain decisions to be made (e.g., a pay rise, an increased headcount, a reorganization, a new supplier?
	❑ How fast are decisions that affect the whole organization implemented?
Management style	❑ How would the style generally be characterized—in terms of its focus on people and task; short and long term; customers and internal issues—supportive or controlling, directive or consultative?
	❑ Is there a recognizable commonality of style, or a considerable diversity?
Authority	❑ What are the levels of authority and how are they expressed?
	❑ What is the extent of empowerment at different levels?
	❑ Do people generally feel that they have the authority matching that needed for their responsibility?
Communications	❑ What methods exist for upwards and downwards communication?
	❑ How effective are they judged to be?
	❑ How often does senior management talk with front-line employees?
	❑ Do people feel they get to hear what they need and have a voice upwards?
Pride and satisfaction	❑ What evidence is there of employee pride in the company?
	❑ What proportion of employees have been with the company for more than 10 years?
	❑ What evidence is there of overall satisfaction with the organization? Do you know what the causes of the evidence are?

CULTURAL AREA	ITEMS TO CHECK
Innovation and creativity	❑ To what extent are these clearly valued in written statements?
	❑ What mechanisms actively encourage experimentation and new ideas?
	❑ What happens when things go wrong?
	❑ How often are existing processes and methodologies rigorously questioned?
Resourcing	❑ Is there a stated policy on internal promotion, and if not what is the reality?
	❑ To what extent are non-permanent employees used?
Reporting	❑ What regular reports are prepared, on what and how often?
	❑ What happens to them?
	❑ What do people feel about the usefulness of reporting disciplines?
Promotion policies	❑ What are the practices regarding internal promotion vs. external recruitment?
	❑ How are people selected for positions?
Work flexibility	❑ What variation exists in employment contracts?
	❑ How flexible is the organization in work time and space options?
Rituals and symbols	❑ What rituals and symbols take place in the organization, and what are their origins?
	❑ Which of these are linked to particular individuals in the company?
	❑ Do any involve the families of employees?

Clashes in these cultural areas are the biggest cause of failure of a merger. They are most likely in cross-border situations and where the degree of integration is high.

Some of the most potent polarizations to be aware of are outlined in Table 10.5 overleaf.

Table 10.5 *Significant cultural polarizations*

The bureaucracy of the large organization, with complex controls, lengthy decision processes and heavy reporting	vs.	Informality and flexibility, pragmatism and few rules
Detailed financial focus and budgetary control	vs.	Customer and market focus
Layers of management	vs.	Flat, with empowered people
Short termism	vs.	Building for the long term
Focus on individual performance	vs.	Focus on teamwork and team rewards
Cultural mindset rooted in that of the home base—xenophobic	vs.	Multicultural international outlook—cosmopolitan

Stage 3: Announcements

Deciding the timing and content of announcements absorbs considerable effort. The messages are eagerly seized on by the media, by customers and suppliers, and of course by employees. Everyone puts their own interpretation on the official words. What messages would the value-creating organization want to feature in its announcements about a merger or acquisition?

❏ The strategic goals of the merger, with special emphasis on how long-term value will be created for each of the main stakeholders

❏ Without denying that cost savings can be expected, emphasize the importance of the acquired intangible assets—particularly the skills, expertise, experience, and key relationships held by the acquired company.

Stage 4: Due diligence

Due diligence is not a term deployed in every country. Before a deal is confirmed, even though it may have been agreed in principle, it will be subject to a process of careful scrutiny of relevant data and facts. There may be adjustments to the price based on what is found through this due diligence. In short, it is the thorough examination of the detail about the organization, and permission is usually given to talk to anyone deemed relevant to the enquiry.

In addition to its legal and financial checks and balances, the process is an opportunity to fill in the missing elements from the earlier checklists, and indeed to double-check the accuracy of what we have so far. From our particular standpoint of interest, we want to be sure we understand the following:

❏ The answers to our checklist questions, including those on culture, translated wherever possible into some idea of whether we have human capital or cultural assets or liabilities.
❏ Where cultural clashes are likely to arise (complete Table 10.3).
❏ Which intellectual assets are critical to our goals (complete Tables 10.1 and 10.2).
❏ Even though it is unlikely that we will find an equivalent of the Human Asset Register, the people and teams who are involved in the critical intellectual assets identified above should be valued according to the Human Asset Worth outlined in Chapter 4.
❏ We also want to find out where the key centers of added value lie. This is different from Tables 10.1 and 10.2, which are about the aspirations of the combined company. Who are the people really behind creating value for customers and other stakeholders in the proposed target?

The more information we have on these questions, the better armed we will be to make balanced decisions when it comes to the vital next stage of integration.

Stage 5: Integration

This is where successes and failures are created. In 1999, a study by the Boston Consulting Group of 200 postmerger integrations was summarized in the *Financial Times* under the heading of "Seven Deadly Sins." These were as follows:

❏ Missing strategic opportunities from the merger. Too often the focus is on cost savings, and meanwhile opportunities to create much greater value from new revenue synergies are missed

❏ Preoccupation with managing change, and failing to lead, to create a vision, and provide united direction

❏ Delaying decisions about the future shape of the business, causing uncertainty and missing opportunities that arise from the period when people expect change

❏ Trying to be fair to both partners and give equal treatment—as we observed earlier, this will not work out practically

❏ Applying a universal integration process to all units regardless of differences in size or difficulty—the integration in the homebase of a multinational will always require more extensive attention than in smaller units

❏ Trying to get all details of the new company and its organization agreed before initiating action and change—this uncertainty potentially loses customers and employees

❏ Declaring completion too soon, and failing to follow through and track changes. Integration is not over just because the project plans are complete.

Many guides have been written on how to do integration successfully. There is a balance to be struck between speed and thoroughness, since both are desirable. Depending on the time available in the previous stages, it may be possible to have a fully fledged, thorough integration plan ready to implement at the official time of integration. This is the ideal balance if it can be achieved.

The value-creating organization will have an overriding priority not to lose value-creating assets. It is very easy to do this with the cost focus of traditional management accounting, and without any real under-standing of how and where value is created.

What is proved time and time again is that inexperienced integra-tors always make mistakes. Overwhelmed with the volume of tasks to be done, often under pressure to make savings quickly, fired up with the excitement of something new and different from everyday work—all these factors can work together to cause the initial objectives to fail. A very experienced integration director from the erstwhile prestigious com-pany ITT told me at the time of one of my very early experiences in acqui-sition: "Never put a person in charge of an integration who is out to make a name for him- or herself." In other words, wisdom and experience will serve you best.

One key question is: "How vital is integration anyway?" It is often the case that an acquisition can continue with its own branding and its previous management. Their unique capability is available to the parent, and the latter's expertise and services can help efficiency in the new fam-ily member. At least in the early days, unless the strategic goals are all about synergy from combination, this may be the best strategy to retain the intangible assets. Haspelagh and Jemison list three integration approaches based on the two key parameters of the need for strategic interdependence, and the need for organizational autonomy:

❏   Absorption—the anticipated value is dependent on full consolida-tion of the constituent parties
❏   Preservation—there is a low need for interdependence; the acquired company is nurtured. As far as possible its own culture and methodologies are left intact
❏   Symbiotic—this is a combination of a high need for both strategic interdependence and for organizational autonomy, and is the most complex scenario.

Research showed that two other factors may influence the integration approach: the quality of the acquired company and the absolute and rel-ative sizes involved. If the acquired company lacks quality of manage-ment, it is natural to supplement it from the parent. This is fine if the two are in similar businesses; risky if the acquired company is in a new market. On the size issue, if the parent is very much larger it runs two risks, either overdomination or neglect. Whatever the right approach, a clear set of integration objectives should be set up.

Integration is typically done by setting up functional and market-based project teams, made up of members from each constituent company, coordinated by an integration director. They reflect the traditional silos of the organization. The value-creating organization would want coordinating teams linked not to functions or departments, but to stakeholder interests. There will also be one concerned with overall intellectual capital, and subsets of this such as a team responsible for knowledge assets. This is the heart of integration: the transfer of intangible asset value in terms of capabilities, knowledge, and methodologies.

Common difficulties and pitfalls in integration

This is a major subject and space does not allow for the treatment it deserves. Below we list just some of the problems that commonly arise with particular reference to human capital, and suggested responses from the value-creating organization.

Table 10.6 *Typical difficulties in managing human capital in integrating mergers and acquisitions*

DIFFICULTY	POSSIBLE RESPONSE
In the interests of cost synergy, sales offices are combined and the sales-forces "rationalized"	The issue here is how important customer relationships are. If we lose customers, we may save cost, but that is little benefit if the revenue goes with it. So there is a vital analysis of key (= loyal, profitable, high-potential) customers and whether they are strongly linked to individuals in the acquired firm
The appointment of general managers is done on the basis of the best person available. Then we find that results are not what we expected, or the person suddenly quits	The question here is what we mean by "best." Having the best track record of bottom-line results in the previous culture does not guarantee a continuing record if (a) a local merging of cultures has to take place; and (b) the individual

DIFFICULTY	POSSIBLE RESPONSE
	finds him- or herself subject to the demands of an alien culture. High emotional intelligence and sensitivity may, for a while, be more necessary characteristics than a successful business record
Sending in managers from the parent to help the acquired management teams, and finding that they are unable to influence what goes on	Such a person may be seen in many negative lights: as a spy, or an "I-know-better," or a political commissar. Potentially they can be a real help, but it is all about trust and confidence. When Fujitsu took over ICL it sent one senior man to act as liaison director. He quickly managed to create a feeling that his role was primarily to help the management team in what they wanted to do and smooth their path through the Japanese decision-making processes. He became highly valued and respected
In rationalizing offices and systems, vital data, information, and knowledge are lost	Many an integration has stalled on the desire to move to common IT systems. HQ executives become paranoid about having their management information in the same format, as if they have lost control. Especially if the people who really know those systems leave, it may be too late before the asset loss is realized. An early integration task must be to identify where the real knowledge assets are, who owns and maintains them
After power struggles, key senior people resign. Other people follow in their wake	The makeup of "tribes" must be understood and mapped. Where are the networks of loyalty in the acquired organization?
Information and knowledge are closely guarded from the new parent	This will happen if suspicion, distrust, and insecurity prevail. In a positive

DIFFICULTY	POSSIBLE RESPONSE
	atmosphere, people are keen to learn from each other and exchange for mutual benefit. Building this atmosphere must be a priority for any integrating manager
	Everybody expects the new management to come round and explain all the benefits of the merger. But people believe what they see, not what they are told
The people involved in creating future value stop work until they see what is happening and the way the future will unfold. As projects are abandoned, disillusion sets in and greener pastures rapidly claim the best people	The acquired firm was a going concern. It had people working on new products or services, marketing campaigns, management development, better logistics, new IT systems. All these value-creating activities may come to a halt, pet projects be abandoned, and people leave.
	These are the value-creating people, for whom we will have paid part of our intangible asset premium. Hence it is important to identify who and where they are as part of the due diligence exercise.
	Attention needs to be given as a priority to the value-creating teams in different functions. In the rush to make short-term savings from administration and operations, it may become too late—exit value
People lack direction, so they do what they feel will best enhance their own position	Providing a clear vision of where the new organization is going is much more important than unraveling the details of integration. It is particularly important that customers see people pulling in the same direction. Vacillation on this leaves people in a vacuum. There is often considerable uncertainty as to where accountabilities lie—these should be clarified along with the direction

A number of targets for managing human capital may need to be reset as a result of the merger. The merger itself is almost certain to lead to a refocusing of the organization's overall strategy. This may affect the cause-and-effect chains, and therefore the measures we use. We may need to create a new cultural vision and template. Although the more powerful partner has a natural tendency to dominate, the combination of cultures can be used to create something new.

We will give the last word on integration to the Economist (1999):

A whole consulting industry thrives by advising companies on post-merger integration, a salvage operation to recover something from the wreckage of impossible promises and ill-considered goals. Companies that agree a clear strategy and management structure before they tie the knot stand a better chance of living happily ever after.

Stage 6: Review

The success of a merger must be reviewed in the light of its original objectives. It is easy for economic analysts to look at results purely in terms of increased profitability or share price. To do so, especially in the short term, invalidates the whole concept of intellectual capital and the premium paid for it. All evaluations should be done against what we set out to do.

Disciplined review is an essential part of the process. The merger or acquisition was an exercise in value transfer and value creation. We must know whether these happened or not. Therefore we need to review:

❏   What happened to value
❏   How our capability to create value has changed
❏   What we learned from the processes we employed.

In the areas that are strategic to the goals of the integration, we would expect to see the Human Asset Worth increase. Thus, if higher market share was our goal, we would expect the HAW of the teams related to that market to have increased: sales, marketing, or product development. If our goal was to improve our technological capability in a particular field, again we would expect to see a measurable increase—and the percentage increase should relate to the original merger goals (see Table 10.7).

Table 10.7 *Increases in HAW as a result of merger*

AREA OF STRATEGIC HUMAN CAPITAL	PREVIOUS HUMAN ASSET WORTH	CURRENT HUMAN ASSET WORTH	% PLANNED	% ACHIEVED
E-business logistics	250	780	+500	+212
Salespeople in Hungary	160	360	+100	+125
Etc.				

The learning from each such event is absolutely critical. This is a risky activity, with immense opportunity for things to go wrong. It is an area fraught with politics, reputation protection, and power games. There may be many interpretations of what went well and what did not. However, as much learning as possible needs to be captured and put into the explicit knowledge memory. If the next team involved is able to access such a memory it could save many mistakes, although this is not guaranteed in the excitement of the moment. In the value-creating organization, it should be normal procedure.

SUMMARY

The restructuring of organizational boundaries continues all the time, through acquisitions, disposals, mergers, and alliances. Many plans and aspirations fail to be realized, and value is not only lost to shareholders but to other stakeholders as well. The desire for synergy is too often expressed in cost terms alone, when it is value-adding synergy that is more often than not the real goal.

Understanding the components of intellectual capital in the target organization is one challenge. It is highly likely that an acquirer will have paid multiples of the book value for this intellectual capital, and the first priority is to retain it. Each strategic goal for the acquisition or alliance needs to be linked, through cause-and-effect chains, to those aspects of intellectual capital that are critical to success.

The process follows defined stages, and we have suggested six. At each link, the opportunity is there to expand our knowledge and understanding of the people and their capability, of the culture and knowledge assets that are to be acquired.

Finally, we will want to see what has happened to our stock of human capital as a result of the merger or acquisition. It is likely that in headcount terms it will be less than that of the original partners—but its strength and quality should have increased in critical areas.

CHALLENGES FOR ACTION

❏ If you have been involved in any mergers, acquisitions, and alliances, what were their original objectives and to what extent were they achieved, to the best of your knowledge? List the positive and negative aspects of each.
❏ How would you describe the value added to stakeholders from each event?
❏ In particular, how would you describe any culture clashes? What effects did they have on the success of the merger?
❏ If people were lost from the new company, who you would regard as real assets, and what caused them to be so?

11

Telling the World

A
N ANNUAL REPORT IS INTENDED TO PROVIDE SHAREHOLDERS, current and potential, with an accurate picture of a particular company. The information given conforms to statutory requirements, which vary country by country. A major part always consists of detailed figures concerning the trading position, and the assets and liabilities of the company (as at the end of the trading period). But, as we know, this usually only represents a minor part of the real value of the organization.

THERE IS, IN THE ERA WHERE KNOWLEDGE IS KING, A MAJOR GAP IN THE PROVISION OF AN ACCURATE AND HELPFUL GUIDE FOR INVESTORS AND THE PUBLIC ON HOW VALUE IS BEING CREATED.

This final chapter looks at the developments that are happening in statutory requirements for disclosure, and at some of the ways in which companies are voluntarily disclosing information about human capital.

THE GAP THAT NEEDS TO BE FILLED

In the UK alone, more than one billion pounds a year is spent on the production of annual reports—and this is not counting the time spent compiling them. Reports are almost entirely retrospective. To find out about the future prospects, we are dependent largely on the narrative that accompanies the figures, and these are often stale clichés of anodyne optimism and selected "good news."

Amazon.com's 1999 annual report provided only the following information about its employees:

> *As of December 31, 1999, the Company employed approximately 7,600 full-time and part-time employees. The Company also employs independent contractors and temporary personnel. None of the Company's employees is represented by a labor union, and the Company considers its employee relations to be good. Competition for qualified personnel in the Company's industry is intense, particularly for software development and other technical staff. The Company believes that its future success will depend in part on its continued ability to attract, hire and retain qualified personnel.*

This comes from a company that knows full well how vital its people are to their success. Investors know this too, but what did they learn from this paragraph? They are not alone. Bassi and others studied the reports of 40 large companies in detail in 1999, and found no disclosures *at all* of relevant quantitative data about their people, except for the frequent statement: "Our employees are our most important asset."

An investor needs confidence that:

❏   There is a coherent strategy to take the company forward
❏   Customers have continuing confidence and loyalty
❏   New products and services come at a rate at least as good as that of the competition
❏   The quality of people is high
❏   The loss of good people is low
❏   Employees feel good about the company and their work
❏   The level of investment in training and people development is appropriate
❏   Investment in new systems and processes is continual
❏   There are successful business partnerships
❏   There is appropriate care for the environment.

The publication of an annual report itself rarely influences the share valuation, but announcements about any of the above certainly do. Positive statements are fine, but what we really need are comparisons that indicate progress. In what direction is this company moving? Is it getting more or less effective in its use of intellectual and human capital?

Steven Wallman, former Commissioner of the US Securities and Exchange Commission, makes the case for a new approach:

> *Some of the most useful information is not necessarily the most reliable; and some of the most reliable is not necessarily the most useful. A great deal of time is spent aggregating information, according to increasingly complex rules, and then a great deal of time and money is spent by analysts disaggregating the information to try and understand the company and what the real strengths are behind it.*

And Brian Birkenhead, vice-chairman of the UK's Hundred Group of Finance Directors, was quoted in *Director* magazine as saying:

> *Annual reports are becoming unreadable. Accounts in their current format are not actually telling people what they want to know.*

For newly qualified young people the excitement lies in knowledge-based industry. It is hard for firms in traditional industries to compete. Top graduates seek accounting firms, management consultancies, financial services, software development, telecommunications, and internet-based companies. In all of these the traditional balance sheet has practically no value or use. Even Bill Gates said, in a speech at London Business School in 2000, that nobody would find out much about Microsoft from its annual financial report (the value placed on intellectual capital being about 97 percent of the total).

Companies that Go Beyond the Minimum

Some companies provide the absolute minimum required; others have become sensitive to their image on some issues and have lengthy sections on their approach to the environment and the community. Dow Chemical, for example, states in its 1999 report:

> *Today, we measure our progress and success by the standards of the new century—balancing environmental concerns, economic growth*

and social responsibility, which is known as the "triple bottom line" of sustainable development.

Worldwide, we are gaining an industry advantage by delivering more of what our customers want. With our accelerated implementation of Six Sigma, customers will realize the difference in Dow as we respond to their needs and deliver on our promises. Our transformation is revealing a new Dow:

❏ *Providing innovative products, technologies and solutions that meet our customers' needs today and tomorrow.*
❏ *Demonstrating our commitment to making the world a better place—balancing environmental integrity, social responsibility and economic prosperity.*
❏ *Elevating the thinking and skills of our employees—making connections and sharing ideas worldwide.*
❏ *Creating long-term shareholder value—differentiating Dow as one of the best investment values in the chemical industry.*
❏ *Excellence. Growth. Value. That's the promise and the power of transformation.*

These fine statements would not be untypical of any major corporation. Several pages emphasize the company's commitment to innovation and give examples of success. Specific, quantified goals are published for environment, health, and safety. The reader is left feeling very positive about the company.

Dow was one of the pioneers in trying to harness intellectual capital in a managed way, but we see very few figures that tell us about this. In 1996 it published *Visualising Intellectual Property in Dow*, a report on how the company evaluates and uses all its intellectual property. This openness does not seem to have been continued, however.

In 1999, mobile phone company Nokia built its report around the theme of "no limits." This is full of information about the future—and there was an exciting tale to tell. Some 25 percent of the company's 55,000 employees are involved in R&D in 14 countries, and it reports on the number of patents and "invention reports" (nearly 3,000 in 1999). Its financial statements are a pullout document separated from the annual report, which concentrates on the future.

Internet portal and information services company Yahoo! accompanied its 1999 report with a set of artistic postcards on a 1930s theme, each with a fact about the company on the back. Its report gets fairly close to an intellectual capital balance sheet, but only with narrative. After a great deal of detail about its services and alliances, it devotes nine pages to no fewer than 24 "risk factors," analyzing the company's capability to meet its future strategies. For example, "We will continue to expand into international markets in which we have limited experience" is one heading, and the factors working for this and against this are discussed. This level of honesty is rarely seen, but is immensely helpful to would-be investors.

Energy company BP, in its annual report for 2000, summarized performance highlights on pages 2 and 3. In addition to financial data, four other charts are set out, for environmental emissions, workforce days lost, employee satisfaction, and community investment (see Figure 11.1). The small section headed "employees" in the main body of the report shows a distribution of gender and ethnicity.

LEADERS IN PUBLIC INFORMATION ABOUT HUMAN CAPITAL

When it comes to openness, most of the serious attempts to provide information and measures of intellectual capital have come from Scandinavia. The world's first intellectual capital report was produced by Skandia Assurance, the largest insurance and financial services company in Scandinavia, in 1995 as a supplement to the traditional financial report. It was called *Visualizing Intellectual Capital*. This was followed by a series featuring different aspects: *Value Creating Processes* (1995), *Renewal and Development* (1996), *Customer Value* (1996), *The Power of Innovation* (1997), *Intelligent Enterprising* (1997) and *Human Capital in Transformation* (1998). Leif Edvinsson spent four years setting up and testing a new measurement structure for the company.

Skandia started its work in 1992 with the evolution of the Skandia Navigator, and its sister tool called the Dolphin Navigator began in 1998.

environmental emissions

	2000		1999
	BP	Underlying[a]	BP
Greenhouse gas emissions (million tonnes)[b]	80.7	72.2[c]	79.8
Hydrocarbon emissions to air ('000 tonnes)	688	636	845
Discharges to water ('000 tonnes)	58	52	46
Number of spills reaching land or water (>1 barrel)[d]	503	413	732

[a] BP operations excluding ARCO and Burmah Castrol.
[b] BP share of emissions of carbon dioxide and methane, expressed as an equivalent mass of carbon dioxide.
[c] 9.5% decrease from 1999 comprises 3% in respect of continuing operations and 6.5% due to asset divestment and other changes.
[d] 1 barrel = 159 litres = 42 US gallons.

workforce days away from work case frequency[a]

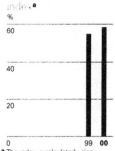

0.50	
0.40	
0.30	
0.20	
0.10	
0 96 97 98 99 00	

[a] An injury or illness that results in a person being unable to work for a day (shift) or more. The frequency is per 200,000 hours. Workforce includes employees and contractors.

employee satisfaction index[a]
%

60	
40	
20	
0 99 00	

[a] The index is calculated using responses to the People Assurance Survey sent annually to BP staff worldwide, covering leadership, diversity, staff development and recognition.

community investment
$ million

	2000	1999
By region		
UK	15.4	10.4
(including UK charities	4.1	5.3)
Rest of Europe	5.3	3.5
USA	46.0	36.4
Rest of World	14.9	17.1
Total	**81.6**	67.4
By theme		
Community development	28.2	29.5
Education	21.3	14.8
Environment	8.3	4.7
Arts and culture	15.0	11.0
Other	8.8	7.4
Total	**81.6**	67.4

Figure 11.1 *Extract from the BP Annual Report 2000*

This is intranet-based and aimed at knowledge sharing, and at replacing budgeting with a more dynamic performance management of all intellectual capital and financial indicators.

Celemi AB has also become well known for its Intangible Assets Monitor, commencing in 1996. Advised by Dr. Karl Erik Sveiby, pioneer and author in this field, Celemi says of its Monitor: "As a rapidly growing international knowledge organization, Celemi does a yearly audit of its intangible assets to guide company management and support long term planning." Its series of 25 measures covers Our Customers (6), Our Organization (9), and Our People (10) under each of three aspects: Growth/Renewal; Efficiency; and Stability. Each measure is clearly defined in the report.

The people column for 1999 is reproduced in Figure 11.2. The company suffered in profitability for both 1998 and 1999, but said this was due to making significant investments. Margareta Barchan, chief executive, commented: "When people ask 'Is it worth the trouble?' we point to an array of uncovered 'hidden' assets now being converted into tangible advantages, all in line with strategic initiatives."

Our People (competence)

	1999	1998	1997
(overall rating year)			
Growth/Renewal			
Average Professional Experience, Years (3,9)	9.2	8.3	8.2
Competence Enhancing Customers (4, 5)	27%	59%	65%
Growth in Professional Competence (11)	38%	8%	49%
Experts with Tertiary Degree (6, 8)	80%	67%	68%
Efficiency			
Value Added per Expert TSEK (9, 17, 30)	892	802	759
Value Added Margin on Sales TSEK (30)	49%	47%	42%
People Satisfaction Index (31)	5.00	4.62	
Expert Turnover (7, 9)	14%	13%	6%
Expert Seniority, Years (9, 28)	4.0	3.3	2.8
Median Age All Employees, Years (17)	37	37	36

© 2000 Celemiab Group AB

Figure 11.2 *Extract from Celemi Intangible Assets Monitor 1999*

Note: The figures in brackets refer to notes in the annual report from which this was taken.

WM-Data is a Sweden-based IT services company with about 8,000 employees. It aims to be "a leading European supplier for the new network economy ... benefits for customers are achieved through supporting customers' business objectives. Benefits for employees are achieved through supporting them in their professional objectives. By creating benefits we can attract and develop the right customers and the right employees in the long term. And, in the process, continue to grow." Its annual reports feature the "four capitals," illustrated as a circle with structural capital in the center and individual, financial, and customer capital surrounding it. Reports include sections on:

❏ Customer capital—a distribution of revenues by geographical area
❏ Structure capital—a distribution of revenues and value added between the four operating divisions of the company
❏ Individual capital—distribution of employees; revenue-generating people, employee turnover, and revenue/value added/income adjusted for depreciation, each per employee; educational levels.

In the 1999 report the three pages devoted to "8,180 Valuable Employees" discuss the breakdown of employees, turnover and expertise, the employer brand, people development, and so on. Some 3,700 employees subscribed to a convertible share program in 1999.

Yet another Swedish company is Lightlab, which has developed a mercury-free low energy lamp. Its report has one page headed "Intellectual Capital," and brief notes on human and structural capital (as yet it has no customers). The focus on human capital is to list the expertise of well-known researchers available to the company.

Systematic A/S

Systematic is a company headquartered in Aarhus, Denmark, founded and run by its managing director, Michael Holm. The company creates and licenses software systems for application integration, communications, and data security. It has developed pioneering systems for the military sector and for electronic data interchange. It is one of 18 companies that participated in a three-year project managed by the Danish Agency for Trade and Industry for the development of an Intellectual Capital Report. Systematic produced its first such report in spring 1999, and based it on the Business Excellence model popularized by the Foundation for European Quality Management (see page 50). In the second report produced in 2000, Holm says:

> *We regard this report as a supplement to the financial accounts and a valuable management tool. In the preparation we have achieved higher self-knowledge and consciousness about:*
>
> ❏ *our knowledge and capabilities*
> ❏ *our shortcomings*
> ❏ *the correlation between the individual knowledge elements.*
>
> *This report is a useful communications tool for our stakeholders, i.e. customers, employees, suppliers, co-operation partners etc., and at the same time a management tool that facilitates our strategies and objectives.*

Systematic's report features commentary and measures in four areas, described below.

Customers

The report includes the results of six parameters of customer satisfaction, including "employee competence" that scored 5.4 on a scale of 6. There are a number of measures on the customer profile over a three-year period. Among these indicators are the number of active project customers, new strategic customers, duration of existing customer relationships, percentage of customers who would recommend Systematic (88 percent) and details of license sales.

Processes and infrastructure

In this section their goals are to be in the top 10 percent of quality software companies, as externally assessed, and to implement a system of knowledge management.

Indicators include process improvement, computer capacity, office premises, and an externally monitored telephone service.

Innovation

The figures shown here include investment in both product development and process improvement, and the number of new products.

The report includes special sections on knowledge management (and quotes a "cola index," which appears to be the number of cokes consumed per employee); cooperation with clients (with a "pizza index"), and competence development (with a "carrot index"). These sections describe in detail processes and targets for making the three areas effective.

Employees

The section on employees is reproduced below and in Figure 11.3.

Employee Satisfaction

We attach great importance to employee job satisfaction. We measure this through staff turnover and specific job satisfaction surveys.

Last year showed an intake of 29 and a reduction of 11 software engineers. This staff turnover of approximately 16% may seem high, but the high demand for IT employees—not least for skilled computer scientists and systems engineers—should be taken into consideration. Besides, a job at Systematic is the first after graduation for many of our employees.

It is our goal to keep the staff turnover down below 15%, which corresponds to an average employment period of seven years.

Employee satisfaction surveys are conducted annually. The latest survey from September 1999 consisted of 35 questions to be answered anonymously on a scale from 1 to 5 with a view to both importance and satisfaction. The response rate to the questionnaire was 97%.

The survey revealed a high satisfaction level, increasing from 3.47 in the first survey in 1997, to 3.61 in 1998 and now to 3.69 in the 1999 survey. Areas of improvement were identified though, and initiatives will be taken to remedy these. The employees are involved in the planning of these activities through department meetings and half-yearly performance reviews.

Training and Education

Last year's investment in training and education amounted to 19,830 DKK per employee. The average number of training days per full-time employee was 7.8.

The variety of internal courses is continuously increasing and comprises both professional and "soft" fields, including courses in team building, presentation technique, speed reading and language. Courses in project management are increasingly integrated with our business values, processes and procedures. Finally, a large number of employees participate in external education and various workshops, seminars and conferences, in Denmark and abroad.

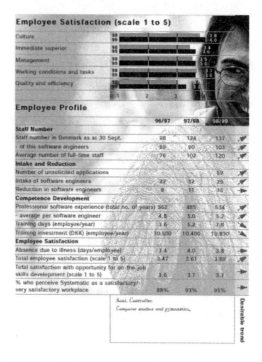

Figure 11.3 *Extract from Systematic Software Engineering* Intellectual Capital Report 2000, *Theme: Knowledge Management*

This example is the best role model found at the time of writing.

FUTURE REPORTING FOR INTELLECTUAL CAPITAL

Both Systematic and Celemi are new, young, knowledge-based and relatively small companies. They are refreshingly open and reading their reports gives a comprehensive visualization of what each company is like. The value to potential recruits is enormous. They also, of course, have positive messages to share—there are not too many intellectual "liabilities" to be talked about. Large, complex companies are likely to be more selective in what they reveal on a voluntary basis.

It is much harder to show continual improvement, as is expected with financial figures such as growth and profitability. Improvement is naturally desirable, but to maintain a target level on many parameters will still give good signals. Also, the return on intellectual capital will generally be a lower figure than the traditional "return on capital employed," although it is arguably more relevant, especially for low capital-intensive companies.

We can predict with some confidence that during the first decade of the twenty-first century, firms will be required statutorily to report on their intangible assets. However, this may come in stages. Accounting bodies will focus first on their own definition of intangible assets, which excludes people and many other aspects such as brands.

Unless forced to do so, we may expect companies to stay with telling the world what they want them to know, that is, about their really positive assets. This could be a misleading presentation of the truth.

In the UK, a body called the Centre for Tomorrow's Company, with over 50 member companies, was set up "with a vision of a world in which business success is spoken about and measured in inclusive terms." It seeks to influence business, investors, educators, and public policy makers. One thrust of its work is to emphasize the need for an annual report that communicates to all stakeholders what they want to know. The perfect report, they argue, describes "how the company has generated—and will continue to generate—value for its shareholders while at the same time identifying and measuring the party played by customers, employees, suppliers and the community in creating and sustaining value." Sebastian Berry, in the Centre's publication *The Future of Business Reporting*, argues that reports should contain:

❏   Benchmarks on environmental and social performance against other companies

❏   Rolling five-year emissions reports

❏   Ethical and reputations issues and policies

❏   Reports on annual consultations with stakeholders

❏   Secondary environmental impacts, such as sites and community affairs

❏   Staff surveys and detailed comparative information on diversity.

He also maintains that websites should be interactive. While this is all beneficial, the importance of human capital is nevertheless understated.

Chris Swinson, President of the UK's Accounting Standards Board, wrote the following:

Many people are beginning to talk about the efficiency and the effectiveness of corporate reporting. It is easy at times not to think about what other people are saying about us accountants and to shut our eyes to the siren voices, some of which may lead us on the rocks, but some of which would improve what we are actually doing.

The long and the short of this is that accountants have long known that historical cost financial reports do not attempt to meet the information needs of all users of accounts. Yet, for all this, the marketplace has gone on using those financial reports.

We ought to ask how we can encourage financial reporting to meet the changing information needs of business and society. It is not that we should reject historical cost financial reporting but that we are not serving anyone if we do not pay attention to calls for change. There is no point in accountants working overtime to produce more and more accounting standards which serve simply to over-specify an old technology. The time is ripe for issues of corporate reporting to be the subject of a formal and broad review. We ought to be hard-nosed and calculating about what are the real permanent sustainable needs which require a real permanent sustainable answer on the form of the corporate reporting system in this country. I would suggest that we learn from experience of the past.

In some countries more direct initiatives are being taken. The Danish Finance Ministry commenced a 10-year plan for development of intellectual capital accounts in 1999. The project includes political reference groups, financial institutions, Copenhagen Business School, accountants Arthur Andersen, technical experts, and 23 knowledge-intensive companies. The various participants collaborate in knowledge sharing and conferences, learning all they can about best practice.

The project group used the four components of employees, customers, business processes, and technology. Its premise is that reporting should be in three parts:

❑ What there is—the resources available
❑ What is done—input measures, or performance drivers
❑ What happens—output measures.

At the time of writing, for employees, the measurement template was as in Table 11.1.

Table 11.1 *The Danish Ministry Framework (published March 2000)*

"WHAT THERE IS" (STATISTICAL INFORMATION)	"WHAT IS DONE" (PERFORMANCE DRIVERS)	"WHAT HAPPENS" (OUTCOMES)
• Seniority	• Share of employees with development plan	• Employee satisfaction
• Education	• Development days per employee	• Employee behavior
• Turnover	• Education costs per employee	• Increase in value per employee

The Canadian Institute of Chartered Accountants has a Corporate Reporting Initiative that is examining how to report intellectual capital and value creation effectively. It decided in June 1999 that it should refrain from mandating reporting requirements for at least three years; that it should encourage experimentation in both internal and external reporting, and develop ways to enhance research collaboration toward an overall common framework.

WHAT SHOULD WE DO?

If we are convinced that the value-creating organization is the route to success and we want to be ahead of the game, what stages should we go through in moving toward external visibility?

- ❏ First, we should decide on the information that it would be strategically advantageous for us to publish, and consider what medium to use
- ❏ Then we should keep an eye on the recommendations of accountancy bodies and other relevant institutions, and what other countries are doing
- ❏ We might want to see how others in our industry sector were looking at the question and what plans they had, and even agree some mutual reporting
- ❏ Last, we need to decide whether we want to be leading or lagging in disclosure.

The Canadian Institute of Chartered Accountants has developed some self-assessment tests that can be undertaken to evaluate readiness for intellectual capital management. These can be found on their website (see References).

SUMMARY

It is rare to find a public annual report that tells readers what they really want to know about how value is being created. We cannot expect companies to disclose all their weaknesses voluntarily, but many could do more to emphasize the strengths of their intangible assets.

Some large companies have started to do this, particularly where areas of activity are sensitive, such as those affecting the environment. Information regarding human capital is rare. The leaders in this area are from Sweden and Denmark, and in some cases they have now been able to compare year-on-year data. With the exception of Skandia, these companies are generally small and highly knowledge based.

A number of bodies in Europe and the US are exploring some guidelines for human capital reporting. It is fairly certain that some requirements will emerge over the next 10 years. Therefore it makes sense for companies to set up internal measures and reporting as soon as possible and to prepare themselves for the future.

CHALLENGES FOR ACTION

❏ How do you currently tell others outside the company about your intellectual capital and its progress? If you have competitors, what do they do in this regard?

❏ Has your board ever discussed the future disclosure of key data about human capital?

❏ Where would you find it difficult to do so due to the lack of a workable internal system?

Appendix:
The Development and
Measurement of
Intellectual Capital

The first thinkers to apprehend the importance of intellectual capital and the need for a new business model came from Sweden.

Björn Wolrath, CEO of Sweden-based financial services company Skandia Assurance, realized in the late 1980s that a better guide to growing a services organization was required than that provided by traditional measures. In 1991, Skandia was the first organization in the world to appoint a director of intellectual capital, Leif Edvinsson. He was given the task of finding a way to monitor the intangible assets of the company. His intellectual capital mission was defined as follows:

❏   To identify and to enhance the visibility and measurability of intangible and soft assets

❏   To capture and support packaging and accessibility by knowledge transparency and knowledge technologies

❏   To cultivate and channel intellectual capital through professional development, training and IT networking

❏   To capitalize and leverage by adding value through faster recycling of knowledge and increased commercialized transfer of skills and applied experience.

The company's first internal "balanced" annual report was produced in 1995. It was based on a measurement system that Edvinsson derived from the Balanced Scorecard (see Chapter 3) to form the Skandia Navigator. Both Edvinsson and Skandia became evangelists for the importance of intellectual capital, and "went public" in 1995 by producing a supplement to the official annual report.

Dr. Karl-Erik Sveiby was executive chairman of one of Sweden's most successful publishing companies. He later became an author and consultant specializing in knowledge and intangible revenue generation. He first published proposals for a different annual report in 1988, and some six years later the Swedish Council of Service recommended that its members adopt his ideas. In 1989 he published the results of a working group study in *The Invisible Balance Sheet*, and introduced the now widely accepted trio of intellectual capital categories. In 1990 he published (in Swedish) his book *Knowledge Management* and was the first to bring out the importance of this in a systematized way. He compiled the Intangible Assets Monitor that has been in use for some years by the consulting company Celemi. He continues to study the area of measurement.

Sveiby also invented several simulations. One, called Tango!, is marketed by Celemi, and explores the challenges of knowledge-intensive companies through managing projects over several time periods. Decisions about staff and customer choices demonstrate the tension between generating money today and developing know-how that enables bigger projects in the future. Every decision has cash implications and in the long term the goal is to build up maximum cash, or wealth available for distribution. It shows how people and their capabilities link ultimately to creating financial value.

Göran and Johan Roos are brothers, one a consultant and the other a professor at IMD in Lausanne. They have worked extensively in advising companies on intellectual capital management and developed a measuring tool called the IC-index. They distinguish between different generations of intellectual capital thinking:

❑ First generation: concerned with awareness, identifying indicators and developing some kind of report

❏   Second generation: concerned with a focus on changes and flows between different kinds of intellectual capital; develops indices and compares them with market value.

In the US, Thomas Stewart, a journalist with *Fortune* magazine, powerfully highlighted the dilemmas of the knowledge age in a 1994 article, since followed up by his book *Intellectual Capital*. Others in North America who have been protagonists include the following:

❏   Gordon Petrash of Dow Chemical was another early appointee as a director of intellectual capital. He started by examining the protected intellectual assets of the company. He developed value measures in terms of the percentage of current and new business sales that were protected

❏   Patrick Sullivan is a founding partner of the ICM group, a California-based company focused on maximizing the benefits from intellectual capital. He has done much to bring together thinkers and practitioners under the aegis of The ICM Gathering, and has also published books of his own. His focus is on the extraction of financial value from intellectual capital

❏   Hubert St Onge has been particularly active in developing links between knowledge management and intellectual capital, while at the Canadian International Bank of Commerce. He also emphasizes the primacy of customer capital.

TERMS IN USE

There have been many works on the subject of intellectual capital in recent years, many of which are included in the References. As thinkers have sought to categorize the components of intellectual capital, many terms have emerged. Table A.1 is a short summary of some of the terms in use and where they fit together.

Table A.1 *Terms used in describing intellectual capital*

TERM	ORIGIN	MEANING
Intellectual capital	Stewart, Brooking, Edvinsson, Roos, Sveiby	Generally used for the nonphysical/financial component of value
Intellectual property	Longstanding	Used historically for patents, copyrights, proprietary software, etc. Now seen as part of intellectual capital
Structural capital (external)	Edvinsson, Sveiby, St Onge	Anything related to customers, markets, and the public. Can include relationship capital
Structural capital (internal)	Edvinsson, Sveiby	Sveiby defines as "the flow of knowledge within an organization," generally used for infrastructure, processes, culture, explicit knowledge
Human capital	Many academic writers, Schultz, Edvinsson, Sveiby, Davenport	Originally defined by Schultz and is use for a long time, generally referring to the knowledge/competence of an individual. Sometimes used as a synonym for intellectual capital
Relationship capital	Roos, St Onge	The value that comes from productive relationships with others, either externally or internally
Social capital	Schiller et al.	Similar to the above, but emphasis on organizational working rather than individual relationships
Emotional capital	Thompson	The passion and enthusiasm factors that can "make the difference"
Knowledge capital	Sveiby	Often used as a synonym for intellectual capital, e.g., the Roos brothers' definition as "the sum of the knowledge of the members of an organization, and the practical translation of this knowledge, e.g., brands, trade marks, and processes"
Knowledge management	Sveiby and numerous writers since	An integrated set of tools, values, and processes designed to maximize the creation and exchange of knowledge within the organization
Intellectual capacity	Fitz-Enz	Used to describe the ability of a company to extract value from the available intellectual capital

APPROACHES TO DEFINING HUMAN CAPITAL

Roos, Roos, Edvinsson, and Dragonetti divide human capital as follows:

❑   *Competence.* These authors define competence as being essentially about knowledge and skills, and by knowledge they mean specifically the "technical or academic knowledge of things," related to education, something that "has to be taught." Skills they see as its practical counterpart. This approach is reflected in many of the measures used by the pioneering Scandinavian companies.

   In my view, however, competence is more complex than this. The most useful knowledge comes though experience, and what a person knows a lot about may be little to do with their formal education. For example, I have a degree in chemical engineering, but how much I could tell you about it decades later is sadly only a fraction of what I once learned.

❏ *Attitude*. This, say Roos *et al.*, depends mostly on personality traits and can be changed very little. It is influenced by "motivation, behavior and conduct." The Human Capital Monitor argues that these are strongly dependent on the environment in which people work.

❏ *Intellectual agility*. This is used to cover innovation, flexibility, and adaptability—traits seen at a group or organizational level as much as in individuals.

Sveiby uses the heading "professional competence" for human capital. This he defines as a combination of educational attainment levels and years of experience. He then breaks it down, as for the other components of intellectual capital, into aspects of growth/renewal, efficiency, and stability, defining his overall framework for measuring intellectual capital components.

Thomas O Davenport, in his book *Human Capital*, sees human capital as owned and invested by the individual, and the task of the organization as to harness it, keep it, and grow it while it is available. Davenport builds his approach on the increased level of control that people have taken of their own lives, and the norm of people staying with an employer only for as long as their conditions are satisfied. Europeans may question this very US attitude to employment, but it does not invalidate the basic concepts.

Davenport breaks human capital down into three elements:

❏ Ability. This is subdivided into knowledge—"the intellectual context in which a person performs"; skill—"the means of performing tasks"; and talent. By the latter he means a specific aptitude, such as being a very good surgeon or a teacher

❏ Behavior. This is the way in which the task is performed, and embraces attitudes and personal traits

❏ Effort. By this is meant *application* of the ability. It relates to motivation and commitment, but has overtones of productivity.

These categories concern the individual's human capital. An organization brings individuals together, however, and makes something greater than their own independent contribution. The way in which people collaborate toward common goals is also part of human capital.

APPROACHES TO VALUING INTELLECTUAL CAPITAL

Here are some of the ways that have been proposed in the last few years for measuring intellectual capital.

Tobin's "q"

The Nobel prize-winning economist James Tobin developed a theory that firms will continue to invest as long as their market value exceeds the total replacement value of their tangible assets. He was the first to recognize the changing relationship between tangible assets and market value. His "q" is the ratio of these two numbers. If "q" is 1, this is a signal for expansion; if less than 1, a pointer toward divestment.

The problem with this ratio is that it does not work well as an investment guide for knowledge-intensive companies. However, it is one way to describe and compare the differences between market and book value, especially over a long period, and it neutralizes the effect of different asset replacement policies.

The Calculated Intangible Value (CIV)

NCI Research in the US, an affiliate of the Kellogg School of Business at Northwestern University, set up a project group to find a way of measuring intangibles. It defined the value of intangible assets as the company's ability to outperform an average competitor that has similar tangible assets. The method calculates first the return on assets for a particular company over a three-year period. The average for the industry is then ascertained. Based on the assets of the company in question, the excess (or deficit) of earnings is calculated, and compared with what would be produced by the average company. Tax is deducted and the outcome is the premium of earnings attributable to the company's intangible assets. That premium is then resolved to its net present value to give a capital value.

This is not the market value, of course. However, it is a useful figure for judging whether the market price is reflecting the "hidden value," or indeed is excessive

People Value Added (PVA)

This ratio is defined as the Economic Value Added (EVA) divided by the capitalized value of employee costs. It recognizes that financial value is ultimately dependent on human capital. PVA is used by AT&T Network Systems, which conducts regular employee surveys under the same name.

Management Value Added and Information Productivity Index

Paul Strassmann, previously chief information officer at Xerox, has studied the productivity and value of intellectual assets for many years. He sees EVA as a measure of the *return* on intellectual capital, and Management Value Added (MVA) as equivalent to its *capital value*. Strassmann asserts that the cost of managing knowledge is—in nearly every case today— greater than the cost of managing capital. He suggests that a relevant ratio is Management Value Added, "what is left over after absolutely all costs are fully accounted for." The methods suggested for calculation are onerous, however, and a more accessible ratio suggested by him is:

$$\text{Information Productivity Index} = \frac{\text{Return on intellectual assets (profits after tax } \textit{less } \text{cost of capital)}}{\text{Management costs (sales and general administration + R\&D)}}$$

This estimates how much of management costs has been converted into intellectual assets. Strassmann has made a number of calculations for specific companies, and also analyzed 7,224 companies worldwide to give a weighted average IP Index by country. Sweden and Finland came top; countries, as it happens, where interest in intellectual capital monitoring has been pioneered.

Organizational Intellectual Capital

Leif Edvinsson, while at Skandia, studied the problem of measuring intellectual capital in great depth. He has used some 170 indicators to describe it in detail, but as a summary introduced the Organizational Intellectual Capital (OIC) indicator. This is calculated as:

Organizational Intellectual Capital (OIC) = i x C

Where i = intellectual capital coefficient of efficiency
and   C = the intellectual capital absolute measure
　　　C is not in this case the difference between market value and tangible assets. It is derived by Edvinsson adding up the 20 or so of his measures that have a calculable monetary value.
　　　i is the average of the indices in his set that are ratios of efficiency expressed as percentages. Edvinsson has nine of these.
　　　There are many objections to this approach, particularly the assumption that each ratio has the same importance. Thus, the nine indices include "market share" and the "training hours index," useful in their own right although it would be hard to demonstrate their equal contribution.

Value Added Intellectual Coefficient

Ante Pulic of the Austrian Intellectual Capital Research Centre argues that to create value added, we must effectively utilize the physical capital we have, as well as the intellectual potential. This concept narrows down intellectual capital to the employees only, i.e., not including structural capital. His expression of value for intellectual potential is the sum of expenditure for employees' salaries. His argument is that this is defined by the market and therefore has validity as an expression of value. As a result, he developed the formula:

VAIC™ (Value Added Intellectual Coefficient) *is the sum of*
VACA = the value added from one unit of physical capital *and*
VAIP = the value added from each $ (for example) spent on employees

The author of this method is unashamedly enthusiastic for his approach, as it is based on published monetary measures and therefore enables comparisons between companies and within one company over time. It is also not subject to the vagaries of stock market gyration, but works essentially from the value that is added.

Because the key divider is the total costs that are spent on employees, the VAIC is increased as the costs of employees fall. As an overall company success measure it has the same dangers as profitability targets, focusing on the short term. It also does not tell us the proportion of value that has come from the physical or the human assets, and therefore does not make the task of managing intellectual capital any easier.

IC Multiplier and IC Rating

These factors have been developed by Leif Edvinsson under the auspices of his company Intellectual Capital Sweden AB. The IC Rating™ is based on data collected through comprehensive interviews with employees and other stakeholders and a rating is applied to each element of intellectual capital. The IC Multiplier is the ratio of structural capital to human capital. Where this is below 1.0 a high risk is implied, in the sense that more of the intellectual capital can "walk away" than is embedded in the infrastructure of the organization.

In a paper presented in May 2001, a study of 43 companies in Sweden (mostly in IT) compared the IC Multiplier with business ratios such as net sales per employee and profit per employee, finding some significant correlations. The average Multiplier found was 0.93, in a range from 1.05 to 0.79.

IC-Index

We referred earlier to Johan and Göran Roos and their first and second generations of intellectual capital. They concluded that because it was so difficult to measure intellectual capital itself, the focus should be on measuring *changes*. To this end they developed a tool called the IC-Index.

Their distinguishing concept is that it is the flows between components of intellectual capital and financial capital that matter. As they put it: "Balance sheets are still photographs. What drives an organization is the movie—each frame different from its predecessor. It's a dynamic where different kinds of capital growth feed into each other." What they call second-generation IC, as opposed to the more simplistic formula of the first generation, is about carefully selected measures and the interaction between them. Roos and Roos recognize that financial and intellectual capital must be balanced—one is consumed to maintain the other.

They therefore break down the overall intellectual capital into subsections, using the categories of human, customers and relationships, processes and infrastructure, and renewal and innovation. For each category a small set of indicators is carefully chosen. These indicators are each weighted to form a category index, and the category indices are themselves weighted to form an overall IC-Index.

This approach is customized based on an organization's specific strategies, and the factors that will make or break each key strategy. Indicators that will track these factors are then grouped in the four categories to make the indices.

Figure A.1 *Example of an IC-Index*

	w1	w2		w1	w2
Customer and Relationship Capital-*Index*	30		Process/Infrastructure Capital-*Index*	20	
• *Growth in numbers of relationships*		20	• *Efficiency*		25
• *Growth in trust*		25	• *Effectiveness*		35
• *Customer retention*		30	• *Key success factor utilization*		30
• *Distribution channel productivity and quality*		25	• *Distribution efficiency*		30
Human Capital-*Index*	25		Renewal/Innovation Capital-*Index*	25	
• *Fulfillment of key success factors*		25	• *Ability to generate new business*		40
• *Value creation per employee*		40	• *Ability to generate good products*		25
• *Training efficiency and effectiveness*		35	• *Growth*		20
			• *Ability to productify*		15

w! = weighting of category index, w2 = weighting within a category

The knowledge bank

The late Alan Benjamin, former director of SEMA group and ICL, developed a measure for the Tomorrow's Company initiative under the auspices of the Royal Society for the Encouragement of Arts, Manufactures and Commerce, a UK "club" of intellectually minded people from all professions. His premise was that investors had no interest in the physical asset side of a company; only in the capability of the people in it.

Benjamin treated all traditional capital spending as an expense. He then evaluated that part of salaries that was dedicated to the future rather than maintaining the present. For a few people this may be all their time; for most it would be a proportion. This part of employee costs Benjamin capitalized, using standard accounting valuation techniques. He then gave a special value to the replacement costs of highly skilled technical people, and also estimated the net present value of future products from R&D. Without going into all the fine detail, the net result of the sum of capitalized pay and R&D value added is termed the knowledge bank.

Valuing knowledge

Knowledge takes many forms. There are technically generated patents, copyrights and formulae, some of which may be directly associated with discrete future revenue streams, as for example in a drug patent or in licensing agreements. Others provide commercial advantage in systems, processes, and methodologies. Another form of knowledge is the creation of databases such as customer details. There is a market in mailing lists, but most companies would not want to share such information.

There are two questions in this regard:

❑   Is the knowledge of such a nature that other people would pay for it if they could?
❑   Is the knowledge of unique value to us, in that it would be hard to replicate, but nevertheless gives us commercial advantage?

One approach is to look at the replacement cost of reproducing the knowledge. However, this may not reflect its real contribution to value.

What matters is not the absolute monetary value—which will always be subject to assumptions—but the nature of the asset and how it is harnessed. We would therefore look for measures that tell us the extent to which it is useful in improving productivity; whether strategic knowledge assets are increasing; and any benchmarks that we could have against competition.

Baruch Lev has suggested a way of calculating knowledge capital. Taking an average of past earnings over, say, three years, and an average of expected future earnings over a similar period, he calculated a "normalized earnings" figure. Subtract the return on physical assets and the return on financial assets and the surplus is that earned as a result of "knowledge," which can then be capitalized as "knowledge capital."

In a study of the US pharmaceutical industry, Merck had the highest figure, with a ratio to book value of 4.8 (where the ratio of overall market value to book value was 12.1), and knowledge-related earnings / sales being 22 percent. This compares with an average figure for the industry of 17.7 percent. Studying the chemical industry showed a much lower average, at 6.8 percent.

Intangible Assets Monitor

Karl Erik Sveiby developed the Intangible Assets Monitor, which we illustrated in Figures 3.6 and 3.7. Against the three main categories of intellectual capital—external structure, internal structure, and competence—he chose indicators that illustrated growth/renewal, efficiency, and stability. An extract from Celemi, one of his user companies, was shown in Chapter 11 for the competence dimension.

ACCOUNTANTS' VALUATION OF INTANGIBLE ASSETS

"Intellectual capital has been considered by many, defined by some, understood by a select few, and valued by practically no one," says Nick Bontis of the National Centre for Management Research and Development in Canada.

The debate on valuing intangible assets goes back many years. It was highlighted in early 1988 when food group Nestlé bid for confectionery company Rowntree, offering twice its pre-bid market capitalization to reflect the value of the brands that it was purchasing. Later that year Grand Metropolitan announced that it had decided to capitalize the brands it had purchased since 1986. All of this led to an accounting standard in 1990 that purchased "goodwill" should be capitalized and depreciated systematically, normally over 20 years. There are two main issues here: this figure can be enormous (IBM paid seven times the book value of Lotus); and the policy of depreciating intangibles is often contrary to the reality of what actually happens in terms of market valuation.

Partly as a result of these dilemmas, 11 major companies sponsored a significant study by Arthur Andersen in 1992 into the valuation of intangibles. This comprehensive report considered several different valuation methodologies, and focused particularly on brands, publishing rights, intellectual property, and licenses.

Professional accountancy bodies have not been idle, albeit their deliberations move slowly. Standard 38 of the International Accounting Standards Committee was the result of more than 10 years' struggle to account for the measurement and amortization of intangible assets and purchased goodwill.

According to this standard, an intangible asset is defined as "an identifiable non-monetary asset without substance held for use in the production or supply of goods and services, for rental to others, or for administrative purposes." The fair value of an asset is the amount for which that asset could be exchanged between knowledgeable willing parties in an arm's-length transaction.

IAS 38 was published in 1998 to be applied from 1 July 1999. The areas covered are advertising, training, startup, and R&D.

The "asset" has to be identifiable and controlled; its cost has to be measured reliably, and it has to be one that is expected to generate future economic benefits to the organization. Otherwise it must be treated as an expense. The standard prohibits internally generated goodwill, brands, publishing titles, customer lists, and similar items. The standard insists that the asset should normally be amortized over the best estimate of the useful life, with a maximum of 20 years.

Anthony Carey, UK staff adviser to the Accounting Standards Committee, recognized in the *Financial Times* that "many enterprises' most valuable assets, their people and the corporate culture, will rarely qualify for inclusion on the balance sheet yet will have a far greater influence on results than many that are recorded."

A comprehensive report was commissioned by the Dutch Ministry of Economic Affairs called *Balancing Accounts with Knowledge*, presented in 1999. In it four consultancies—PricewaterhouseCoopers, KPMG, Ernst and Young, and Walgemoed—studied several companies and drew conclusions regarding the valuation of intangible assets. Only the last one tackled human resources, mentioned in Chapter 4.

Valuing Intangible Liabilities

There are many examples of firms who have gone bankrupt or been subject to other ignominious deaths due to their failure to recognize or deal with intangible liabilities. It is possible to have a negative intangible valuation where the tangible exceeds the market valuation. The Finnish chemicals and energy company Fortum, in late 1999, was showing such a negativity. It was formed of two state enterprises, Neste and Ivo, both of which had undoubted intellectual assets, and yet the market valuation did not reflect them positively at all. What the market was showing was a lack of confidence in their ability to compete in a privatized world and to survive internationally.

Just as we saw the difficulties of valuing assets in absolute monetary terms, so we may expect the same problem with liabilities. However, sometimes it is easier to evaluate what we do not want, rather than what we have. Many "liabilities" actually cost money and this can be calculated.

Harvey and Lusch of the University of Oklahoma attempted to categorize such liabilities and argued rightly that any statement of intangible assets on a balance sheet must be derived from offsetting the negatives. They distinguish between internal and external factors, and within these have four categories for balancing:

❏ Process issues—systems and methodologies
❏ Human issues—people and organization; externally they include customer behaviors

❑ Informational issues—internally this is about knowledge; externally about brand and reputation
❑ Configuration issues—organizational structure, locations, distribution channels.

Theoretically, every liability should be valued at the present value of the services of assets that must be given up to settle the obligation. However, this will be a very difficult task in most cases.

SUMMARY

Which of the methodologies described above are in regular use? Baruch Lev commented in 2000 that his ideas had not generally been taken up, except by one or two Indian companies (Infosys, for example). The IC-Index is being applied through the Roos Brothers in their consultancy work. Celemi is the most consistent user of the Intellectual Capital Monitor, although other firms in Scandinavia have developed their own approaches along similar lines. Although not featured in this Appendix, we must note that the Balanced Scorecard in practice provides significant focus on intellectual capital, and this has been the most popular approach of all.

Until the regulatory bodies exert some muscle, it is unlikely that many organizations outside the open cultures of Scandinavia will voluntarily disclose data on intellectual capital. There is no doubt that methodologies for measuring many aspects of intellectual capital will become standardized in the next 10 years. Meanwhile, we would recommend a combination of a market-based overview model, which highlights the monetary value of intellectual capital as a whole, combined with a scorecard approach that tracks a set of indicators driving the organization's performance in adding value. Of the scorecard approaches, we believe that those derived from the intellectual capital approach represent best the knowledge era that is replacing the industrial business model.

The Human Capital Monitor is a comprehensive way forward, and the only one that links the intrinsic worth of people with the value that they produce.

References

Ansoff, HI (1986) *Corporate Strategy*, McGraw-Hill, New York.

Arthur Andersen (1992) *The Valuation of Intangible Assets*, Special Report no P254, January.

Bartram, P (1998) "Are you being read?," *Director*, November.

Bassi, L (1999) "Measuring corporate investment in human capital," in M Blair & T Kochan (eds), *The New Relationship*, Brookings Institution.

Becker, BE, Huselid, MA, & Ulrich, D (2001) *The HR Scorecard: Linking People, Strategy, and Performance*, Harvard Business School Press, Boston.

Bedingham, K (1999) "The measurement of organisational culture," *Journal of Human Resource Management*, January.

Bontis, N (1998) "Intellectual capital: An exploratory study that develops measures and models," *Management Decision*, 36(2): 63–76.

Brand, A, VanderMerwe, A, & Boshoff, A (1974) "The measurement of investment in human resources," *Personnel Review*, 3(2, Spring).

Brooking, A (1996) *Intellectual Capital*, Thomson Business Press, London.

Brouthers, KD, van Hastenburg, P, & van den Ven, J (1998) "If most mergers fail, why are they so popular?," *Long Range Planning*, 31(3): 347–53.

Brown, T (1996) "Value migration: The key to tomorrow?," *Management Review*, March.

Buckingham, M & Coffman, C (1999) *First Break All the Rules*, Simon and Schuster, New York.

Bühner, R (1997) "Increasing shareholder value through human asset management," *Long Range Planning*, 30(October).

Bukowitz, WR & Petrash, GP (1997) "Visualising, Measuring and Managing Knowledge," *Research and Technology Management*, July/August.

Bukowitz, WR & Williams, RL (1997) "New metrics for hidden assets," *Journal of Strategic Measurement* (Arthur Andersen), February/March.

Capron, L (1999) "Horizontal acquisitions: The benefits and risks to long term performance, *Financial Times*, "Mastering Strategy," Part 7, November.

Carey, A (1997) "The real value of hidden assets," *Financial Times*, 6 November.

Case, J (1998) *The Open Book Management Experience*, Nicholas Brealey Publishing, London.

Chambers, E (1998) "Winning the war for talent," *McKinsey Quarterly*, 3.

Cohen, DJ & Prusak, L (2001) *In Good Company: How Social Capital Makes Organizations Work*, Harvard Business School Press, Boston.

Cooper, C (2000) "In for the count," *People Management*, 12 October: 28–34.

Cope, M (2000) *Know Your Value?*, Financial Times/Prentice Hall, London.

Cunningham, I (1993) *The Wisdom of Strategic Learning*, McGraw-Hill Maidenhead.

Danish Ministry of Finance (2000) *Knowledge Management and Intellectual Capital: Statement within the State.*

Davenport, TO (1999) *Human Capital*, Jossey Bass, San Francisco.

De Bono, E (1971) *Lateral Thinking for Management*, McGraw-Hill, Maidenhead.

DiFrancesco, JM & Berman, SJ (2000) "Human productivity: The new American frontier," *National Productivity Review*, Summer.

Dixon, N (2000) *Common Knowledge: How Companies Thrive by Sharing What They Know*, Harvard Business School Press, Boston.

Dobson, P (1996) "The dark side of competence: Building cultures in the air," *Journal of Professional HRM*, April: 3–9.

Drucker, P (1992) *Managing for the Future*, Butterworth Heinemann, Oxford.

Dunn, A (1995) "The poverty of accountancy," *Transformation* (Gemini Consulting), Winter.

Eccles, RG, Herz, R, Keegan, EM & Phillips, DMH (2001) *The Value Reporting Revolution*, John Wiley, New York.

Economist (1997) "Valuing companies," *Economist*, 2 August: 61–3.

Economist (1999) "How to merge," *Economist*, 9 January: 15–23.

Economist (1999) "A price on the priceless, *Economist*, 12 June: 94–8.

Edvinsson, L (1997) "Developing intellectual capital at Skandia," *Long Range Planning*, 30(June): 366–73.

Edvinsson, L & Malone, MS (1997) *Intellectual Capital*, Piatkus, London.

Edvinsson, L & Øberg, D (2001) "The IC Multiplier and the importance of structural capital," paper presented at the *4th Intangibles Conference on Measurement of Intellectual Capital*, New York, May, available at www.intellectualcapital.se.

Epstein, M & Manzoni, J-F (1998) "Implementing corporate strategy: From tableaux de bord to balanced scorecards," *European Management Journal*, 16(2, April).

Fitz-Enz, J (1995) *How to Measure Human Resource Management*, 2nd edn, McGraw-Hill, New York.

Fitz-Enz, J (2000) *The ROI of Human Capital*, Amacom, New York.

Flamholz, EG (1999) *Human Resource Accounting: Advances in Concepts, Methods and Applications*, 3rd edn, Kluwer, Amsterdam.

Friedman, B, Hatch, J, & Walker, D (1998) *Delivering on the Promise: How to Attract, Manage and Retain Human Capital*, Free Press, New York.

Giles, WJ & Robinson, DF (1972) *Human Asset Accounting*, IPM/ICMA, London.

Goffee, R & Jones, G (1999) *The Character of the Corporation*, HarperCollins, London.

Goffee, R & Jones, G (2000) "Why should anyone be led by you?," *Harvard Business Review*, September–October.

Goold, M, Campbell, A, & Alexander, M (1993) *Corporate Level Strategy: Creating Value in Multibusiness Companies*, John Wiley, Chichester.

Gratton, L (2000) *Living Strategy*, FT-Prentice Hall, London.

Hamel, G & Prahalad, CK (1994) *Competing for the Future*, Harvard Business School Press, Cambridge, MA.

Hammer, M & Champy, J (1993) *Reengineering the Corporation: A Manifesto for Business Revolution*, Nicholas Brealey Publishing, London.

Harman, C & Brelade, S (2000) *Knowledge Management and the Role of HR*, FT Prentice Hall, London.

Haspeslagh, PC & Jemison, DB (1991) *Managing Acquisitions: Creating Value Through Corporate Renewal*, Free Press, New York.

Her Majesty's Stationery Office (1977) *The Future of Company Reports*, HMSO, London.

Heskett, JL, Sasser, WE, Jr, & Schlesinger, LA (1997) *The Service Profit Chain*, Free Press, New York.

Honey, P & Mumford, A (1995) *Using Your Learning Styles*, 3rd edn, Peter Honey Publications, Maidenhead.

Hope, J & Hope, T (1995) *Transforming the Bottom Line*, Nicholas Brealey Publishing, London.

Huselid, M (1995) "The impact of human resource management practices on turnover, productivity and corporate financial performance," *Academy of Management Journal*, 38: 635–72.

Huselid, M, Becker, B, & Ulrich, D (2001) *The HR Scorecard: Linking People, Strategy, and Performance*, Harvard Business School Press, Boston, MA.

Institute of Personnel and Development (1997) *The Impact of People Management Practices on Business Performance*, IPD Research Report, London.

Jackson, T (1997) "Winning minds not hearts," *Financial Times*, 27 October.

Jackson, T (1998) "The art of taking the unknown into account," *Financial Times*, 3 December.

Johnson, HT & Bröms, A (2000) *Profit Beyond Measure*, Free Press, New York.

Johnson, HT & Kaplan, RS (1987) *Relevance Lost: The Rise and Fall of Management Accounting*, Harvard Business School Press, Boston.

Kaplan, RS & Norton, DP (1996) *The Balanced Scorecard*, Harvard Business School Press, Boston.

Kaplan, RS & Norton, DP (2000) *The Strategy-Focused Organization*, Harvard Business School Press, Boston.

Katzenbach, J & Smith, D (1993) *The Wisdom of Teams*, Harvard Business School Press, Boston.

Kearns, P (1995) *Measuring Human Resources and the Impact on Bottom Line Improvements*, Technical Communications, Hitchin.

Kennedy, A (2000) *The End of Shareholder Value*, Orion, London.

Lank, E (1997) "Leveraging invisible assets: The human factor," *Long Range Planning*, June: 406–12.

Lester, T (1996) "Accounting for knowledge assets," *Financial Times*, 20 February.

Lester, T (1996) "Measuring human capital," *Human Resources*, May/June.

Lev, B (2000) "Intangibles, management, measurement and reporting," Stern School of Business, December.

Lev, B & Schwartz, A (1971) "On the use of the economic concept of human capital in financial statements," *The Accounting Review*, January.

Likert, RM & Bowers, DG (1973) "Improving the accuracy of P&L reports by estimating the changes in dollar value of the human organization," *Michigan Business Review*, 25(3): 15–24.

Markides, C & Oyon, D (1998) "International acquisitions: Do they create value for shareholders?," *European Management Journal*, 16(2, April).

Mathur, S & Kenyon, A (1997) *Creating Value*, Butterworth Heinemann, Oxford.

Mayo, AJ & Hadaway, AJ (1994) "Cultural adaptation from an Anglo-Nordic merger," *Journal of Management Development*, 13(2, June).

Mayo, AJ & Lank, E (1994) *The Power of Learning*, Institute of Personnel and Development, London.

McGregor, D (1960) *The Human Side of Enterprise*, McGraw-Hill, New York.

Ministry of Economic Affairs in cooperation with Bak, GGM (1999) *Balancing Accounts with Knowledge*, The Hague, October, available from www.minez.nl.

Monnery, N & Malchione, R (2000) "Seven deadly sins of mergers," *Financial Times*, 2 March.

Monti-Belkaoui, J & Riahi-Belkaoui, M (1995) *Human Resource Valuation: A Guide to Strategies and Techniques*, Quorum Books, Westport, CT.

Mooraj, S, Oyon, D, & Hostettler, D (1999) "The balanced scorecard: A necessary good or an unnecessary evil?," *European Management Journal*, 17(5, October).

Nahapiet, J & Ghoshal, S (1999) "Social capital, intellectual capital, and the organizational advantage," *Academy of Management Review*, 23(3): 242–66.

Olve, N-G, Roy, J, & Wetter, M (1997) *Performance Drivers: A Practical Guide to Using the Balanced Scorecard*, John Wiley, Chichester.

Patterson, F (2000) "Maximising innovation in the workplace," *Training Journal*, August.

Peters, T (1987) *Thriving on Chaos*, Macmillan, New York.

Peters, T (1992) *Liberation Management*, Knopf, New York.

Pfeffer, J (1997) "Pitfalls on the road to measurement: The dangerous liaison of human resources with the ideas of accounting and finance," *Human Resource Management*, 36(Fall): 357–65.

Pfeffer, J (1998) *The Human Equation*, Harvard Business School Press, Boston.

Porras, JI & Collins, JC (1994) *Built to Last*, Harper Business, New York.

Pulic, A (1998) "Measuring the performance of intellectual potential in the knowledge economy," paper from the Austrian Intellectual Capital Research Centre.

Quinn, JB, Anderson, P, & Finkelstein, S (1996) "Making the most of the best," *Harvard Business Review*, March–April.

Rajan, A, Lank, E, & Chapple, K (1999) *Good Practices in Knowledge Creation and Exchange*, CREATE, Tunbridge Wells.

Roos, J (1998) "Exploring the concept of intellectual capital," *Long Range Planning*, 31(1): 150–3.

Roos, J & Roos, G (1997) "Intellectual capital: The next generation," *Financial Times*, "Mastering Management," May.

Roos, J & Roos, G (1997) "Measuring your company's intellectual performance," *Long Range Planning*, June.

Roos, J, Roos, G, Edvinsson, L, & Dragonetti, NC (1997) *Intellectual Capital*, Macmillan, Basingstoke.

Roy, S (1999) "Managing intellectual capital: The work with the Navigator in the Skandia Group," *Journal of Human Resource Costing and Accounting*, 4(1, Spring).

Sadler, P (1993) *Managing Talent*, Economist Books, London.

Schuller, T (1996) "Social and human capital: Twins, siblings or rivals?," paper submitted as part of *ESRC/EU Conference on Lifelong Learning*, Newcastle, November.

Senge, P (1990) *The Fifth Discipline*, Doubleday, New York.

Steffy, B & Maurer, S (1988) "Conceptualizing and measuring the economic effectiveness of human resource activities," *Academy of Management Review*, April: 271–86.

Stewart, T (1997) *Intellectual Capital*, Nicholas Brealey Publishing, London.

Strassmann, P (1996) "The value of computers, information and knowledge," January, www.strassmann.com.

Sullivan, P (2000) *Value Driven Intellectual Capital*, John Wiley, New York.

Sveiby, KE (1997) *The New Organizational Wealth*, Berrett-Koehler, San Francisco.

Thatcher, M (1998) "All about EVA," *People Management*, October.

Thomson, K (1998) *Emotional Capital*, Capstone, Oxford.

Ulrich, D (1997) *Human Resource Champions*, Harvard Business School Press, Boston.

Ulrich, D (1997) "Measuring human resources: An overview of practice and a prescription for results," *Human Resources Management*, 36(3, Fall): 303–20.

Whiteley, P (2001) "Is an employee an asset or a liability?," *Times*, 8 February.

Williams, M (2000) *The War for Talent*, Chartered Institute of Personnel and Development, London.

Wilson, B (1979) "Creating and sharing wealth," *Employee Relations*, 1(1 & 2).

Yeung, AK & Berman, B (1997) "Adding value through human resources: Reorientating resource measurement to drive business performance," *Human Resource Management*, 36(3, Fall): 321–35.

Websites

www.cam-i.org/bb	Beyond Budgeting Round Table, a consortium dedicated to an alternative to budgeting
www.celemi.se	Celemi AB
www.cpri.matrixlinks.ca	Canadian Institute of Chartered Accountants Performance and Reporting Initiative
www.efqm.org	European Foundation for Quality Management
www.fm.dk	Danish Ministry of Finance (for publications)

www.iasb.org.uk	International Accounting Standards Board
www.intellectualcapital.se	For details of the IC Multiplier
www.lewisham.gov.uk	Lewisham Council
www.mliltd.com	Mayo Learning International, the author's site
www.measuring-ip.at	Austrian Intellectual Capital Research Center
www.quality.nist.gov	Baldrige National Quality Program
www.skandia.se	Skandia Assurance
www.strassmann.com	Paul Strassmann
www.sveiby.com.au	The very informative website of Karl Erik Sveiby
www.systematic.dk	Systematic A/S
www.tomorrowscompany.com	Centre for Tomorrow's Company
www.unic.net	Universal Networking Intellectual Capital, the site of Leif Edvinsson
www.watsonwyatt.com	For the Human Capital Index

Index